The State, Justice, and the Common Good

An Introduction to
Social and Political Philosophy

Edited by **B. J. Diggs**
University of Illinois, Urbana

Scott, Foresman and Company
Glenview, Illinois   Brighton, England

Academic Editor: **William K. Frankena**
University of Michigan

Library of Congress Catalog Card Number: 73–89430
ISBN:0–673–05198–6

Regional offices of Scott, Foresman and Company are located in
Dallas, Texas; Glenview, Illinois; Oakland, New Jersey; Palo Alto,
California; Tucker, Georgia; and Brighton, England.

FOREWORD

This volume is an introduction to political and social philosophy for the student and general reader. As Professor Diggs says, political and social philosophy have usually been treated together with ethics or moral philosophy, and this is also true in this book. The selections are all modern or contemporary, but Professor Diggs provides an illuminating review of pre-Hobbesian political and social philosophy, nicely combining quotation, exposition, and narrative. The arrangement is chronological, from Hobbes to Rawls, but these selections are so made and the introductions so written that the problems and topics are also covered in a systematic way.

The introductions and selections are carefully designed to form a well integrated whole. Moreover, taken together, they present Professor Diggs' own political and social philosophy as well as those of the authors selected. As a result, a reflective reading of this book will not only introduce one to the field it represents, but also lead one to evolve a position of one's own.

This book is suitable for use in a general introductory philosophy course or in specific courses in political or social philosophy. It can provide a background for a discussion of contemporary social issues or for special topics in upper-level courses. It may also be used in political science courses concerned with the theory of the state, and advanced students and the educated reader in general will find that it gives an excellent historical and systematic survey of this field.

William K. Frankena

PREFACE

This book is designed to provide a systematic and historical introduction for beginning readers of political and social philosophy. Three classical philosophies of the modern state—Locke's theory of natural rights, Hume's utilitarianism, and Rousseau's theory of the social contract—are presented in their historical settings, and their similarities and differences, their strengths and weaknesses, are explored. Against this background, some major conflicting philosophies of the nineteenth and twentieth centuries are briefly examined, with special attention given to justice and the common good. Rawls' recently proposed theory of justice weaves together a number of these themes and contributions of the past; the outline of its elementary features is not only of intrinsic interest, but also lends unity to this volume. The critical introductions, together with the substantial selections from carefully chosen texts, presented in a partly historical and partly dialectical order, should give the attentive reader a good working knowledge of some of the major issues and points of view in social and political philosophy.

This book is so arranged that parts of it can be used independently. Part II can be used alone, with Part I as background; and Part I and the critical introduction to Part II can be used as background for an independent treatment of Part III.

In preparing this book I have incurred a substantial debt to Louis Werner and William Frankena, who read the whole of the manuscript, and to Llewellyn Diggs and Richard Schacht, who read parts of it, for their many suggestions and helpful advice. I am even more indebted to Max Fisch, John Rawls, and Frederick L. Will, who in different ways have contributed greatly to the development of the underlying views. None of these people should be held responsible for the blunders.

I am also indebted to Martha Friedman of the University of Illinois Library; Linda Hermann, Sandy Davison, Diane Hiither, and Marjorie Beasley of the secretarial staff of my Department; and Thomas Easton, Diane Ratcliffe, Paul Rohe, and Joanne Tinsley of Scott, Foresman—all of whom gave me substantial assistance in preparing the manuscript for publication.

Grateful acknowledgment is made to The Belknap Press and Harvard University Press, The Clarendon Press, Oxford, and The Hafner Publishing Company for permission to reprint from their publications. More exact acknowledgments will be found accompanying the selections below.

B. J. D.

CONTENTS

I

Introduction

The Individual and Society

That each person born into this world is greatly dependent on his fellow human beings and on society is a commonplace, but not one that has always been appreciated. Recognition of this dependence, although it is difficult to set its limits, is essential to any sane social and political philosophy. It is obvious that if a person had to rely wholly on himself, and mysteriously survived, his food gathering, shelter, medicine, etc., would be extremely primitive. It should be equally obvious that with little or no language, no companions, no community of experience, and no history, such a person could scarcely be said to have a view of the world or of himself. A person may wish to reject society, perhaps in disgust at its evils, but he can have this desire only after he has enjoyed some of society's blessings.

In order to gain such goods as life in society has to offer, a price must be paid. As many social theorists now observe, if each individual has needs that only a society of individuals can satisfy, so also each society has needs that only individuals can satisfy.[1] If a society is to exist, its members must learn a common language and must share within broad limits a common view of the world; it is not easy for two persons to live together if there is little to eat and only one of them re-

[1] For an introductory account of social needs, see D. F. Aberle, A. K. Cohen, A. K. Davis, M. J. Levy, Jr., and F. X. Sutton, "The Functional Prerequisites of a Society," *Ethics,* 60 (January 1950): 100–111. See also T. Parsons and E. Shils (Eds.), *Toward a General Theory of Action* (Cambridge, Mass.: Harvard University Press, 1951), esp. I, 1, 6; II, 4; M. Levy, Jr., *The Structure of Society* (Princeton: Princeton University Press, 1952); and the anthropological writings mentioned in footnote 5 below.

1

gards cows as sacred. There must also be care of offspring in infancy and "socialization," or education in the "ways of the society." These ways constitute a social order that allows each person to act on the expectation that others will behave in certain ways. Without this system of expectations, a person could not so much as make a promise and certainly could not engage in cooperative schemes or compete with others. And since each person must be able to count on others to conform to this order and to the rules and conventions that specify it, some degree of mutual trust, some sort of social morality, is ordinarily required.

Many writers have called attention to the native weakness of individuals and the strength that they achieve in society, as well as to morality as a functional requirement of a society, but none more colorfully than the Greek philosopher Plato (429–347 B.C.), in one of whose dialogues the great sophist Protagoras tells the following "myth" or story of the creation.

Once upon a time there were gods only, and no mortal creatures. But when the appointed time came that these also should be created, the gods fashioned them out of earth and fire and various mixtures of both elements in the interior of the earth; and when they were about to bring them into the light of day, they ordered Prometheus and Epimetheus to equip them, and to distribute to them severally their proper qualities. Epimetheus said to Prometheus: "Let me distribute, and do you inspect." This was agreed, and Epimetheus made the distribution. There were some to whom he gave strength without swiftness, while he equipped the weaker with swiftness; some he armed, and others he left unarmed; and devised for the latter some other means of preservation. Upon those whom he clothed in diminutive bodies, he bestowed winged flight or subterranean habitation: those which he aggrandized with magnitude, he protected by their very size: and similarly with the rest of his distribution, always compensating. These devices he used as precautions that no race should be destroyed. And when he had provided against their destruction by one another, he contrived also a means of protecting them against the seasons of heaven; . . . And some he made to have few young ones, while those who were their prey were very prolific; and in this manner the race was pre-

served. Thus did Epimetheus, who, not being very wise, forgot that he had distributed among the brute animals all the qualities which he had to give,—and when he came to man, who was still unprovided, he was terribly perplexed. Now while he was in this perplexity, Prometheus came to inspect the distribution, and he found that the other animals were quite suitably furnished, but that man was naked and shoeless, and had neither bed nor arms of defence. The appointed hour was approaching when man in his turn was to emerge from earth into the light of day; and Prometheus, not knowing how he could devise his salvation, stole the mechanical arts of Hephaestus and Athene, and fire with them (they could neither have been acquired nor used without fire), and gave them to man. Thus man had the wisdom necessary to the support of life, but political wisdom he had not; for that was in the keeping of Zeus. . . .

Now man, having a share of the divine attributes, was at first the only one of the animals who had any gods, because he alone was of their kindred; and he would raise altars and images of them. He was not long in inventing articulate speech and names; and he also constructed houses and clothes and shoes and beds, and drew sustenance from the earth. Thus provided, mankind at first lived dispersed, and there were no cities. But the consequence was that they were destroyed by the wild beasts. . . . After a while the desire of self-preservation gathered them into cities; but when they were gathered together, having no art of government, they evil entreated one another, and were again in process of dispersion and destruction. Zeus feared that the entire race would be exterminated, and so he sent Hermes to them, bearing reverence and justice to be the ordering principles of cities and the bonds of friendship and conciliation. Hermes asked Zeus how he should impart justice and reverence among men:—Should he distribute them as the arts are distributed; that is to say, to a favoured few only, one skilled individual having enough of medicine or of any other art for many unskilled ones? "Shall this be the manner in which I am to distribute justice and reverence among men, or shall I give them to all?" "To all," said Zeus; "I should like them all to have a share; for cities cannot exist, if a few only share in the virtues, as in the arts. And further, make a law by my order, that he who has no part in reverence and justice shall be put to death, for he is a plague of the state."

And this is the reason, Socrates, why the Athenians and mankind in general, when the question relates to carpentering or any other mechanical art, allow but a few to share in their deliberations; and when anyone else interferes, then, as you say, they object, if he be not of the favoured few; which, as I reply, is very natural. But when they meet to deliberate about political virtue, which proceeds only by way of justice and wisdom, they are patient enough of any man who speaks of them, as is also natural, because they think that every man ought to share in this sort of virtue, and that states could not exist if this were otherwise. Such, Socrates, is the reason of this phenomenon.[2]

The State as Sovereign Power

It would be happy indeed if the moral sense of human beings were strong enough to secure order with justice. The members of a society would then live under rules that they accepted voluntarily and enforced through their own consciences. But however much we may admire and even be astonished by the extent to which persons voluntarily accept restraints, keep faith with one another, and respect one another, nevertheless human beings seem, and certainly have been thought to be, too selfish, too much attracted by immediate gain and pleasure, and too unenlightened to live under a system of wholly voluntary social control. It has been generally thought that if society is not to disintegrate, or give way, as it was traditionally put, to "a state of nature," then in addition to morality there must be a political order and a juridical system charged with the enforcement of at least the essential core of morality. This is one basic argument for the necessity of the state and one view of its primary function.

---

[2] *The Dialogues of Plato,* 4th ed., trans. Benjamin Jowett (Oxford: The Clarendon Press, 1953), Vol. 1, pp. 145–148. By permission of The Clarendon Press, Oxford.

This view was held in an extreme form by Thomas Hobbes (1588–1679), who regarded each human being as a kind of egoistic machine and the "state of nature" as a state of war "of every man against every man." But a somewhat similar view was also held in less extreme forms by modern classical political philosophers, such as Locke (1632–1704) and Hume (1711–1776) in Britain and Kant (1724–1804) in Germany, who took a much more affirmative view of human nature. These philosophers were able to discern, much more clearly than Hobbes, the distinction between society and the state, morality and law; but from them and others, in spite of considerable differences among themselves, we have received as a legacy the general view that the state, or the political system within society, is primarily needed and perhaps most fittingly characterized as the power in a society recognized as having supreme authority to lay down rules and use legitimate physical coercion in enforcing them.

This characterization of the state runs persistently through much recent social theory. The German sociologist Max Weber (1881–1961), as part of his general theory of institutions, defined the state as:

A compulsory political association with continuous organization . . . [whose] administrative staff successfully upholds a claim to the monopoly of the legitimate use of physical force in the enforcement of its order.[3]

He also remarked that "the right to use physical force is ascribed to other institutions or to individuals only to the extent to which the state permits it."[4] Many political theorists have followed Weber more or less closely. Robert Dahl, for example, defines a political system as "any persistent pattern of human relationships that involves, to a significant extent, power, rule, or authority," and government as "the collection of offices in a political system." He then defines *"the* Government," on Weber's pattern, as "any government that successfully upholds a claim to

---

[3] Max Weber, *The Theory of Social and Economic Organization,* trans. A. M. Henderson and T. Parsons (New York: Oxford University Press, 1947), p. 154.

[4] H. H. Gerth and C. W. Mills (Trans. and Ed.), *From Max Weber: Essays in Sociology* (New York: Oxford University Press, 1946), p. 78.

the exclusive regulation of the legitimate use of physical force in enforcing its rules within a given territorial area." [5] A number of anthropologists, stressing the need for an agency to maintain social order, hold somewhat similar views.[6]

However, we should have reservations about and qualify this common view that the state is the governing power having supreme authority to use legitimate coercion to enforce its rules. For one thing, the view must not be interpreted to mean that the state has a monopoly of power. There are many power centers in a complex society, and a stable political system depends on a considerable degree of popular acceptance and consensus.[7] Second, the view of the state as the authoritative governing and coercive power is not as negative as it may appear to be, since the political system may be (and in some cases is) greatly responsive to the will of its citizens. Third, the view should not be tied to a negative or protectionist view of the functions and purposes of the state. Weber explicitly divorced his definition of the state from any statement of its ends on the grounds that "there is scarcely any task that some political association has not taken in hand, and there is no task that one could say has always been exclusive and peculiar" to such associations.[8] Although some of the modern classical political philosophers have a strong tendency to regard the protection of rights and enforcement of elementary moral rules as the principal business of the state, others have taken a much broader view, using such concepts as the

[5] R. Dahl, *Modern Political Analysis,* 2nd ed. (Englewood Cliffs, N.J.: Prentice-Hall, Inc., 1970), pp. 6, 11–12. See also, for example, G. Almond and G. Powell, Jr., *Comparative Politics* (Boston: Little, Brown and Company, 1966), pp. 17–18, and A. Downs, *An Economic Theory of Democracy* (New York: Harper & Row, Publishers, 1957), Ch. 2.

[6] M. Fortes and E. E. Evans-Pritchard (Eds.), *African Political Systems* (London: Oxford University Press, 1940), Preface and Introduction. See also L. Mair, *Primitive Government* (Baltimore, Md.: Penguin Books, Inc., 1962), Introduction; M. Sahlins, *Tribesmen* (Englewood Cliffs, N.J.: Prentice-Hall, Inc., 1968), Ch. 1; B. Malinowski, *Crime and Custom in Savage Society* (London: Routledge & Kegan Paul Ltd., 1926); and R. Firth, "Social Anthropology," *Encyclopaedia Britannica* (Chicago: 1964), Vol. 20, pp. 862–870 (with references).

[7] See S. I. Benn and R. S. Peters, *The Principles of Political Thought* (New York: The Free Press, 1965) (originally published as *Social Principles and the Democratic State,* London: George Allen & Unwin Ltd., 1959), Ch. 12.

[8] Gerth and Mills, *From Max Weber,* p. 77. See also Weber, *Theory of Social and Economic Organization,* p. 155.

"general happiness" and the "public interest" to justify and legitimize a great extension of the use of political power. Moreover, the idea that the primary function of the state is to promote to the fullest extent possible the well-being of its citizens is more ancient than the idea that it should first of all protect or preserve rights and enforce law. The more limited and more negative view became prominent after the birth of the modern nation-state. In order to understand this change and to provide a setting for the political philosophy of the modern state, we shall go back to the beginnings of Western political theory in Greece, where we find no mention of "political rights," and then briefly review the development of political concepts up to the time of Hobbes, with whom the readings in this volume begin.

The Philosophy of the Polis: Plato and Aristotle

The political writings of Plato and Aristotle (384–322 B.C.) are so trenchant, timeless, and pertinent that there is a tendency to think of these two ancient philosophers as writing as much for us today as they did for the Greeks of the fourth century B.C. However, we should bear in mind that they lived in the city-state Athens, a *polis,* whose democratic form of government of the fifth century had become famous and only partially survived the disastrous war with Sparta. Actually the democracy of Athens was limited to its citizens, who with the members of their families numbered about a half of its two or three hundred thousand inhabitants, the remainder being made up largely of resident aliens, of whom Aristotle was one, and slaves. Partly because they often had occasion to compare themselves to the rude barbarians in armies opposed to their own and to compare their government to the much more autocratic governments of neighboring states, the citizens of Athens commonly took great pride in their citizenship and their democratic heritage. Considerable numbers of them attended the regular (though infrequent) meetings of the Assembly, which were open to all citizens, and shared in the extensive business of the courts. They had a great respect for law, constituted largely by accepted custom as reviewed by the courts, and a great love of liberty. Citizenship offered an opportunity for a fine mixture of rhetorical, political, social, and religious activity.

In their ethical and political writings, Plato and Aristotle were primarily concerned with the good life of persons living together in the *polis.* In the *Republic,* Plato sought to determine what a just person is by considering what justice is in the *polis;* he concluded that an individual and a *polis* are good in virtue of the same qualities.[9] Inspired by Socrates, Plato critically examined custom and popular opinion, both with an eye toward determining the true or ideal nature of the *polis* and with the hope that Athens could be saved from demagoguery, oligarchy, and tyranny. His account is found largely in the *Republic,* the *Statesman,* and the *Laws.* Aristotle, for his part, argued that the excellence of the good citizen and of the good person are identical, provided that the citizen shares in the ruling function under a good constitution; all agree, he said, that the well-being of the *polis* and of the individual are of the same kind.[10] He undertook, principally in the *Nicomachean Ethics* and the *Politics,* to construct a science of the *polis.*

Both Plato and Aristotle maintained that the good life can be had only in the *polis,* because they regarded the *polis* as the self-sufficient social unit; it arises from the most elementary needs of human beings and is naturally designed to enable persons living together to become "self-sufficient in goods" and to live well. This goal can be attained, however, only if there is a proper ordering of the elements that compose both the individual and the *polis.* According to Plato there are three basic elements: In the *psyche,* or "soul," of each individual there are "appetites" for objects that afford pleasure; a "spirited" element that expresses itself in such passions as anger and fear; and a "rational" or "reflective" element whose nature is to seek understanding and use it in directing the other elements. In the *polis* there correspond, respectively, a class of farmers, artisans, and traders that serves to satisfy the appetites, a class of warriors that protects the *polis,* and a class of rulers. The fundamental problem both for the individual and the *polis* is to bring about an order or harmony of these elements by having each element

---

[9] *Republic,* II, 368–369; IV, 441.
[10] *Politics,* III, 4; VII, 2.

achieve its appropriate "excellence" or "virtue," namely, temperance, courage, or wisdom. When this is accomplished, each element performs its proper function in the whole, each receives its "due," and justice is achieved. Plato summarized as follows:

And so, after a stormy passage, we have reached the land. We are fairly agreed that the same three elements exist alike in the state and in the individual soul.

That is so.

Does it not follow at once that state and individual will be wise or brave by virtue of the same element in each and in the same way? Both will possess in the same manner any quality that makes for excellence.

That must be true.

Then it applies to justice: we shall conclude that a man is just in the same way that a state was just. And we have surely not forgotten that justice in the state meant that each of the three orders in it was doing its own proper work. So we may henceforth bear in mind that each one of us likewise will be a just person, fulfilling his proper function, only if the several parts of our nature fulfil theirs.

Certainly.

And it will be the business of reason to rule with wisdom and forethought on behalf of the entire soul; while the spirited element ought to act as its subordinate and ally. The two will be brought into accord, as we said earlier, by that combination of mental and bodily training which will tune up one string of the instrument and relax the other, nourishing the reasoning part on the study of noble literature and allaying the other's wildness by harmony and rhythm. When both have been thus nurtured and trained to know their own true functions, they must be set in command over the appetites, which form the greater part of each man's soul and are by nature insatiably covetous. They must keep watch lest this part, by battening on the pleasures that are called bodily, should grow so great and powerful that it will no longer keep to its own work, but will try to enslave the others and usurp a dominion to which it has no right, thus turning the whole of life upside down. At the same time, those two together will be the best of guardians for the entire soul and for the body against all enemies from without: the one will take counsel,

*while the other will do battle, following its ruler's commands
and by its own bravery giving effect to the ruler's designs.*

. . .

*And so our dream has come true—I mean the inkling we
had that, by some happy chance, we had lighted upon a rudimen-
tary form of justice from the very moment when we set about
founding our commonwealth. Our principle that the born shoe-
maker or carpenter had better stick to his trade turns out to have
been an adumbration of justice; and that is why it has helped us.
But in reality justice, though evidently analogous to this principle, is not a matter of external behaviour, but of the inward
self and of attending to all that is, in the fullest sense, a man's
proper concern. The just man does not allow the several elements in his soul to usurp one another's functions; he is indeed
one who sets his house in order, by self-mastery and discipline
coming to be at peace with himself, and bringing into tune those
three parts, like the terms in the proportion of a musical scale,
the highest and lowest notes and the mean between them, with
all the intermediate intervals. Only when he has linked these
parts together in well-tempered harmony and has made himself
one man instead of many, will he be ready to go about whatever
he may have to do, whether it be making money and satisfying
bodily wants, or business transactions, or the affairs of state. In
all these fields when he speaks of just and honourable conduct,
he will mean the behaviour that helps to produce and to preserve
this habit of mind; and by wisdom he will mean the knowledge
which presides over such conduct. Any action which tends to
break down this habit will be for him unjust; and the notions
governing it he will call ignorance and folly.*[11]

Aristotle wrote from a general point of view much like that
of his teacher, Plato, but Aristotle was (among other things)
one of the first biologists, and his approach was more that of a
naturalist:

. . . § 3. There is one classification of the constituent elements

[11] *The Republic of Plato*, trans. F. M. Cornford (London: The Oxford
University Press, 1941), pp. 139–142. By permission of The Clarendon
Press, Oxford.

*of the best life which it is certain that no one would challenge.
This is the classification of these elements into external goods;
goods of the body; and goods of the soul. It will also be generally agreed that all of these different "goods" should belong to
the happy man. § 4. No one would call a man happy who had
no particle of fortitude, temperance, justice, or wisdom [i.e.,
none of the goods of the soul]: who feared the flies buzzing
about his head; who abstained from none of the extremest forms
of extravagance whenever he felt hungry or thirsty; who would
ruin his dearest friends for the sake of a farthing; whose mind
was as senseless, and as much astray, as that of a child or a mad-
man. § 5. These are all propositions which would be accepted
by nearly everybody as soon as they were stated. But differences
begin to arise when we ask, "How much of each good should
men have? And what is the relative superiority of one good over
another?" Any modicum of goodness [i.e., of the "goods of the
soul"] is regarded as adequate; but wealth and property, power,
reputation, and all such things, are coveted to an excess which
knows no bounds or limits. § 6. There is an answer which can
be given to men who act in this way. "The facts themselves
make it easy for you to assure yourselves on these issues. You
can see for yourselves that the goods of the soul are not gained
or maintained by external goods. It is the other way round. You
can see for yourselves that felicity—no matter whether men find
it in pleasure, or goodness, or both of the two—belongs more to
those who have cultivated their character and mind to the utter-
most, and kept acquisition of external goods within moderate
limits, than it does to those who have managed to acquire more
external goods than they can possibly use, and are lacking in the
goods of the soul."* [12]

Aristotle devoted the *Nicomachean Ethics* to describing
these "goods of the soul." Unlike Plato, he did not regard the
soul as immortal; the soul is the source of life in all living things,
the source of sensation, desires, feelings in all animals, and the
source of thinking in humans. The goods of the human soul are
to be attained by developing the right habits, or habits of
"virtue." The "morally virtuous" habits shape desires, actions,

[12] *The Politics of Aristotle*, trans. E. Barker (Oxford: The Clarendon
Press, 1946), p. 280. By permission of The Clarendon Press, Oxford.

and passions; they lie in a mean between excess and defect, as determined by reason. However, reason itself requires virtuous habits; these are the "intellectual virtues" of the consummate scientist, and those of the statesman and the artist. The fundamental problem for the statesman is to make the citizenry self-sufficient in goods, and primarily in these goods of the soul. This is the goal of the *polis*.

Both Plato and Aristotle were deeply interested in different constitutional forms and in determining what kind of constitution would produce the best persons and the best *polis*. Plato regarded government by the wise and good ruler "exercising his art" as best of all, but this is an unattainable ideal, and government under law is "second best." In the *Statesman,* he classified good and bad constitutions according to whether they respect or fail to respect the law. Kingship, aristocracy, and lawful democracy are respectively governments by one, a few, and many observing the law. Tyranny, oligarchy, and lawless democracy are the corresponding bad forms that fail to observe law.[13] Aristotle wrote in a similar vein, but he put the principle of division between good and bad constitutions differently. Under good constitutions the rulers govern for the sake of the citizens, rather than for the sake of themselves.[14] Although something can be said for personal rule by an exceptionally wise person, in light of the difficulty of finding one, the rule of law is preferable. Law, which Aristotle defined as "reason free from all passion," should be sovereign.[15] A constitution gives the *polis* its identity.

Both Plato and Aristotle favored rule under law by those who are "wisest and best"; and they tended to view democracy either as too libertarian and indulgent or too much dominated by the poor desiring wealth. However, Plato in the *Laws* chose a form of government with an extensive electorate. And Aristotle argued with conviction that the "many" may excel the "few" in wisdom; that ideally all citizens are equals; and that any stable constitution depends on its being, in a sense, voluntarily accepted by the citizenry.[16] For Aristotle, citizenship was characterized, as one modern author stresses, by its being a relation-

[13] *Statesman,* 297–303.
[14] *Politics,* III, 6–7. See also Plato's *Laws,* IV, 715.
[15] *Politics,* III, 11, 16–17; VII, 14; III, 3, 9.
[16] *Laws,* V–VI. *Politics,* II, 9; III, 11; IV, 9; V, 9; VII, 3, 4, 8, 14.

ship between equals, each rendering voluntary loyalty to a government having lawful authority.[17] Another scholar speaks of "constitutionalism" as the essential legacy that the *Politics* bequeathed to the common thought of Europe.[18]

From the foregoing it is clear that the *polis* is radically different from the modern state, and not merely in size. A *polis*, as Aristotle put it, is a body of persons who, under a constitution, share in deliberative and judicial offices for the purpose of achieving together a perfect and self-sufficient existence.[19] And for both Aristotle and Plato, a perfect and self-sufficient existence was a life of virtue and well-being. It is common enough to think of the modern state as having as its aim the *welfare* of its citizens, but it would be most uncommon to interpret this welfare as the *virtue* of the citizens. Confusion over this fundamental difference is at least partly responsible for the charge that Plato especially was a totalitarian thinker who not only advocated rule by a few and condoned slavery, but went so far as to have the "state" outlaw art forms that he found unpalatable. This charge is not *wholly* beside the mark, but it cannot be assessed without taking into account the vast difference between the city-state of ancient Greece and the modern state. The city-state that both Plato and Aristotle were talking about has been said to be "a church as well as a state"; certainly, according to Plato's and Aristotle's conceptions, it is as much concerned as any church with the virtue of its citizens, although the resemblance ends soon thereafter. Whereas one might now be inclined to say that a person's *virtue* is the state's business only to the extent to which this is required to guarantee the *rights* of other persons, any such restriction probably would have made no sense to Plato and Aristotle. They did not think of the *polis* in terms of rights, and they would have considered it wrong to limit the welfare at which the modern state supposedly aims to protection of either rights or external goods. They were guilty of a parochialism in looking upon people as divided into classes in the way they did, but they conceived of people as living together in a communal and cooperative life in a way that we, perhaps

---

[17] G. H. Sabine, *History of Political Theory*, 3rd ed. (New York: Holt, Rinehart & Winston, Inc., 1961), p. 144.
[18] Barker, *The Politics of Aristotle*, Introduction, p. lxi.
[19] *Politics*, III, 1, 6, 9.

through our own parochialism, find difficult to imagine. Since the greatest threat to the community of the *polis* was taken by Plato and Aristotle to come from those who conceived of "justice" as the "stronger gaining their own interests," they often seem to have been writing for us today. Their deep sense of what is necessary in order to have a cooperative community, however, is but one of the major lessons they have to offer us.

The Philosophy of the Cosmopolis: Cicero and the Medieval Christians

The city-states of Greece were in a sad decline even as Plato and Aristotle sought to describe their ideal form. Not choosing isolation one from the other, these city-states nevertheless failed to maintain a firm alliance, and no one of them was able to establish permanent hegemony. Larger political units were needed. The Empire of Macedonia filled the natural breach for a time and then gave way to Rome. The ideal of a *cosmopolis,* or world community, succeeded the ideal of the *polis.*

In light of actual events, it became impossible to think realistically of the city-state as a self-sufficient community or of the exercise of citizenship in it as constituting the good life. With the breakdown of the communal ideal of the city-state, and with nothing resembling the modern nation as a political unit, there arose, on the one hand, a new individualism, and, at the opposite extreme, a new universalism. As part of the former, philosophers constructed the hopeless ideal of the individually self-sufficient "wise man," an ideal that was given different forms by the different philosophical schools. But, as Aristotle observed, since only a beast or a god could live apart from the state, some account had to be given of society in place of Plato's and Aristotle's accounts of the city-state. The society that caught the eye of these philosophers, perhaps with the help of Alexander the Great, was the "society of all men." Some of them, the Epicureans and skeptics, impressed by the great differences in customs of different peoples, discarded all notion of an ideal state and came to the view that laws, at best, are useful conventions. The Stoics, on the other hand, took the position that all persons, Greek and barbarian, masters and slaves, belong to the same "herd" and constitute one human society. When Saint Paul said, "There is neither Jew nor Greek, there is neither slave nor free, there is neither male nor female . . ." he expressed an idea as much Stoic as Christian.[20]

This idea of the unity of humanity, although it constituted a fundamental departure from the "politics" of Plato and Aristotle, became joined with that "politics" by the middle period of Stoicism. The two together, somewhat diluted by the mixture, were transmitted to Europe through the great intellectual influence of Cicero (106–43 B.C.) and through their embodiment in Roman law. In the early Stoicism after Aristotle, the unity of all persons was based on the theoretical idea of each person's having the capacity to free himself from all feeling and to follow reason, the Law of Nature, and God. But Cicero recommended kindness, benevolence, and humanitarian feelings as virtues. By the time of Cicero, moreover, there was a tendency to confuse the Law of Nature of the Stoics with the actual law *(jus gentium)* that had grown up in trying to decide equitably those cases to which Roman civil law *(jus civile)* did not apply, namely, cases involving aliens. Cicero the lawyer, much indebted to Stoicism, though he wrote two dialogues on the general plan of Plato, united these influences.[21] He firmly believed in the sovereignty of law, but this was no longer the law of the *polis*. It was primarily the law of reason in which God and human beings share, by which civil law is judged, which gives rights to all, and before which all are equal:

> . . . *True law is right reason in agreement with nature; it is of universal application, unchanging and everlasting; it summons to duty by its commands, and averts from wrongdoing by its prohibitions. And it does not lay its commands or prohibitions upon good men in vain, though neither have any effect on the wicked. It is a sin to try to alter this law, nor is it allowable to attempt to repeal any part of it, and it is impossible to abolish it entirely. We cannot be freed from its obligations by senate or*

[20] Gal. 3:28.
[21] *De Legibus*, I, v. This and the following quotations are from *Cicero: De Re Publica; De Legibus*, trans. C. W. Keyes (Cambridge, Mass.: Harvard University Press, 1928). By permission of the Loeb Classical Library and the Harvard University Press.

people, and we need not look outside ourselves for an expounder or interpreter of it. And there will not be different laws at Rome and at Athens, or different laws now and in the future, but one eternal and unchangeable law will be valid for all nations and all times, and there will be one master and ruler, that is, God, over us all, for he is the author of this law, its promulgator, and its enforcing judge. Whoever is disobedient is fleeing from himself and denying his human nature, and by reason of this very fact he will suffer the worst penalties, even if he escapes what is commonly considered punishment. . . .[22]

. . . Law is the highest reason, implanted in Nature, which commands what ought to be done and forbids the opposite. This reason, when firmly fixed and fully developed in the human mind, is Law.[23]

On the commonwealth Cicero spoke through Scipio as follows:

Well, then, a commonwealth is the property of a people. But a people is not any collection of human beings brought together in any sort of way, but an assemblage of people in large numbers associated in an agreement with respect to justice and a partnership for the common good. The first cause of such an association is not so much the weakness of the individual as a certain social spirit which nature has implanted in man.[24]

And Cicero on the unity of humanity said:

. . . we are born for Justice, and that right is based, not upon men's opinions, but upon Nature. This fact will immediately be plain if you once get a clear conception of man's fellowship and union with his fellow-men. For no single thing is so like another, so exactly its counterpart, as all of us are to one another. Nay, if bad habits and false beliefs did not twist the weaker minds and turn them in whatever direction they are inclined, no one would be so like his own self as all men would be like all others. And so, however we may define man, a single definition will apply to all.[25]

[22] *De Re Publica*, III, xxii.
[23] *De Legibus*, I, vi.
[24] *De Re Publica*, I, xxv.
[25] *De Legibus*, I, x.

. . . From this it is clear that, when a wise man shows toward another endowed with equal virtue the kind of benevolence which is so widely diffused among men, that will then have come to pass which, unbelievable as it seems to some, is after all the inevitable result—namely, that he loves himself no whit more than he loves another. For what difference can there be among things which are all equal? [26]

These ideas were easily adopted by the early Christians. What essentially needed to be added was the completion of the above quotation from Saint Paul: "For ye are all one in Christ Jesus." To the Stoics' Law of Nature, there was added the revealed Word of God, and this Word was thought to be embodied in a new institution, the Church, representing the union of all in Christ. Stoics had spoken of a city of Zeus; this city was converted into a Christian City of God. For Aristotle, persons attained the greatest self-sufficiency through citizenship in the *polis*, and for Cicero, by living according to reason, but for the early Christian, the only self-sufficiency was that of God, and the only way of attaining it was by union with God made possible by the revelation of Christ. The Christian could quote Plato and Cicero in arguing that civil law was subject to the judgment of higher authority; but in claiming that the way to virtue and salvation was in the Church, as distinguished from the state, he broke sharply with both Greek and Roman thought.

As might be expected, all Christians were not of the same mind on the proper role of the state vis-à-vis the Church. Some regarded life in the state as punishment for sin, while others took a much more favorable view of the role of the state, as exemplified later by the reign of Charlemagne. But all agreed that the goods of this world were as nothing compared with the salvation to be gained only within the Church, and the Church was soon declared to have an authority independent of that of the state. The function of the state was thus distinctly limited, a person's greatest good was to be found outside its jurisdiction, and liberty from its encroachments became an issue for the future. As one writer put it recently, ". . . the belief in spiritual autonomy and the right of spiritual freedom left a residuum

[26] *Ibid.*, I, xii.

without which modern ideas of individual privacy and liberty would be scarcely intelligible." [27]

Since every society except perhaps the most primitive requires political organization, a view of the state as essentially evil could hardly predominate. What developed in its place was the doctrine of the two cities, one temporal and the other eternal, each with its own organization, jurisdiction, and interests, each person being subject to the authority of both. This became the accepted doctrine in late antiquity, and it persisted in the Middle Ages. All the major influences we have discussed were united in the intellectual formulation of this doctrine by Saint Thomas Aquinas (1225–1274). First of all, he was a Christian and much influenced by the Church Fathers, especially by Saint Augustine (354–430), author of the *City of God*. But he also had great respect for Aristotle, "The Philosopher," whose works were just becoming known to the Latin West; Saint Thomas wrote extensive commentaries on a number of them, including the *Nicomachean Ethics* and a part of the *Politics*. Finally, he was influenced by Cicero, to some extent directly and through Roman law, much more through the Church Fathers. Saint Thomas, interpreting Aristotle, called the state "a perfect community," whose natural end is to promote the common good of all of its citizens by giving them peace, satisfying their needs, and enabling them to act well. This end is implanted by God in the social nature of human beings; as such it is dictated by the "natural law" laid down by God, and no "human positive law" should violate it. This prescribes the fundamental obligation of any temporal ruling authority, whatever the form of government. If a monarch rules in his own interest, and thus by Aristotle's classification becomes a tyrant, he may be rightfully deposed, provided the common good will be promoted; absolutely speaking, his self-serving edicts are not laws. Within "his own order," however, a nontyrannical prince is supreme; sedition is a sin against nature and the common good.

Law by Saint Thomas' definition is "an ordinance of reason for the common good, promulgated by him who has the care of the community." In addition to natural law and human posi-

[27] Sabine, *History of Political Theory*, p. 196.

tive law, divided into *jus civile* and *jus gentium,* there is the "divine law" which is the revelation of God through Christ, and the Church is its keeper. Thus the state is naturally ordered and subject to the Church, as the body is ordered and subject to the soul. Both state and Church aim at the good of their subjects, and each has its proper domain, but one domain— that concerned with salvation through grace—is superior. As grace presupposes nature, the Church presupposes the state; but the former perfect the latter, not vice versa. If all are properly ordered, however, all will reflect the perfection of the eternal law of God that is manifested in different ways in human law, natural law, and divine law.[28]

In considering the relation of state to Church, Saint Thomas was concerned primarily with a theological, rather than a practical, question. It was inevitable that those writing more with practice in mind would not maintain so delicate a balance. Some, like John of Paris, Marsilius of Padua, and William of Ockham, in the late thirteenth and fourteenth centuries, would stress the state as an independent community and allocate to the Church a strictly spiritual function. Others, like Giles of Rome, would choose the other side, the supremacy of the Church over temporal as well as spiritual matters, and emphasize the supreme sovereignty of the pope as its head. Opposite sides were taken on various questions, the investiture of bishops, the right of the Church to veto the choice of emperor, the limits on papal authority, etc. Elaborate arguments developed for the divine right of the pope, a right that was challenged on the traditional ground that any authority a ruler has is conferred by law with the consent of all. To support their arguments, opponents of papal supremacy could draw not only on classical sources, which they did, but also on feudal custom, according to which the "lord" is bound by obligations to his vassals and holds his office under the law which belongs to all. Both these traditions are expressed in the words of the thirteenth-century lawyer Bracton: "Let [the king] therefore bestow upon the law what

---

[28] See especially, *De Regno* (or the part of *De Regimine Principum* by Saint Thomas) and the Treatise on Law in *Summa Theologiae,* I, II, Q90 ff. Saint Thomas' political views, however, are scattered throughout his writing, e.g., II, II, Q42, Q60, 6 *ad* 3, etc.

the law bestows upon him, namely, rule and power. For there is no *rex* [king] where will rules rather than *lex* [law]." [29]

After Saint Thomas the new political philosophy of the national state began to develop. Up to this point, it is to be especially noted, the state was generally conceived on the classical model, as having the positive function of serving the needs and promoting the well-being of its citizens. Thirteen centuries after the beginning of the Church of Rome, as indicated above, some spoke of the state as the perfect and self-sufficient society, at least with regard to the goods obtainable in this life. The big change came with the breakdown of feudalism and the rise of national monarchies. The doctrine that popes enjoyed rule by a divine right became less an issue than the doctrine of the divine right of kings. Modern political philosophy began in the sixteenth century, confronted by a new state of affairs: greatly strengthened monarchs, supported by a new class of merchants, in a number of increasingly powerful and competing nation-states. The *cosmopolis,* which for a long time had been revered more in theory than in fact, fell apart.

Some Basic Questions of Political Philosophy

Before proceeding to the philosophy of the modern state it is important to examine, even if only briefly, the character of political philosophy and some of its basic questions. Why should persons living in society give their support to something as inherently powerful and threatening as a political system? Why do they need a "state"? What functions should it perform? What goals should it promote? And who should have supreme political authority and be "sovereign"? These are some of the basic questions that have engaged the attention of political philosophers.

The major ancient and medieval philosophers tried to

[29] H. Bracton, *Legibus et Consuetudinibus Angliae (On the Laws and Customs of England),* Samuel Thorne and G. E. Woodbine (Eds.) (Cambridge, Mass.: published in association with the Selden Society by the Belknap Press of Harvard University Press, 1968), II, p. 33; see also pp. 305–306.

answer such questions. Plato and Aristotle saw the *polis* as designed by nature to make a society of individuals self-sufficient in goods, fully developed in talents and virtues. As Cicero saw it, the Roman Empire should promote justice and the common good, in accord with the law of reason and nature. The medieval kingship, on Saint Thomas' view, should provide a sufficiency of earthly goods and virtues and, in harmony with the Church, lead persons to God. The goals assigned by seventeenth- and eighteenth-century philosophers to the modern state, as we shall see, were considerably less grand. In keeping with a new individualism, these philosophers thought of the state as more specialized and more limited. Large areas of people's lives—their science, their art, and much of their social lives—were increasingly regarded as outside the domain of the state and politics.

This fundamental change in political philosophy reveals a decided ambiguity in many basic questions in political philosophy. Expressions such as "the political system," "government," and the like, take their meaning from the forms of political organization that exist at a given time. Since a *polis* or a medieval principality differs substantially from the modern state, it should not be assumed that they have the same nature, functions, and goals. At the same time, the modern philosophers represented in the readings in this book are perhaps most readily understood, at least in a preliminary way, if one finds their answers to the basic questions. The forms of government they considered are sufficiently similar to make the questions intelligible, and a comparison of their answers with answers to corresponding questions about the *polis* and other early political societies can be very illuminating. Such comparisons reveal important characteristics of modern governments, their strengths as well as their weaknesses. They also yield the kind of characterization of the state, shared by so many, that was referred to on page 5 (we now put it slightly differently): "Government" or "the state" is the system of offices in a society that has supreme power and authority to promulgate laws and to use legitimate coercion. So conceived, a state is an organization of offices within a society; sometimes a society so organized is called a state.

But how, it may be asked, can questions about the functions and goals of the state be well formed, in view of Weber's point above that there are no ends that *all* political organizations have recognized, and there is hardly any end that has not been pursued by some? One reply, as has been suggested, is that many political systems are at least sufficiently similar to make an inquiry into their goals significant. Another reply is that Weber, as he acknowledged, was seeking a *sociological* definition of the state; he was interested in determining the place and nature of political organization in actual societies. The traditional political philosophers, on the other hand, were not simply trying to say what goals states actually pursue—some thought this was all too evident—but also what goals they *ought* to pursue. Similarly, with respect to the functions of the state, they were not primarily asking what functions states *do* perform, but what functions they *ought* to perform; and they were concerned not with who has *de facto* power or sovereignty, but with who *ought* to have power and be the *rightful* sovereign. Some of them were trying to delineate the general character of the *best* form of government, at least for their time and country. As philosophers put it, they often were asking not *factual* questions, but *normative* questions.

This point is even more evident if we raise a group of important questions closely related to those above, such as, "Why and to what extent is one obligated to obey the laws of the state?" or "What is the nature of political obligation?" These questions, which often are of great practical concern, are sometimes said to be the most fundamental of all; the inquiry into the purposes, functions, and nature of the state is a search for the principles relevant to reasoned answers.

If adequate answers to such questions are to be found, the meanings of certain crucial concepts and terms must be analyzed. This has been the major concern of much recent political philosophy. What is meant when it is said that human beings by nature have certain basic rights? What are "rights" and how can some be determined to be "natural"? In the Declaration of Independence it is said:

We hold these truths to be self-evident, that all men are created equal, that they are endowed by their Creator with certain unalienable Rights, that among these are Life, Liberty and the pursuit of Happiness.—That to secure these rights, Govern-

*ments are instituted among Men, deriving their just powers from
the consent of the governed. . . .*

What do the critical terms here mean? How, for example, is
"consent" to be taken? Which of the several theories of consent presented in the readings in this book is most pertinent?
Should "self-evident truths" be taken in the sense of Cicero's
law of reason? (A similar doctrine influenced Jefferson, by way
of the writings of Locke.) Moreover, in characterizing the state
we used the terms *sovereign* and *authority*. What do they mean?
And in what sense are all men "equal"? Some philosophers
claim that the careful analysis of such terms and expressions is
the principal business of political philosophy. We shall participate in the enterprise to some extent when we come to *justice*
and *the common good* in Part III.[30]

Traditionally, however, political philosophy has primarily
been concerned with finding systematic answers to the basic
normative questions. Most of the philosophers represented in
this book have proposed "theories of the state"—usually with
an eye toward either *justifying* political institutions or *criticizing*
them. These theories, generally speaking, give an account not
only of the nature, functions, and goals of the state but also of
the most desirable form of government (especially, who should
have sovereign authority) and the source, character, and limits
of the obligation to obey government. (Like the basic questions,
these points are interrelated.) In this volume our major business
is to become acquainted with these theories and to assess the
reasons and arguments that each theory offers in its defense. A
careful analysis and assessment is essential if one is to develop
a reasoned view of the state in contrast to an *ideology* (taken as
a rationalization of one's political predilections or economic
interests).

Since political philosophy is concerned with normative
questions, it is very closely related to ethics, or moral philosophy,
broadly conceived. It is sometimes said to be an application of
moral philosophy, because it uses moral or ethical principles
in evaluating political organizations and institutions. (It also

[30] For a taste of this "analytical political philosophy," see some of the
papers in A. Quinton (Ed.), *Political Philosophy* (London: Oxford University Press, 1967).

tries to determine what principles should be used.) One should bear in mind, however, that normative questions are often closely tied to factual questions and that the selection of the "relevant facts" for a given case depends on one's moral or political philosophy. For example, if one takes the simple "teleological" view that a state is good, and obedience to it justified, insofar as it promotes a certain goal (such as the welfare of the citizens), then it becomes highly important to consider what measures actually promote this end (assuming that it can be clarified) and what consequences have actually followed when governments have undertaken to promote this and similar ends. On this account, there is no sharp dividing line between political philosophy on the one hand and certain branches of social science (such as political and economic history, political sociology, etc.) on the other.

Although political philosophy depends on moral philosophy, it is a mistake to think that one must get his moral philosophy perfectly straight before his political philosophy can be developed. Often it is the other way around, and most of the political philosophers represented in this volume were doing moral and political philosophy at the same time. The two often go along together. For example, if a political philosopher rejects the "teleological" approach just mentioned and adopts the "deontological" view that a state is justified, or good, insofar as it is in accord wth self-evident natural law, then he will almost certainly subscribe to the ethical view that actions are morally right insofar as they conform to this law.

Part II of this book contains both a discussion and selections from the works of four major political philosophers of the modern state. The first of these, Hobbes, was more than any other person the founder of modern political philosophy. Those before him had made it abundantly and lastingly clear that conventional political forms and the customary use of political power are properly subject to rational criticism and moral control. This was the most important element in the legacy of Socrates and his followers: Plato and Aristotle, Cicero, Saint Augustine, and Saint Thomas. Hobbes conceived his task in a new way: Impressed by the new mathematics and mechanics and the tragedy of the English civil war, he undertook to develop a "scientific" theory of the state and a defense of political power. Both of these were to be based on a "scientific" view of human nature.

The other three philosophers of Part II, Locke, Hume, and Rousseau, are included in order to present three of the most important points of view in modern political philosophy. Locke turned to the natural law tradition of Cicero and Saint Thomas, but he used it in order to establish certain "natural rights," which in turn would require that government should rest on the consent of the governed. Natural law was thus made to serve a social contract and democratic ends. Although very much an eclectic, Locke was a "deontologist" in his natural law theory.

Utilizing Hobbes' insights, but putting them in a more sensible form, Hume vigorously attacked Locke's doctrine of self-evident moral principles. After presenting a series of negative arguments that many still find decisive, he gave his own positive account of rights, rooting them in social conventions or practices, and then proceeded to his teleological view of government. Because Hume regarded the end of both conventions and government as "the happiness of mankind," and because he emphasized their usefulness in promoting this end, he is properly called a "utilitarian." And because he determined the moral rightness of many acts by useful conventional *rules,* not by the usefulness of the *acts* themselves, he may be called a "rule-utilitarian." In most respects Hume differed from Locke.

Rousseau differed from them both; he neither appealed to a self-evident natural law nor took utility to be the primary or only standard of good government. Giving Locke's contract theory a new twist, Rousseau insisted that if people are to act morally, they must live under laws that each one freely accepts. His fundamental emphasis was on personal moral autonomy, the capacity and right of each person to live under laws that he lays down for himself. Thus the fundamental requirement of any morally acceptable government is that all persons freely subscribe to a common body of law. This is Rousseau's "general will," the object of which is the common good.

In Part III the reader will become acquainted with the two most important and influential political philosophies of the nineteenth century: the organic theory of Hegel and his followers and the utilitarianism of Bentham and J. S. Mill. Part III also includes an analytical exercise in sorting out, and trying to give some order to, the many complex elements that enter into our conceptions of justice and the common good. In the selection from Marx, the reader will find an organic radical view of the economic roots of what we call injustice; in J. S. Mill, he will find a classic expression of the liberal utilitarian's defense of liberty; in T. H. Green, he will find an argument for the primacy of "the common good" and, at the same time, a statement of the organic liberalism of a British Hegelian. And finally, he will find in John Rawls the elements of a new theory of justice, the central theme of which was laid down by Rousseau and Kant, and the development of which weaves together many other views presented in this volume. Rawls' theory offers a new synthesis.

Bibliography

Of general interest:

Benn, S. I., and R. S. Peters, *The Principles of Political Thought.* New York: The Free Press, 1965. (Originally published as *Social Principles and the Democratic State.* London: George Allen & Unwin Ltd., 1959.)

Field, G. C., *Political Theory.* London: Methuen & Co. Ltd., 1956.

Friedrich, C. J., "Government," in *Encyclopaedia Britannica,* Vol. 10, pp. 616–623. Chicago: 1964.

Mabbott, J. D., *The State and the Citizen: An Introduction to Political Philosophy.* London: Hutchinson University Library, 1948.

Passerin d'Entrèves, A., *The Notion of the State: An Introduction to Political Theory.* Oxford: The Clarendon Press, 1967.

On political and social theory:

Barry, B., *Political Argument.* London: Routledge & Kegan Paul Ltd., 1965.

Barry, B., *Sociologists, Economists and Democracy.* London: Collier-Macmillan Ltd., 1970.

Berlin, I., "Does Political Theory Still Exist?" in *Philosophy, Politics and Society,* second series, P. Laslett and W. G.

Runciman (Eds.). Oxford: Basil Blackwell & Mott Ltd., 1962.

Easton, D., *The Political System*. New York: Alfred A. Knopf, Inc., 1953.

Gewirth, A., *Political Philosophy,* Introduction. New York: The Macmillan Company, 1965.

MacDonald, M., "The Language of Political Theory," in *Logic and Language,* first series, A. Flew (Ed.). Oxford: Basil Blackwell & Mott Ltd., 1951.

Plamenatz, J., "The Use of Political Theory," in *Political Philosophy,* A. Quinton (Ed.). London: Oxford University Press, 1967.

Strauss, L., *What Is Political Philosophy? And Other Studies.* Glencoe, Ill.: The Free Press, 1959.

Weldon, T. D., *The Vocabulary of Politics.* Baltimore, Md.: Penguin Books, Inc., 1953.

On ancient and medieval social theory:

Friedrich, C. J., *The Philosophy of Law in Historical Perspective,* 2nd ed., Ch. 1–9. Chicago: University of Chicago Press, 1963.

McIlwain, C. H., *The Growth of Political Thought in the West, from the Greeks to the End of the Middle Ages.* New York: The Macmillan Company, 1932.

Sabine, G. H., *A History of Political Theory,* 3rd ed., Parts I and II. New York: Holt, Rinehart & Winston, Inc., 1961.

II

The Classical Philosophy of the Modern State

The State as Sovereign: Hobbes

During the formative period of the modern state, a vigorous individualism, sprung from many seeds, created new ideals that gradually altered almost every major European institution. This individualism took many forms, one notable example of which was the protestant defense of the primacy of conscience and of the right of each person to interpret scripture for himself. Political philosophy was deeply affected, as the writings of Hobbes, Locke, and Hume reveal. The political theories of all three are variants of what might be labeled "the individualist philosophy of the modern state." [1]

The new individualism was expressed in the sixteenth century not only in the protestant opposition to traditional Catholic doctrine, but in a thoroughly secular view of human nature. On this view, a human being is not an image of the Christian God but a self-seeking animal born with the fundamental problem of how to use his intelligence to advance his own egoistic ends. Machiavelli (1469–1527)—with many examples of such animals in high places around him—has usually been taken to express this view in *The Prince*. Thomas Hobbes (1588–1679), however, was the first to present a fully developed philosophical statement of this new view.

Hobbes wrote his *Leviathan* during the period of the En-

---

[1] In the eighteenth century, modern individualism took a still different form in Adam Smith's theory of "natural liberty" and the "invisible hand," Smith's expression of the doctrine of laissez-faire (according to which economic well-being naturally emerges from each individual's pursuing his own self-interest). And in the nineteenth century, as we shall see in Part III, laissez-faire itself had a variant form in the political individualism of some early utilitarians.

glish civil war in order to support strong government. More important, he undertook to give a scientific account of the state, one based not on ancient or medieval ideas, but on the "new" science. Tremendously impressed by mathematics and mechanics, Hobbes regarded the whole of the natural world as a vast array of moving bodies, and he undertook to develop a philosophy in which all human behavior, political included, was to be explained on mechanical principles. In the Introduction to the *Leviathan,* which is Hobbes' name for the Commonwealth or State, he said "life is but a motion of limbs, the beginning whereof is in some principal part within." He then proceeded to account for those motions within us, beginning with the motions of "sense," from which all "thoughts" as well as all acts or "external motions" arise.

Hobbes did not stop there, however. Instead of regarding human beings, in accordance with traditional doctrine, as naturally social, he regarded each person as mechanically geared to seek self-satisfaction, and thereby to "corroborate his vital motion." And since people are much alike, and compete for the same things, he assumed that power in the hands of one individual is a threat to the others and that each naturally seeks domination over others. Human beings are thus so many opposed forces, natural enemies, in a condition of "war of every man against every man." However, their fears and desires lead them to hope for something better; and reason, by discovering precepts for their "conservation and defense," points the way. Hobbes called these precepts "natural laws"; although calling them "laws" is improper, he suggests, since they are not "commands of a sovereign."

This was a new interpretation of the traditional doctrine of natural law. For Hobbes, a natural law was still an "ordinance of reason," but it was no longer primarily or directly for the common good in the sense of Saint Thomas' definition of law. It was, instead, a rule for the enlightenment of self-interest, a precept for attaining one's natural end. He nevertheless saw the laws of nature as promoting a common good, because every person's self-interest is best served by peace. His first law of nature prescribes that one seek peace if it is possible; fourteen or so other laws prescribe means for attaining it. Since the particular laws prescribe that a person be just, grateful, sociable, merciful, and the like, Hobbes also associated them with "moral virtues" and said that the science of them is the "true and only moral philosophy." [2]

With this view of humanity as a foundation, Hobbes completed his "scientific" account of the origin of the state. Reason's laws and whatever virtuous endeavors they may instill are contrary to self-interested natural passion; on account of this contrariety, "covenants, without the sword, are but words." The way to become assured that natural laws will be followed, and thus made effective, is by each individual, through covenant with the others and in accordance with the second law of nature, which prescribes that a person be willing to relinquish rights provided others are equally willing, granting all his power to one person (or one assembly) that will have absolute power and authority to act for him and keep the peace. With the exception of certain elementary rights that cannot be transferred—no individual, for example, can be obliged to kill, maim, or accuse himself—all rights must be granted to this one Person, the Sovereign. This is the only way, apart from conquest, that a commonwealth can be generated. Hobbes' argument for an absolute sovereign power will be found, abridged, in the readings.

In contrast to earlier approaches, Hobbes' view is thoroughly individualistic. The power that must be granted the sovereign is in direct proportion to humanity's self-interestedness. Each individual by nature seeks good for himself; and the state, somewhat paradoxically, is a natural product of the endeavors or forces of the individuals who compose it. Moreover, once constituted, society and the state are nothing other than these individuals; the "commonwealth" is a multitude of individuals united in a sovereign of whose acts they are the author. Finally, the goal of the state is nothing other than the goods of its members. Whereas on Plato's and Aristotle's view, one would attain his good in considerable measure by exercising the "role" or "office" of citizen, for Hobbes, one's good, insofar as this makes sense, is describable in terms of his pleasures or "vital motion," without any reference to the state or any office in it. The state does not constitute the institutional forms that the good life takes; it has become a pure instrument.

[2] This discussion is found in *Leviathan*, XIV and XV, parts of which are included below.

In order to understand Hobbes' thought, it is very important to consider this individualistic analysis of the state. But Hobbes' individualism, although it had a very great influence, was not the striking feature of his thought to his contemporaries. What caught their attention was the mechanical and self-interested view of human nature, and its counterpart, the argument for a sovereign who must be absolute in order to keep the peace and thereby perform the single function in terms of which the state is properly defined. Although many were highly critical, the elementary cogency of Hobbes' argument was not lost; those who came later often rejected the union of "might and right," but they still used a version of the argument to explain the necessity of the state.

One of Hobbes' contributions, however, seems to have been overlooked. "So long as a man is in the condition of mere nature," he said, "private appetite is the measure of good." Morality, on the other hand, is fundamentally social; it is a matter of "what is good and evil, in the conversation and society of mankind." [3] If this includes, on the one hand, natural laws, it also includes, on the other, both the covenant necessary to guarantee the peace and the sovereign's commands that establish "a common rule of good" in the form of civil law. Civil law, consisting in rules for the distinction of right from wrong, is necessary to make natural law externally binding. It is thus a distinctive feature of Hobbes' philosophy that where there is no commonwealth, and no commands of the commonwealth, there nothing is unjust. Although this view of the social and contractual origin and ground of rights, justice, and a society's morality needs critique and revision, Hobbes should be credited with having pointed out an important dimension of social morality that had been left obscure and confused in traditional natural law theory.

Hobbes was perhaps the most original of all philosophers of the modern state. Those who followed him either were influenced by his individualistic account of the state; or were led to adopt some of his positive views, especially those concerning justice, law, and morality; or found him the chief opponent to contend with—sometimes in combination. Many today use his

[3] Hobbes, *Leviathan,* **XV.**

views on such topics as "authority" or "sovereignty" as the start-ing-point for their own analyses. It is probably impossible to escape his influence completely. In assessing this influence, it is especially important to observe, as some adherents of monarchy among Hobbes' contemporaries noted, that he did not require sovereignty to be vested in a monarch. He did insist, however, that if a complex society is to exist, given the natural propensities of human beings, there must be some sovereign political power. This is a position to which many persons subscribe today, as was pointed out in Part I. Interpreted in this general way, the basic point of Hobbes' political doctrine, like the point of view of his psychology, is still with us.

The State as Defender of Natural Rights: Locke

All who prize human rights, especially the right of persons to govern themselves, owe a great debt to John Locke (1632–1704), who more than any other brought these rights to the forefront of political thought. With his usual common sense, Locke saw that the morality of rights and justice cannot be ultimately based on arbitrary will or mere convention. At the same time, he was so intent on the evil of tyranny, and in ap-pealing to the good sense of humanity so much influenced by traditional theory, that he failed to take advantage of Hobbes' contribution, although some of what he said could have been subscribed to by Hobbes. What was needed was a rethinking of the basic problems of political philosophy and a whole new perspective on natural law theory. This was a task too great for any one person, and Locke was not exclusively, or even pri-marily, a political philosopher.

When Locke spoke of natural law as "the right rule of rea-son" and as "the common rule and measure God has given to mankind, . . . as intelligible and plain to a rational creature and a studier of that law as the positive laws of commonwealths . . . which are only so far right as they are founded on the law of nature" (*Second Treatise,* Ch. 2, §§10–12), he might have been taken as a spokesman for either Cicero or Saint Thomas; and similarly when he spoke of one community or society of all humanity under natural law (*Second Treatise,* Ch. 9, §128).

Through the writings of the oft-cited "judicious Hooker," Locke *was* influenced by Saint Thomas, but he made a new use of natural law. He interpreted it as establishing primarily a natural and equal liberty of each person to do what he wills within the limits of natural law, thus to be naturally free from the constraining will of any other. This "perfect freedom," which belongs equally to each individual by nature, is violated whenever anyone infringes on another's life, liberty, or possessions, all three of which Locke usually included within a person's "property." This fundamental requirement of a perfect and equal freedom of each person under natural law is central to Locke's whole political philosophy; it sets the "great and chief end of political society," which is, in Locke's peculiar sense, "the preservation of property."

If "natural liberty" is liberty in what Locke called "the state of nature," and if the latter is the supposed state in which humanity is governed solely by natural law, then it surely follows that a human being has a natural liberty to do anything not proscribed by natural law. The crux of Locke's doctrine depends not so much on his idea that human beings have a "natural liberty," as on what he took natural liberty to include, and this in turn depends on what he assumed natural law to require. The point can be seen by comparing Locke with Hobbes: Hobbes granted humanity a natural right that includes, with some restrictions, a liberty of each person to impose his will on another; for Locke, however, many such impositions of one person's will on another were just what natural liberty, or natural law, most prominently excluded.

It should also be emphasized that when Locke spoke of natural law he was no more speaking of a law descriptive of how men actually behave than was Cicero or Saint Thomas. He was not saying that human beings are equal in fact, but that they are equal from the moral point of view, that each person has an equal moral right to freedom—that is, a moral right not to be subjected to the constraint of another person's will but to be subject as a rational being only to the moral law itself. This is a fundamentally important idea: Freely interpreted, it means that a person can be morally obligated or bound to do something only if reason (and not just the will of another person) requires it. If Locke had developed this idea, he might have ended with a position well ahead of his time. He did pursue it to some extent, but perhaps with more of an eye on practice than on theory: The only way in which a person's natural freedom from another person's will can be preserved is by joining together with others in society under laws to which he gives his consent. Only in this way can a person live under his own will within the limits of natural law. Rightful authority of positive law or government must thus be derived from the consent of the governed; without this consent, law would lack authority and not be law. The consent that is required for the constitution of a lawful community, moreover, is the consent of *everyone*.

Locke did not develop the implications of the idea of moral or natural freedom much beyond this point. Having gone this far toward constructing a theory of rightful authority and government his philosophical imagination retreated before the practical problem of how unanimity is to be achieved. It appeared to Locke that the only rational or sensible course is for everyone to agree to accept majority decisions, but his theory made no clear distinction between "what it is rational to consent to" and "what men consent to," and gave no preference to "rational consent" over "actual consent" as the source of authority. Instead of confronting this kind of difficulty, Locke became embroiled in questions about when persons can be said to give their consent, and to do so "tacitly." His treatment of this problem, like his treatment of many others, hardly makes a tidy package, but then Locke was not the kind of philosopher to suppress difficulties in the interest of tidiness.

Although he viewed the individual differently from Hobbes, Locke was just as much of an individualist. The basic reason for persons to join in political society lies in the "inconveniences of the state of nature," and if these are not so great as in Hobbes' state of war, they are of the same kind. If some persons were not corrupt and vicious, there would be no need of political society. Thus, although Locke gave natural law a central place in his system, and by citing Hooker frequently appealed to traditional doctrine, he did not regard the state as having the positive function that traditional theory assigned it.

Locke conceived of the state negatively, as created in order to preserve and protect something, namely "property," the lives, liberties, and possessions of its members. To be sure, he often mentioned "the public good," and once went so far as to endorse the proposition that "the good of the people is the supreme law." But he interpreted this proposition primarily in terms of fair representation in the legislature; in general, he saw the "great and chief end" of political society as the kind of good of its members that can be adequately described without making any reference either to the state or to society. The chief function of the state is to serve as an instrument for the protection of its members' "property"; its function is not along with other social institutions to help develop "human nature," and certainly not to add anything to it, but to keep certain degenerative tendencies from interfering with its natural development. There is no evidence of a greater perception of what society can offer a person, by offering him cooperative enterprises and opportunities to fill offices and roles in an institutional order, than we attributed to Hobbes. In fact, there is less. On Locke's view, persons can engage in social practices, like speaking, promising, owning and exchanging property, and using money, in a state of nature outside of any actual society. Correspondingly, they can be under obligations to tell the truth, to keep promises, to respect others' property, and to bargain fairly in a state of nature according to a morality which is self-evident to rational beings. He thus conceived the morality of social practices, not as deriving in any sense from rules built into the practices, but as dictated by natural law.

Although Locke's doctrine of a rationally self-evident natural law is not persuasive, his influence, as already remarked, was incalculably great. On the most elementary point he was surely correct: Political organization and power, however much they are needed to maintain and to develop a society, are not always morally legitimate or right in their exercise; in order to be so, they must satisfy certain fundamental requirements of morality. This simple but important point probably accounts for much of Locke's influence. However, when Locke attempted to set out these requirements, he was much less cogent. Although he helped initiate the "empirical approach" of modern British philosophy, his empiricism was so mixed with the rationalism of his time that, after having insisted in the early parts of his *Essay Concerning Human Understanding* that there were no innate ideas, he could go on to say: ". . . I doubt not but from self-evident propositions by necessary consequences, as incontestable as those in mathematics, the measures of right and wrong might be made out to anyone that will apply himself with the same indifference and attention to the one as he does to the other of these sciences" (Book 4, Ch. 3, §18). From a moral point of view all persons surely ought to be accorded fundamental rights; but Locke's doctrine of "self-evidence," notwithstanding its appeal in the age of reason, provides no firmer foundation for these rights than Cicero had found for natural law. One should bear in mind, however, that Locke was not entirely single-minded: "The good of the people," if only he had developed the concept, might have provided a better foundation. Something of the same can be said of his theory of consent, but in this case Locke carried his ideas further and left us an important legacy; his theory contains points of signal importance for both systematic theory and practical politics. Moreover, Locke's many-sided discussion of resistance to tyranny, the limits of legislative power, etc., drawn from his life with Shaftesbury— a discussion omitted from the selections below—is a considerable contribution in itself.

Conventionalism and Utilitarianism: Hume

David Hume (1711–1776) is perhaps best known for his radical criticisms of a number of traditional dogmas, of which the doctrine of natural law was one. These criticisms derive from his attempt "to introduce the experimental method of reasoning into moral subjects," that is, to construct a philosophy of human nature, morals, and society from observation and experience. The result in social philosophy was not primarily destructive. Hume wove important insights of a number of his predecessors into a much more developed and a more nearly acceptable system that included: (1) a theory of morals that has been very influential; (2) an analysis of the nature of common social practices that is used in much contemporary social philosophy; and (3) a theory of government that contains one of the clearest and ablest defenses ever presented of an important view of the state.

Hume's criticism of the Lockean variety of natural law

theory proceeded along two main lines. First, Hume insisted, morality is essentially "practical"; a person's thinking that he ought to do *x,* for example, often leads him to do *x.* But reason by itself cannot motivate; one's rational perception of a truth can lead to action only if some passion or desire is aroused. Thus when one concludes that one *ought* to act in a certain way, the conclusion is not the product of reason alone; in drawing the conclusion, one expresses a certain kind of "feeling" or "sentiment" without which it would not be drawn. Second, Hume challenged the defenders of rationally evident "moral truths" to show the "relation" in virtue of which statements expressing these "truths" are self-evident or capable of demonstration. To say that it is all right for parents to abandon their children may be repugnant to one's "sentiment," but it is not to utter a "self-contradictory" statement. In virtue of *what* relation is a "moral truth" intuitively or demonstrably certain? Hume said that he could find no such relation.

By a similar line of reasoning, Hume argued that so-called "moral truths" cannot be established by observation or experience. If one observes parents mistreating their children, one may be "pained" and may express one's disapproval by saying that they ought not to do that. But how is it possible to *observe* that one *ought* not to do something? And how can one decide from statements of observable fact what one ought to do? It is this line of reasoning that has led many to extol Hume as the father of the distinction between statements of fact and statements of value, a distinction that has had an enormous vogue and inestimable effects—not all good—both on philosophy and on much of our social science.

Hume concluded that sentiment, not reason, is the source of moral distinctions. Reason can influence action only by pointing out certain matters of fact relevant to our passions and desires; in this sense, as Hume provocatively put it, "reason is, and ought only to be, the slave of the passions . . . ."

But what kind of sentiment produces moral distinctions? After considering personal qualities that human beings find virtuous, Hume decided that we approve the more important, such as justice and benevolence, because they promote the interests of humanity. Thus, although self-interest is the strongest human motive, contrary to Hobbes, it is not the only one.

Through a certain natural *sympathy,* each person is moved to approve what is agreeable or beneficial to mankind. Or as Hume put it later, along with self-interest,

> . . . *there is some benevolence, however small, infused into our bosom; some spark of friendship for human kind; some particle of the dove kneaded into our frame, along with the elements of the wolf and serpent. Let these generous sentiments be supposed ever so weak; let them be insufficient to move even a hand or finger of our body, they must still direct the determinations of our mind, and where everything else is equal, produce a cool preference of what is useful and serviceable to mankind, above what is pernicious and dangerous. A moral distinction, therefore, immediately arises; a general sentiment of blame and approbation . . . .*[4]

In the course of his argument, Hume made an additional distinction. Persons naturally develop some of the virtues, such as beneficence and generosity, that may be called "natural virtues." A person cannot, however, have a natural disposition to be "just," for a virtue of this kind depends on a kind of "artifice" or "human contrivance," or, more specifically, on "conventions" constituted by persons' coming to act according to certain general rules. In discussing justice, Hume both clarified what he meant by the "artificial virtues" and gave his analysis of social practices and the rights which depend on them. This analysis was central to his theory of both society and government, which he clearly distinguished.

Hume's view of the origin of social practices is similar to that found in Protagoras' great speech, partially quoted above, although there is more emphasis on self-interest. Society enables human beings to overcome their natural infirmities, but, in order to unite in society, they must overcome the "incommodious" conjunction of natural partiality to self and the scarcity and instability of possessions. The remedy lies in the development of conventions, or commonly accepted rules, that determine who shall have the use or enjoyment of what objects. These rules establish "rights" and "obligations" of persons relative to one another with respect to external goods; they constitute external

---

[4] *Enquiry Concerning the Principles of Morals,* IX, 1.

objects as a person's "property," as distinguished from what he physically "possesses." The notions of "rights" and "property" are thus correlative with the notion of "convention" and are unintelligible apart from it. Any notion of a "natural right" or "natural property" is absurd. Similarly, since "making a promise" is impossible without conventional rules governing promising, the notion of individuals in a state of nature "contracting" to enter society is equally absurd. Conventions are naturally entered into, out of natural needs, in the way persons might come to row a boat together, or speak according to the rules of a common language; since self-interest requires one to follow conventional rules, sometimes contrary to inclination, one may even speak of a "natural obligation of interest" to follow them. Nevertheless, conventions are "artifices" or "creations" of human beings, and until they are constituted there are no rights and no justice. This is Hume's constructive argument against natural rights.

Self-interest is so strong in human nature that it can be controlled only by itself: It is an enlightened self-interest that leads persons to form and live under conventions. As one discovers that, by rowing in unison with another, one can benefit, so one learns that by respecting "another's property," on condition that the other respect "his," he can enjoy a greater security and prosperity. Thus the first obligation to follow conventional rules is "the natural obligation of interest." But once these conventions have been established their general utility is so apparent that another affection comes into play. Through sympathy with or benevolence toward one another, persons develop a sense of the public good or common interest. This sense of the public good is the source of one's feeling a new and moral obligation to follow conventional rules and of one's morally disapproving anyone who breaks them. It is also the source of justice as a moral and not simply a conventional virtue.

The "general scheme" of conventional rules, necessary to escape the "savage condition" outside society, is for the most part highly beneficial to all. One should bear in mind, however, that some acts required by the rules do not promote the public good; some violations would promote it more. But on Hume's view, because it is impossible to devise *general* rules that are beneficial in every particular case and yet *general* rules are essential to social existence, every violation of a beneficial rule deserves moral condemnation. Moreover, if each person did what seemed best to him, so great are the differences in private conceptions of good, society would be impossible. The subordination of private conceptions of good to commonly accepted general rules and public moral standards is essential to society and its benefits.

Hume's theory of society and morality provides the foundation for his view of government. Government, which is not found in some primitive societies, arises through the growth of a set of conventional rules which themselves constitute the form, as well as the institutions and procedures, of the government. Hume's view has a constructive side; these conventions, like those governing property and promises, establish new social forms and practices. But Hume, like Hobbes and Locke, and unlike most of their predecessors, said that the primary reason for instituting government is to control the self-interest of individuals and to prevent it from destroying society. By attaching legal sanctions to the moral requirements to follow social conventions, individuals make it in their immediate interest to do what is in their long-range interest, namely, maintain the social practices and institutions necessary for society. As in the case of other conventions, enlightened self-interest leads to the establishment of conventions by which self-interest is controlled. Once instituted, these conventions afford an additional advantage that gives further reason for government. By enforcing other conventional rules, government in effect guarantees expectations and thus permits business to be done with complete strangers. When each person is able to count on everyone, or almost everyone, to follow the rules, vast cooperative schemes are made possible. Hume's constructive view of social practices partially overcomes his initial propensity to take an essentially protectionist view of the state. One purpose of the state is to make society's benefits possible when there is a considerable population and conditions of limited affluence.

Hume's view of political obligation should be noted. One's initial obligation to the state is an "obligation" of self-interest. But as soon as the general utility of government becomes apparent, then, as in the case of the other conventions, a moral obligation is recognized. The primary function of the state is to support the moral obligation to follow the rules of social practices; the state buttresses moral obligation. At the same time, to the extent that the state succeeds in performing this function, it becomes worthy of our moral approval and an additional moral obligation arises. The state thus supports morality, and morality supports the state.

Hume's theory of society and government was a considerable achievement. However much insight may be attributed to Hobbes and Locke, few today would adopt the position of either; Hume, on the other hand, has his contemporary appeal, although his theory as presented contains a serious internal weakness, a weakness that derives from a failure to consider seriously the standard of a just convention. In arguing for the utility of the conventions that constitute property, government, and the like, Hume compared persons living in society under these conventions to persons living outside society. But if this latter class is the standard of comparison, *any* set of social conventions will fare well, since not even Hume's "savages" could survive outside society; what is needed is a standard by which the *relative* justice and worth of conventions can be judged, not one that will make them all look good. And it is at just this point that Hume's presentation, and perhaps his theory, was deficient, more deficient than Locke's. This is not because Hume had nothing to say, but because he never adequately faced the problem of judging conventions and institutions. Sometimes he seemed so impressed by the chaos and destructiveness latent in different persons' conceptions of good (a chaos that had come into the open in the century before him) that the choice of *some* general rule was all that mattered. Sometimes, as in his discussion of the convention that uses "long possession" as the ground for assigning rights to property, he seemed willing to give a purely psychological explanation, instead of an argument or justification, for our having the convention. Sometimes, as in his consideration of quite specific property rules, he found (probably correctly) that although it is essential to have a rule, the choice is often arbitrary. This kind of discussion is often illuminating, sophisticated, and important, but it does not provide a principle for judging the justice of conventions.

Nevertheless, Hume did have a fundamental principle for judging conventions: On his theory, one is obligated to follow conventional rules only because they are useful in contributing to the "public good," the "common interest," or the "happiness of mankind." Jeremy Bentham, the great utilitarian reformer, credited Hume with having taught him that "utility," the "cause of the people," is the foundation of all virtue.[5] Hume, moreover, made fairly regular use of this principle: He defended resistance to tyranny on the ground that the obligation to obey a government ceases when the government no longer serves the common interest. He defended the inheritance of property because it promotes a useful industry and frugality. In his political and economic *Essays*,[6] he used the notion of the public good or common interest in arguing for economic policies, forms of government, the need of controlling factions, civil liberty, the balancing of liberty and authority, and many other topics.

Thus Hume was not without a fundamental principle. But his use of it, as when he argued that "the greatness of the sovereign, and the happiness of the state, are in a great measure united with regard to trade and manufactures,"[7] soon provokes the question: Is the "public good" or the "common interest," in his sense of these terms, an adequate principle for judging the *justice* of institutions? And how to clarify and relate these two great goals of modern government, justice, and the common good has been a major problem for utilitarians and others ever since. It is very close to that with which Rousseau began *The Social Contract*.

The General Will as Sovereign: Rousseau

Jean Jacques Rousseau (1712–1778) was above all else a moralist, deeply disturbed by what so-called civilized human beings had done to one another. His political philosophy was

[5] J. Bentham, *Fragment on Government*, I, paragraph 36, note. Bentham seems to have credited others as well.

[6] These essays made Hume famous at home and abroad, probably influenced his friend Adam Smith, and had an important influence on James Madison and other founders of the American Constitution, especially in their thought about political factions and how they could be controlled.

[7] See his essay "Of Commerce," in almost any collection of his essays.

marked both by the work of his older contemporary Montesquieu and, even more fundamentally, by the influences of Locke and Plato. There has, however, been considerable disagreement even about its central ideas: Rousseau regularly preferred eloquence to clarity, he wrote with passion, and he had a remarkable sympathy for ideas incompatible with one another. But among the moderns, Hobbes was perhaps his only equal in originality.

It is important to recognize that Rousseau's major treatise in political philosophy, *The Social Contract*, was first of all concerned with an ideal. His procedure was thus almost the opposite of Hume's. In his *Confessions* (IX, paragraphs 6–7), he tells us that *The Social Contract* derived from earlier work founded on the conviction that a people would never be other than the nature of their government made them. The central question was, "What is the nature of the government fitted to make the most enlightened, the wisest, and, in short, the best people, taking the word 'best' in its highest sense?" In *Emile,* published at the same time as *The Social Contract,* he said that in judging governments one must know what ought to be in order to judge well of what is. *The Social Contract,* subtitled "Principles of political right," itself undertook to state the conditions of a morally legitimate civil order, one that would unite justice and utility.

One fundamental condition was made clear in the first few chapters. If a civil order is to be morally legitimate, if it is to be one that people ought to support as a matter of right, then there must be a reason for them to accept this civil order other than the threat of force. Might does not make right; moral legitimacy cannot derive from force. Moreover, the general use of force, of the kind that would be required to impose a civil order on society, is incompatible with morality. In depriving persons of their liberty, it deprives them of their humanity, the very character or quality in virtue of which they are human beings. To be sure, there are different kinds of liberty: Natural liberty is a liberty to do whatever one's power permits; civil liberty is a liberty to do what the law allows. But what is in question here is moral liberty, and this does not consist in either of these two kinds, or in a liberty to "do as one pleases," if this means satisfying any appetite at all. Moral liberty consists, rather, in following laws that one prescribes for oneself. To deprive a person of the liberty to determine his own life in the way that he judges best is to deprive him of the possibility of moral action and make him less than human. Thus any argument for the moral legitimacy of a civil or social order presupposes and must respect moral liberty, a right of humanity in each person.

Rousseau probably got the idea for this first and fundamental step in his argument from Locke.[8] He could even have got his idea of moral liberty from Locke (see *Second Treatise,* §§ 22, 57). There is nevertheless a great difference between the ideas of the two men. For Rousseau, moral liberty was not simply, as it was for Locke, a right that persons have; it was a person's very humanity, what makes him human. Moreover, "that men have this liberty" is not a self-evident pronouncement of a Lockean natural law, although it is a fundamental moral principle; in order to be moral, according to what amounts to a new or revived concept of morality, a person must follow laws that he prescribes for himself. Finally, at least in its full sense, moral liberty does not consist in one's not being subject to the will of another and *having the liberty* to do one's own will; it consists in *doing* it, actually following the laws that one legislates for oneself. Rousseau did not conceive of this kind of freedom primarily in terms of abilities, or a lack of restrictions; to him it was not a means, but a goal. Thus, in the first few chapters of *The Social Contract,* we find, in however unsystematic a form, distinctive views of human nature, morality, and freedom. The German philosopher, Kant (1724–1804), deeply affected by these ideas, used them a short time later in trying systematically to lay out the foundations of morality and politics—small wonder that he spoke of Rousseau as having done for the moral world what Sir Isaac Newton had done for the physical.[9]

So far we have been concerned with a fundamental condition that any morally legitimate civil order must satisfy: Such an order must permit each person to live under precepts and laws

---

[8] See Rousseau, *Letters Written from the Mountain,* VI, *ad fin.*
[9] See the quotation of Kant in E. Cassirer, *Rousseau, Kant, Goethe: Two Essays,* trans. J. Gutmann, P. O. Kristeller, and J. H. Randall, Jr. (reprint ed., New York: Harper & Row, Publishers), p. 18. (Originally published by Princeton University Press, 1945.)

that he lays down for himself. An additional point deserves special emphasis: On Rousseau's view, civil society is indispensable to the individual. Notwithstanding his having glorified the goodness of "the natural man," [10] Rousseau believed that without social goods, a person would be guided wholly by instinct or inclination; it is from society that one acquires language, imagination, intelligence, nobility of feeling, and, most important of all, one's sense of justice and morality. Thus persons to a considerable extent must live in society, and from the standpoint of morality each person must "legislate" for himself. These two demands inescapably set the problem of a moral social order: How can each person, while uniting himself to every other, still obey only himself, and remain as free as before?

For this question to have an answer, for a moral civil order to be possible, there apparently must be either a natural harmony of interests of all persons in a society, leading all to agree on laws that each legislates in common with every other; or, because of the importance of the moral order, they must create such a harmony by contracting to follow common laws, even at the sacrifice of particular interests. For Rousseau, in either case, individuals will have particular interests not included in the common interest, but when there is conflict, laws in the common interest will take priority over special interests. Otherwise, one person (or group) would impose his (or its) will on the others (in some manner or other) and thus violate the basic condition of a moral civil order. In laying down this requirement, Rousseau first said that each person must totally "alienate" (give jurisdiction over) himself and all his rights to the whole community (the kind of statement that probably had a great effect on Hegel). Rousseau's idea, however, was probably more accurately expressed later: A person must alienate only those powers, goods, and liberties which the general will requires.

Rousseau's name for the legislative body of all, laying down laws to all, is the sovereign, or the general will. Having rightful authority, it should also have power—if necessary—to "force

[10] Rousseau's praise of the savage prompted Voltaire to write, "One longs in reading your book to walk on all fours." For Rousseau's actual view, see the "Discourse on the Origin and Foundations of Inequality Among Men" in J. J. Rousseau, *The First and Second Discourses*, R. D. Masters (Ed.) (New York: St. Martin's Press, 1964).

men to be free." Hobbes ("a great genius" with a "horrible sys-tem")[11] has left his mark; although now the general will of the citizens, rather than an absolute monarch, is sovereign. The object of the general will, the tie that binds persons together, is the common good, for the sake of which the civil order exists. In the interest of living morally with others, each person must live under the legislation of the general will; each is subject to its power and authority. On the other hand, each person in common with every other is a legislator, and as much so as any other. A civil equality is established in place of physical inequal-ity, civil liberty replaces natural liberty, rights in property are established, and without coercion; in the moral sense, each re-mains as free as he was before. And each then has society's blessings; each enjoys a good in common with the others.

So much for a statement of Rousseau's ideal. But as soon as the essential features of this ideal are set down, difficulties arise. May not some persons persuade others to accept legisla-tion that is not in the common interest? Is legislation just, and right, simply because it passes unanimously? Rousseau's first reply to this kind of objection is in keeping with his ideal: The general will is always everything it ought to be; it cannot err, it cannot be corrupted. On this account, it must be distinguished not only from "particular wills," guided by special interests, but also from the "will of all," which is either a hodgepodge of all interests, or a unanimous but deceived will. Kant adopted the same view: He made what he called the United Will intrinsically rational.

Now, however, the difficulties seem even greater. Is not this ideal of a general will hopelessly impractical? And, in view of the great and interesting differences between people, is it even the kind of ideal to which one would wish to subscribe? (But let it be noted that if one rejects the ideal, as an ideal, one is also rejecting Rousseau's argument that the conditions of a *moral* civil order or a *moral* political system require it to be acceptable to a general will or its equivalent; one should be willing to try to state what conditions one would substitute.)

Rousseau's own answer to the former question is the source of many difficulties in interpreting his writings. He himself ar-

[11] See "The State of War."

gued, on the one hand, that the task of legislation is beyond human powers, that to get people to see "the good they will" requires a divinely inspired legislator who, paradoxically, is without any authority. He set out conditions for realizing the general will—for example, every citizen should know every other—that are wholly unrealizable in a modern state. On the other hand, he sometimes eloquently argued that persons who are simple and upright have a natural wisdom, and wrote as if the ideal is realizable in certain forms of society. At still other times, he seemed to compromise his fundamental ideal in order to make the general will a practical political ideal. Perhaps the root difficulty was that Rousseau undertook both to state the ideal conditions of a perfectly moral government, and at the same time to say something significant about how best to approach this ideal in practice, without always distinguishing the two tasks. *The Social Contract* certainly presents a curious and stark contrast: There are passages, on the one hand, in which ideal principles require unanimous legislation without even the possibility of representation, this requirement making the whole populace the legislature and what we call government a purely administrative arm. And juxtaposed are passages (largely omitted below) in which this ideal seems to have vanished; here we find discussion of the importance of climate and fertility of soil, the impracticability of democracy, and legitimate rule by majority, and we are almost told that "majority tyranny" is a simple conceptual confusion.

Notwithstanding his faults, such as his tendency to savor paradox and write philosophy from the heart, Rousseau has a very important place among political philosophers. If we agree that the institutions and conventions of our society, which so largely shape our lives, are at least sometimes no surer guide to right than Hobbes' sovereign, and yet reject, as we must, Locke's theory of natural law, then by what principles are these institutions and conventions to be judged? If there are no principles, but some institutions are to be judged by others, on which do we rely? If there are principles, but they do not constitute a simple measure of institutions, how are they to be applied? The first of these was Rousseau's question: Whether he gave the essentially correct answer is still being debated. In any case, his influence is undeniable, and it was exercised in several directions. If, as in the account above, one emphasizes the general will as a standard for judging institutions, one sees the source of Rousseau's influence on Kant—and on many others who use the notion of a social contract as a ground of judgment. The influence is apparent in Kant's statement that the "idea [of the social contract] alone enables us to conceive of the legitimacy of the state." [12] The depth of the influence is even more apparent when Kant says that although such a contract is not even possible, this "mere idea of reason . . . obligates every lawgiver to promulgate his laws in such a way that they could have arisen from the united will of an entire people, and to regard every subject, insofar as he desires to be a citizen, as though he had joined in assenting to such a will. For that is the touchstone of the legitimacy of every public enactment." [13] We shall see a new version of "contract theory" in the selection from Rawls' *A Theory of Justice* in Part III.

On the other hand, if in giving an account of Rousseau's thought, one emphasizes the doctrine of freedom as a goal, and the dependence of human beings on civil society for their intelligence, imagination, morality, and even humanity—perhaps interpreting his requirement of "total alienation" as implying this dependence—then one sees the source of his influence on Hegel. It is difficult to think that Rousseau's *The Social Contract* was far from Hegel's thought when he wrote: "Hence in this identity of the universal will with the particular will, right and duty coalesce, and by being in the ethical order a man has rights in so far as he has duties, and duties in so far as he has rights." [14]

Finally, if in his reading of Rousseau one emphasizes "the common good" as the goal of civil society, and the need of an all-wise legislator, one is apt to interpret Rousseau as harking back to Plato and the ideal of the *polis*. The British Idealists in the nineteenth century, influenced by Kant and Hegel, but taking much of their inspiration from the Greeks, found Rousseau

---

[12] I. Kant, *Metaphysical Elements of Justice*, trans. J. Ladd (Indianapolis: The Bobbs-Merrill Co., Inc., 1965), p. 80.

[13] Quoted in E. Cassirer, *Rousseau, Kant and Goethe*, p. 35.

[14] G. W. F. Hegel, *Philosophy of Right*, trans. T. M. Knox (London: Oxford University Press, 1952), paragraph 155. See also paragraph 258, in the course of which Rousseau's view of the general will is discussed. By permission of The Clarendon Press, Oxford.

exceptionally important and his idea of the common good perhaps his greatest contribution. Bosanquet devoted two chapters of his *Philosophical Theory of the State* to Rousseau, and T. H. Green maintained that Rousseau's conception of the social contract was essentially (although not literally) true, since ". . . only through a recognition by certain men of a common interest, and through the expression of that recognition in certain regulations of their dealings with each other, could morality originate, or any meaning be gained for such terms as 'ought' and 'right' and their equivalents." [15] We shall see more of what Green has to say on the common good and justice in Part III.

Rousseau had other influences, theoretical and practical, on individualists and on collectivists, as might be expected from a man whose mind was so little of one piece. His importance as a political philosopher derives most of all from his having insisted on raising questions about the *morality* of institutions— the kind of questions that Hume passed by—and from his attempt to locate the source of morality in the individual "self-legislative will." The kind of answer that Rousseau gave, however, and the kind that he stimulated, would have to contend with the "utilitarian" or "greatest happiness" principle, which Bentham found in Hume, and with a new interpretation of freedom that was soon to be brought forward by Hegel.

Bibliography

Aiken, H. (Ed.), *Hume's Moral and Political Philosophy*, Introduction. New York: Hafner Publishing Co., Inc., 1948.

Brown, K. (Ed.), *Hobbes Studies*. Cambridge, Mass.: Harvard University Press, 1965.

Carritt, E. F., *Morals and Politics: Theories of Their Relation from Hobbes and Spinoza to Marx and Bosanquet*. Oxford: The Clarendon Press, 1935.

Cranston, M., and R. S. Peters (Eds.), *Hobbes and Rousseau: A Collection of Critical Essays* (on Rousseau, note especially R. B. Masters' "The Structure of Rousseau's Political

[15] T. H. Green, *Lectures on the Principles of Political Obligation*, paragraph 116, in *Works*, Vol. 2, 5th impression, R. L. Nettleship (Ed.) (London and New York: Longmans, Green, 1906).

Thought"). Garden City, N.Y.: Doubleday & Company, Inc., 1972.

Dunn, J., *The Political Thought of John Locke: An Historical Account of the Argument of the "Two Treatises of Government."* Cambridge, England: The University Press, 1969.

Gauthier, D. P., *The Logic of Leviathan.* Oxford: The Clarendon Press, 1969.

Gierke, O., *Natural Law and the Theory of Society, 1500–1800,* trans. E. Barker. Cambridge, England: The University Press, 1934.

Gough, J. W., *The Social Contract: A Critical Study of Its Development,* 2nd ed. Oxford: The Clarendon Press, 1957.

Gough, J. W., *John Locke's Political Philosophy: Eight Studies,* 2nd ed. Oxford: The Clarendon Press, 1973.

Hayek, F. A., "The Legal and Political Philosophy of David Hume," in *Hume,* V. C. Chappell (Ed.), pp. 335–360. Garden City, N.Y.: Doubleday & Company, Inc., 1966.

Masters, R. D., *The Political Philosophy of Rousseau.* Princeton, N.J.: Princeton University Press, 1968.

Passerin d'Entrèves, A., *Natural Law: An Introduction to Legal Philosophy,* 2nd ed. London: Hutchinson University Library, 1970.

Plamenatz, J., *Man and Society,* Vol. 1. London: Longmans, Green & Co. Ltd., 1963.

Sabine, G. H., *A History of Political Theory,* 3rd ed., Part III, Ch. 17–29. New York: Holt, Rinehart & Winston, Inc., 1961.

Stewart, J. B., *The Moral and Political Philosophy of David Hume.* New York and London: Columbia University Press, 1963.

Warrender, H., *The Political Philosophy of Hobbes: His Theory of Obligation.* Oxford: The Clarendon Press, 1957.

1 SELECTIONS FROM

Leviathan, or the Matter, Form, and Power of a Common-
wealth, Ecclesiastical and Civil

THOMAS HOBBES

*Thomas Hobbes was born in 1588, entered Magdalen Hall,
Oxford, at the age of fifteen, and, upon graduating in 1608, became a tutor in the Cavendish family. He began his scholarly
career as a classicist, publishing a translation of Thucydides
in 1629, but in his middle years, stimulated by extensive visits
to the Continent and meetings with Père Mersenne and Galileo,
he was greatly attracted to philosophy, science, and mathematics.
He then began his trilogy,* De Corpore, De Homine, De Cive,
*but as the political crises heralding the English civil wars began
to brew, he interrupted that work to write a defense of royal
power,* The Elements of Law, Natural and Politic. *In 1640,
believing that his political views made him suspect, he fled to
France, where he completed* De Cive *(1642), and wrote* Leviathan *(1651), his major work. These works antagonized many,
including royalists, and soon after his return to England in 1651
he was embroiled in controversy.* De Corpore *(1655) and* De
Homine *(1658) only added fuel to the flames, and even though
he was later befriended and intermittently pensioned by Charles
II, whom he had tutored in France, his* Behemoth, *on the civil
wars, had to be published clandestinely. In his later years, he
returned to his classical studies and published translations of
Homer. He died in 1679.*

The standard edition of Hobbes' English and Latin works is that of
Sir William Molesworth (London: John Bohn, 1839), from Volume III
of which the following selections are taken. A new and probably more
authentic version of the complete *Leviathan* (from which these selections
do not materially differ) has been edited by C. B. Macpherson and published by Penguin Books.

Part 1. Of Man

Chapter 6: Of the Interior Beginnings of Voluntary Motions.
There be in animals, two sorts of *motions* peculiar to them : one
called *vital;* begun in generation, and continued without inter-
ruption through their whole life ; such as are the *course* of the
blood, the *pulse,* the *breathing,* the *concoction, nutrition, excre-
tion,* etc. to which motions there needs no help of imagination :
the other is *animal motion,* otherwise called *voluntary motion ;*
as to *go,* to *speak,* to *move* any of our limbs, in such manner
as is first fancied in our minds. That sense is motion in the
organs and interior parts of man's body, caused by the action
of the things we see, hear, etc. ; and that fancy is but the relics
of the same motion, remaining after sense, has been already
said in the first and second chapters. And because *going, speaking,* and the like voluntary motions, depend always upon a
precedent thought of *whither, which way,* and *what ;* it is evident,
that the imagination is the first internal beginning of all voluntary
motion. And although unstudied men do not conceive any motion at all to be there, where the thing moved is invisible ; or the
space it is moved in is, for the shortness of it, insensible ; yet
that doth not hinder, but that such motions are.

. . .

As, in sense, that which is really within us, is, as I have
said before, only motion, caused by the action of external objects, but in apparence ; to the sight, light and colour ; to the
ear, sound ; to the nostril, odour, etc.: so, when the action of the
same object is continued from the eyes, ears, and other organs
to the heart, the real effect there is nothing but motion, or endeavour ; which consisteth in appetite, or aversion, to or from
the object moving. But the apparence, or sense of that motion,
is that we either call *delight,* or *trouble of mind.*
This motion, which is called appetite, and for the apparence of it *delight,* and *pleasure,* seemeth to be a corroboration
of vital motion, and a help thereunto ; and therefore such things
as caused delight, were not improperly called *jucunda, à juvando,*
from helping or fortifying ; and the contrary, *molesta, offensive,*
from hindering, and troubling the motion vital.

. . .

Continual success in obtaining those things which a man from time to time desireth, that is to say, continual prospering, is that men call FELICITY ; I mean the felicity of this life. For there is no such thing as perpetual tranquillity of mind, while we live here; because life itself is but motion, and can never be without desire, nor without fear, no more than without sense. . . .

. . .

Chapter 13: Of the Natural Condition of Mankind as Concerning Their Felicity, and Misery. Nature hath made men so equal, in the faculties of the body, and mind ; as that though there be found one man sometimes manifestly stronger in body, or of quicker mind than another ; yet when all is reckoned together, the difference between man, and man, is not so considerable, as that one man can thereupon claim to himself any benefit, to which another may not pretend, as well as he. For as to the strength of body, the weakest has strength enough to kill the strongest, either by secret machination, or by confederacy with others, that are in the same danger with himself.

And as to the faculties of the mind, setting aside the arts grounded upon words, and especially that skill of proceeding upon general, and infallible rules, called science ; which very few have, and but in few things ; as being not a native faculty, born with us ; nor attained, as prudence, while we look after somewhat else, I find yet a greater equality amongst men, than that of strength. For prudence, is but experience ; which equal time, equally bestows on all men, in those things they equally apply themselves unto. That which may perhaps make such equality incredible, is but a vain conceit of one's own wisdom, which almost all men think they have in a greater degree, than the vulgar ; that is, than all men but themselves, and a few others, whom by fame, or for concurring with themselves, they approve. . . .

From this equality of ability, ariseth equality of hope in the attaining of our ends. And therefore if any two men desire the same thing, which nevertheless they cannot both enjoy, they become enemies ; and in the way to their end, which is principally their own conservation, and sometimes their delectation only, endeavour to destroy, or subdue one another. And from hence it comes to pass, that where an invader hath no more to fear, than another man's single power ; if one plant, sow, build, or possess a convenient seat, others may probably be expected to come prepared with forces united, to dispossess, and deprive him, not only of the fruit of his labour, but also of his life, or liberty. And the invader again is in the like danger of another.

And from this diffidence of one another, there is no way for any man to secure himself, so reasonable, as anticipation ; that is, by force, or wiles, to master the persons of all men he can, so long, till he see no other power great enough to endanger him : and this is no more than his own conservation requireth, and is generally allowed. Also because there be some, that taking pleasure in contemplating their own power in the acts of conquest, which they pursue farther than their security requires ; if others, that otherwise would be glad to be at ease within modest bounds, should not by invasion increase their power, they would not be able, long time, by standing only on their defence, to subsist. And by consequence, such augmentation of dominion over men being necessary to a man's conservation, it ought to be allowed him.

Again, men have no pleasure, but on the contrary a great deal of grief, in keeping company, where there is no power able to over-awe them all. For every man looketh that his companion should value him, at the same rate he sets upon himself : and upon all signs of contempt, or undervaluing, naturally endeavours, as far as he dares, (which amongst them that have no common power to keep them in quiet, is far enough to make them destroy each other), to extort a greater value from his contemners, by damage; and from others, by the example.

So that in the nature of man, we find three principal causes of quarrel. First, competition ; secondly, diffidence ; thirdly, glory.

The first, maketh men invade for gain ; the second, for safety ; and the third, for reputation. The first use violence, to make themselves masters of other men's persons, wives, children, and cattle ; the second, to defend them ; the third, for trifles, as a word, a smile, a different opinion, and any other sign of undervalue, either direct in their persons, or by reflection in their kindred, their friends, their nation, their profession, or their name.

Hereby it is manifest, that during the time men live without a common power to keep them all in awe, they are in that condition which is called war ; and such a war, as is of every man, against every man. For WAR, consisteth not in battle only, or the act of fighting ; but in a tract of time, wherein the will to contend by battle is sufficiently known : and therefore the notion of *time,* is to be considered in the nature of war ; as it is in the nature of weather. For as the nature of foul weather, lieth not in a shower or two of rain ; but in an inclination thereto of many days together : so the nature of war, consisteth not in actual fighting ; but in the known disposition thereto, during all the time there is no assurance to the contrary. All other time is PEACE.

Whatsoever therefore is consequent to a time of war, where every man is enemy to every man ; the same is consequent to the time, wherein men live without other security, than what their own strength, and their own invention shall furnish them withal. In such condition, there is no place for industry ; because the fruit thereof is uncertain : and consequently no culture of the earth ; no navigation, nor use of the commodities that may be imported by sea ; no commodious building ; no instruments of moving, and removing, such things as require much force ; no knowledge of the face of the earth; no account of time ; no arts ; no letters ; no society ; and which is worst of all, continual fear, and danger of violent death ; and the life of man, solitary, poor, nasty, brutish, and short.

It may seem strange to some man, that has not well weighed these things; that nature should thus dissociate, and render men apt to invade, and destroy one another : and he may therefore, not trusting to this inference, made from the passions, desire perhaps to have the same confirmed by experience. Let him therefore consider with himself, when taking a journey, he arms himself, and seeks to go well accompanied ; when going to sleep, he locks his doors ; when even in his house he locks his chests. . . . Does he not there as much accuse mankind by his actions, as I do by my words ? But neither of us accuse man's nature in it. The desires, and other passions of man, are in themselves no sin. . . .

It may peradventure be thought, there was never such a time, nor condition of war as this ; and I believe it was never generally so, over all the world : but there are many places, where they live so now. For the savage people in many places of America, except the government of small families, the concord whereof dependeth on natural lust, have no government at all ; and live at this day in that brutish manner, as I said before. Howsoever, it may be perceived what manner of life there would be, where there were no common power to fear, by the manner of life, which men that have formerly lived under a peaceful government, use to degenerate into, in a civil war.

. . .

To this war of every man, against every man, this also is consequent ; that nothing can be unjust. The notions of right and wrong, justice and injustice have there no place. Where there is no common power, there is no law : where no law, no injustice. Force, and fraud, are in war the two cardinal virtues. Justice, and injustice are none of the faculties neither of the body, nor mind. If they were, they might be in a man that were alone in the world, as well as his senses, and passions. They are qualities, that relate to men in society, not in solitude. It is consequent also to the same condition, that there be no propriety, no dominion, no *mine* and *thine* distinct ; but only that to be every man's, that he can get ; and for so long, as he can keep it. And thus much for the ill condition, which man by mere nature is actually placed in ; though with a possibility to come out of it, consisting partly in the passions, partly in his reason.

The passions that incline men to peace, are fear of death ; desire of such things as are necessary to commodious living ; and a hope by their industry to obtain them. And reason suggesteth convenient articles of peace, upon which men may be drawn to agreement. These articles, are they, which otherwise are called the Laws of Nature : whereof I shall speak more particularly, in the two following chapters.

Chapter 14: Of the First and Second Natural Laws, and of Contracts. The RIGHT OF NATURE, which writers commonly call *jus naturale,* is the liberty each man hath, to use his own power, as he will himself, for the preservation of his own nature ; that is to say, of his own life ; and consequently, of doing any thing, which in his own judgment, and reason, he shall conceive to be the aptest means thereunto.

By LIBERTY, is understood, according to the proper signification of the word, the absence of external impediments : which impediments, may oft take away part of a man's power to do what he would ; but cannot hinder him from using the power left him, according as his judgment, and reason shall dictate to him.

A LAW OF NATURE, *lex naturalis,* is a precept or general rule, found out by reason, by which a man is forbidden to do that, which is destructive of his life, or taketh away the means of preserving the same ; and to omit that, by which he thinketh it may be best preserved. For though they that speak of this subject, use to confound *jus,* and *lex, right* and *law :* yet they ought to be distinguished ; because RIGHT, consisteth in liberty to do, or to forbear ; whereas LAW, determineth, and bindeth to one of them : so that law, and right, differ as much, as obligation, and liberty ; which in one and the same matter are inconsistent.

And because the condition of man, as hath been declared in the precedent chapter, is a condition of war of every one against every one ; in which case every one is governed by his own reason ; and there is nothing he can make use of, that may not be a help unto him, in preserving his life against his enemies ; it followeth, that in such a condition, every man has a right to every thing; even to one another's body. And therefore, as long as this natural right of every man to every thing endureth, there can be no security to any man, how strong or wise soever he be, of living out the time, which nature ordinarily alloweth men to live. And consequently it is a precept, or general rule of reason, *that every man, ought to endeavour peace, as far as he has hope of obtaining it ; and when he cannot obtain it, that he may seek, and use, all helps, and advantages of war.* The first branch of which rule, containeth the first, and fundamental law of nature ; which is, *to seek peace, and follow it.* The second, the sum of the right of nature ; which is, *by all means we can, to defend ourselves.*

From this fundamental law of nature, by which men are commanded to endeavour peace, is derived this second law ; *that a man be willing, when others are so too, as far-forth, as*

*for peace, and defence of himself he shall think it necessary, to
lay down this right to all things ; and be contented with so much
liberty against other men, as he would allow other men against
himself.* For as long as every man holdeth this right, of doing
any thing he liketh ; so long are all men in the condition of war.
But if other men will not lay down their right, as well as he ;
then there is no reason for any one, to divest himself of his : for
that were to expose himself to prey, which no man is bound to,
rather than to dispose himself to peace. This is that law of the
Gospel ; *whatsoever you require that others should do to you,
that do ye to them.* And that law of all men, *quod tibi fieri non
vis, alteri ne feceris.*

. . .

Right is laid aside, either by simply renouncing it ; or by
transferring it to another. By *simply* RENOUNCING ; when he
cares not to whom the benefit thereof redoundeth. By TRANSFER-
RING ; when he intendeth the benefit thereof to some certain
person, or persons. And when a man hath in either manner
abandoned, or granted away his right ; then is he said to be
OBLIGED, or BOUND, not to hinder those, to whom such right is
granted, or abandoned, from the benefit of it : and that he *ought,*
and it is his DUTY, not to make void that voluntary act of his
own : and that such hindrance is INJUSTICE, and INJURY, as
being *sine jure ;* the right being before renounced, or transferred. . . .
Whensoever a man transferreth his right, or renounceth it ;
it is either in consideration of some right reciprocally transferred
to himself ; or for some other good he hopeth for thereby. For
it is a voluntary act : and of the voluntary acts of every man,
the object is some *good to himself.* And therefore there be some
rights, which no man can be understood by any words, or other
signs, to have abandoned, or transferred. As first a man cannot
lay down the right of resisting them, that assault him by force,
to take away his life ; because he cannot be understood to aim
thereby, at any good to himself. The same may be said of
wounds, and chains, and imprisonment ; both because there is
no benefit consequent to such patience ; as there is to the patience of suffering another to be wounded, or imprisoned : as

also because a man cannot tell, when he seeth men proceed against him by violence, whether they intend his death or not. And lastly the motive, and end for which this renouncing, and transferring of right is introduced, is nothing else but the security of a man's person, in his life, and in the means of so preserving life, as not to be weary of it. And therefore if a man by words, or other signs, seem to despoil himself of the end, for which those signs were intended ; he is not to be understood as if he meant it, or that it was his will ; but that he was ignorant of how such words and actions were to be interpreted.

The mutual transferring of right, is that which men call CONTRACT.

. . .

Chapter 15: Of Other Laws of Nature.   From that law of nature, by which we are obliged to transfer to another, such rights, as being retained, hinder the peace of mankind, there followeth a third ; which is this, *that men perform their covenants made :* without which, covenants are in vain, and but empty words ; and the right of all men to all things remaining, we are still in the condition of war.

And in this law of nature, consisteth the fountain and original of JUSTICE. For where no covenant hath preceded, there hath no right been transferred, and every man has right to every thing; and consequently, no action can be unjust. But when a covenant is made, then to break it is *unjust :* and the definition of INJUSTICE, is no other than *the not performance of covenant.* And whatsoever is not unjust, is *just.*

But because covenants of mutual trust, where there is a fear of not performance on either part, as hath been said in the former chapter, are invalid ; though the original of justice be the making of covenants ; yet injustice actually there can be none, till the cause of such fear be taken away ; which while men are in the natural condition of war, cannot be done. Therefore before the names of just, and unjust can have place, there must be some coercive power, to compel men equally to the performance of their covenants, by the terror of some punishment, greater than the benefit they expect by the breach of their covenant ; and to make good that propriety, which by mutual contract men acquire, in recompense of the universal right they abandon : and such power there is none before the erection of a commonwealth. And this is also to be gathered out of the ordinary definition of justice in the Schools : for they say, that *justice is the constant will of giving to every man his own.* And therefore where there is no *own,* that is no propriety, there is no injustice ; and where there is no coercive power erected, that is, where there is no commonwealth, there is no propriety ; all men having right to all things: therefore where there is no commonwealth, there nothing is unjust. So that the nature of justice, consisteth in keeping of valid covenants : but the validity of covenants begins not but with the constitution of a civil power, sufficient to compel men to keep them : and then it is also that propriety begins.

. . .

Part 2. Of Commonwealth

Chapter 17: Of the Causes, Generation, and Definition of a Commonwealth. The final cause, end, or design of men, who naturally love liberty, and dominion over others, in the introduction of that restraint upon themselves, in which we see them live in commonwealths, is the foresight of their own preservation, and of a more contented life thereby ; that is to say, of getting themselves out from that miserable condition of war, which is necessarily consequent, as hath been shown in chapter XIII, to the natural passions of men, when there is no visible power to keep them in awe, and tie them by fear of punishment to the performance of their covenants, and observation of those laws of nature set down in the fourteenth and fifteenth chapters.

For the laws of nature, as *justice, equity, modesty, mercy,* and, in sum, *doing to others, as we would be done to,* of themselves, without the terror of some power, to cause them to be observed, are contrary to our natural passions, that carry us to partiality, pride, revenge, and the like. And covenants, without the sword, are but words, and of no strength to secure a man at all. Therefore notwithstanding the laws of nature, which every one hath then kept, when he has the will to keep them, when he can do it safely, if there be no power erected, or not great enough for our security ; every man will, and may lawfully rely on his own strength and art, for caution against all other men. . . .

The only way to erect such a common power, as may be able to defend them from the invasion of foreigners, and the injuries of one another, and thereby to secure them in such sort, as that by their own industry, and by the fruits of the earth, they may nourish themselves and live contentedly ; is, to confer all their power and strength upon one man, or upon one assembly of men, that may reduce all their wills, by plurality of voices, unto one will : which is as much as to say, to appoint one man, or assembly of men, to bear their person ; and every one to own, and acknowledge himself to be author of whatsoever he that so beareth their person, shall act, or cause to be acted, in those things which concern the common peace and safety ; and therein to submit their wills, every one to his will, and their judgments, to his judgment. This is more than consent, or concord ; it is a real unity of them all, in one and the same person, made by covenant of every man with every man, in such manner, as if every man should say to every man, *I authorise and give up my right of governing myself, to this man, or to this assembly of men, on this condition, that thou give up thy right to him, and authorize all his actions in like manner.* This done, the multitude so united in one person, is called a COMMONWEALTH, in Latin CIVITAS. This is the generation of that great LEVIATHAN, or rather, to speak more reverently, of that *mortal god,* to which we owe under the *immortal God,* our peace and defence. For by this authority, given him by every particular man in the commonwealth, he hath the use of so much power and strength conferred on him, that by terror thereof, he is enabled to perform the wills of them all, to peace at home, and mutual aid against their enemies abroad. And in him consisteth the essence of the commonwealth ; which, to define it, is *one person, of whose acts a great multitude, by mutual covenants one with another, have made themselves every one the author, to the end he may use the strength and means of them all, as he shall think expedient, for their peace and common defence.*

And he that carrieth this person, is called SOVEREIGN, and

said to have *sovereign power ;* and every one besides, his SUB-JECT.

. . .

Chapter 18: *Of the Rights of Sovereigns by Institution.* A com-monwealth is said to be *instituted,* when a *multitude* of men do agree, and *covenant, every one, with every one,* that to whatsoever *man,* or *assembly of men,* shall be given by the major part, the *right* to *present* the person of them all, that is to say, to be their *representative ;* every one, as well he that *voted for it,* as he that *voted against it,* shall *authorize* all the actions and judgments, of that man, or assembly of men, in the same manner, as if they were his own, to the end, to live peaceably amongst themselves, and be protected against other men.

From this institution of a commonwealth are derived all the *rights,* and *faculties* of him, or them, on whom sovereign power is conferred by the consent of the people assembled.

First, because they covenant, it is to be understood, they are not obliged by former covenant to anything repugnant here-unto. And consequently they that have already instituted a commonwealth, being thereby bound by covenant, to own the actions, and judgments of one, cannot lawfully make a new covenant, amongst themselves, to be obedient to any other, in any thing whatsoever, without his permission. . . .

Secondly, because the right of bearing the person of them all, is given to him they make sovereign, by covenant only of one to another, and not of him to any of them ; there can happen no breach of covenant on the part of the sovereign ; and consequently none of his subjects, by any pretence of forfeiture, can be freed from his subjection. . . . The opinion that any monarch receiveth his power by covenant, that is to say, on condition, proceedeth from want of understanding this easy truth, that covenants being but words and breath, have no force to oblige, contain, constrain, or protect any man, but what it has from the public sword ; that is, from the untied hands of that man, or assembly of men that hath the sovereignty, and whose actions are avouched by them all, and performed by the strength of them all, in him united. . . .

Thirdly, because the major part hath by consenting voices declared a sovereign ; he that dissented must now consent with the rest ; that is, be contented to avow all the actions he shall do, or else justly be destroyed by the rest. . . .

Fourthly, because every subject is by this institution author of all the actions, and judgments of the sovereign instituted ; it follows, that whatsoever he doth, it can be no injury to any of his subjects ; nor ought he to be by any of them accused of injustice. . . .

Fifthly, . . . no man that hath sovereign power can justly be put to death, or otherwise in any manner by his subjects punished. For seeing every subject is author of the actions of his sovereign ; he punisheth another for the actions committed by himself.

And because the end of this institution, is the peace and defence of them all ; and whosoever has right to the end, has right to the means ; it belongeth of right, to whatsoever man, or assembly that hath the sovereignty, to be judge both of the means of peace and defence, and also of the hindrances, and disturbances of the same. . . .

Sixthly, it is annexed to the sovereignty, to be judge of what opinions and doctrines are averse, and what conducing to peace ; and consequently, on what occasions, how far, and what men are to be trusted withal, in speaking to multitudes of people ; and who shall examine the doctrines of all books before they be published. For the actions of men proceed from their opinions. . . .

Seventhly, is annexed to the sovereignty, the whole power of prescribing the rules, whereby every man may know, what goods he may enjoy, and what actions he may do, without being molested by any of his fellow-subjects ; and this is it men call *propriety*. . . .

Eighthly, is annexed to the sovereignty, the right of judicature ; that is to say, of hearing and deciding all controversies, which may arise concerning law, either civil, or natural ; or concerning fact. For without the decision of controversies, there is no protection of one subject, against the injuries of another. . . .

. . .

But a man may here object, that the condition of subjects is very miserable ; as being obnoxious to the lusts, and other irregular passions of him, or them that have so unlimited a power in their hands. And commonly they that live under a monarch, think it the fault of monarchy ; and they that live under the government of democracy, or other sovereign assembly, attribute all the inconvenience to that form of commonwealth ; whereas the power in all forms, if they be perfect enough to protect them, is the same : not considering that the state of man can never be without some incommodity or other ; and that the greatest, that in any form of government can possibly happen to the people in general, is scarce sensible, in respect of the miseries, and horrible calamities, that accompany a civil war, or that dissolute condition of masterless men, without subjection to laws, and a coercive power to tie their hands from rapine and revenge : nor considering that the greatest pressure of sovereign governors, proceedeth not from any delight, or profit they can expect in the damage or weakening of their subjects, in whose vigour, consisteth their own strength and glory ; but in the restiveness of themselves, that unwillingly contributing to their own defence, make it necessary for their governors to draw from them what they can in time of peace, that they may have means on any emergent occasion, or sudden need, to resist, or take advantage on their enemies. For all men are by nature provided of notable multiplying glasses, that is their passions and self-love, through which, every little payment appeareth a great grievance ; but are destitute of those prospective glasses, namely moral and civil science, to see afar off the miseries that hang over them, and cannot without such payments be avoided.

Chapter 21: Of the Liberty of Subjects.

. . .

First therefore, seeing sovereignty by institution, is by covenant of every one to every one ; and sovereignty by acquisition, by covenants of the vanquished to the victor, or child to the parent ; it is manifest, that every subject has liberty in all those things, the right whereof cannot by covenant be transferred. . . .[1]

As for other liberties, they depend on the silence of the law. In cases where the sovereign has prescribed no rule, there the subject hath the liberty to do, or forbear, according to his own discretion. And therefore such liberty is in some places more, and in some less ; and in some times more, in other times less, according as they that have the sovereignty shall think most convenient. . . .

The obligation of subjects to the sovereign, is understood to last as long, and no longer, than the power lasteth, by which he is able to protect them. For the right men have by nature to protect themselves, when none else can protect them, can by no covenant be relinquished. . . .

.   .   .

Chapter 26: Of Civil Laws.   By CIVIL LAWS, I understand the laws, that men are therefore bound to observe, because they are members, not of this, or that commonwealth in particular, but of a commonwealth. . . . [My design is] not to show what is law here, and there ; but what is law ; as Plato, Aristotle, Cicero, and divers others have done, without taking upon them the profession of the study of the law.

And first it is manifest, that law in general, is not counsel, but command ; nor a command of any man to any man ; but only of him, whose command is addressed to one formerly obliged to obey him. And as for civil law, it addeth only the name of the person commanding, which is *persona civitatis,* the person of the commonwealth.

Which considered, I define civil law in this manner. CIVIL LAW, *is to every subject, those rules, which the commonwealth hath commanded him, by word, writing, or other sufficient sign of the will, to make use of, for the distinction of right, and wrong ; that is to say, of what is contrary, and what is not contrary to the rule.*

.   .   .

[1] The nontransferable rights enumerated by Hobbes (see Chapter 14) are rights to disobey commands: to kill or wound oneself, not to resist assault, to abstain from necessities, to accuse oneself, and (in some cases) to fight.—ED.

JOHN LOCKE

John Locke was born in 1632, entered Oxford at twenty, and was associated with Christ Church College, as a student and, later, as a lecturer, until 1684. At Oxford, his continuing interest in philosophy was sparked by the works of Descartes, and medical studies brought him in touch with the noted scientists Sydenham and Boyle, whose empirical methods distinctly affected his theory of knowledge. In 1666 he directed a serious operation on Anthony Ashley Cooper, and soon thereafter he went to live as a member of Ashley's household, serving as confidential secretary and political counselor. His life was closely tied to Ashley's, who soon became the first Earl of Shaftesbury: He held several political offices, began serious philosophical work in Restoration London, went to France in 1675, and returned to help the Earl in opposition to the Crown from 1679 to 1683. Then, suspected with the Earl of political plotting, he chose self-exile in Holland. On his return to England in 1689, A Letter Concerning Toleration *and* Two Treatises of Government *were published anonymously.* An Essay Concerning Human Understanding, *begun twenty years earlier, appeared in 1690. Two more letters on* Toleration, The Reasonableness of Christianity, Some Thoughts Concerning Education, *and numerous minor writings added to his growing fame, and in the latter years of his life he exercised some considerable influence on the affairs of the state. He died in 1704.*

The following selections are reprinted from Book 2 of the 1764 edition of *Two Treatises of Government* (London: A. Millar et al., 1764). For the history of the text, see the critical edition of Peter Laslett, published by Cambridge University Press and available as a Mentor paperback.

Book 2: An Essay Concerning the True Original, Extent, and End of Civil Government

Chapter 1

.   .

§. 2. . . . I think it may not be amiss, to set down what I take to be political power; that the power of a *magistrate* over a subject may be distinguished from that of a *father* over his children, a *master* over his servant, a *husband* over his wife, and a *lord* over his slave. All which distinct powers happening sometimes together in the same man, if he be considered under these different relations, it may help us to distinguish these powers one from another, and show the difference betwixt a ruler of a common-wealth, a father of a family, and a captain of a galley.

§. 3. *Political power,* then, I take to be a *right* of making laws with penalties of death, and consequently all less penalties, for the regulating and preserving of property, and of employing the force of the community, in the execution of such laws, and in the defence of the common-wealth from foreign injury ; and all this only for the public good.

Chapter 2: Of the State of Nature.   §. 4. To understand political power right, and derive it from its original, we must consider, what state all men are naturally in, and that is, a *state of perfect freedom* to order their actions, and dispose of their possessions and persons, as they think fit, within the bounds of the law of nature, without asking leave, or depending upon the will of any other man.

A *state* also *of equality,* wherein all the power and jurisdiction is reciprocal, no one having more than another ; there being nothing more evident, than that creatures of the same species and rank, promiscuously born to all the same advantages of nature, and the use of the same faculties, should also be equal one amongst another without subordination or subjection, unless the lord and master of them all should, by any manifest declaration of his will, set one above another, and confer on him, by an evident and clear appointment, an undoubted right to dominion and sovereignty.

. . .

§. 6. But though this be *a state of liberty,* yet *it is not a state of licence :* though man in that state have an uncontroulable liberty to dispose of his person or possessions, yet he has not liberty to destroy himself, or so much as any creature in his possession, but where some nobler use than its bare preservation calls for it. The *state of nature* has a law of nature to govern it, which obliges every one : and reason, which is that law, teaches all mankind, who will but consult it, that being all *equal and independent,* no one ought to harm another in his life, health, liberty, or possessions : for men being all the workmanship of one omnipotent, and infinitely wise maker ; all the servants of one sovereign master, sent into the world by his order, and about his business ; they are his property, whose workmanship they are, made to last during his, not one another's pleasure : and being furnished with like faculties, sharing all in one community of nature, there cannot be supposed any such *subordination* among us, that may authorize us to destroy one another, as if we were made for one another's uses, as the inferior ranks of creatures are for our's. Every one, as he is *bound to preserve himself,* and not to quit his station wilfully, so by the like reason, when his own preservation comes not in competition, ought he, as much as he can, *to preserve the rest of mankind,* and may not, unless it be to do justice on an offender, take away, or impair the life, or what tends to the preservation of the life, the liberty, health, limb, or goods of another.

§. 7. And that all men may be restrained from invading others rights, and from doing hurt to one another, and the law of nature be observed, which willeth the peace and *preservation of all mankind,* the *execution* of the law of nature is, in that state, put into every man's hands, whereby every one has a right to punish the transgressors of that law to such a degree, as may hinder its violation : for the *law of nature* would, as all other laws that concern men in this world, be in vain, if there were no body that in the state of nature had a *power to execute* that law, and thereby preserve the innocent and restrain offenders. And if any one in the state of nature may punish another for any evil he has done, every one may do so : for in that *state of perfect equality,* where naturally there is no superiority or jurisdiction of one over another, what any may do in prosecution of that law, every one must needs have a right to do.

§. 8. And thus, in the state of nature, *one man comes by a power over another ;* but yet no absolute or arbitrary power, to use a criminal, when he has got him in his hands, according to the passionate heats, or boundless extravagancy of his own will ; but only to retribute to him, so far as calm reason and conscience dictate, what is proportionate to his transgression, which is so much as may serve for *reparation* and *restraint :* for these two are the only reasons, why one man may lawfully do harm to another, which is that we call *punishment.* In transgressing the law of nature, the offender declares himself to live by another rule than that of reason and common equity, which is that measure God has set to the actions of men, for their mutual security ; and so he becomes dangerous to mankind, the tye, which is to secure them from injury and violence, being slighted and broken by him. Which being a trespass against the whole species, and the peace and safety of it, provided for by the law of nature, every man upon this score, by the right he hath to preserve mankind in general, may restrain, or where it is necessary, destroy things noxious to them, and so may bring such evil on any one, who hath transgressed that law, as may make him repent the doing of it, and thereby deter him, and by his example others, from doing the like mischief. And in this case, and upon this ground, *every man hath a right to punish the offender, and be executioner of the law of nature.*

. . .

§. 10. Besides the crime which consists in violating the law, and varying from the right rule of reason, whereby a man so far becomes degenerate, and declares himself to quit the principles of human nature, and to be a noxious creature, there is commonly *injury* done to some person or other, and some other man receives damage by his transgression : in which case he who hath received any damage, has, besides the right of punishment common to him with other men, a particular right to seek *reparation* from him that has done it : and any other person, who finds it just, may also join with him that is injured, and assist him in recovering from the offender so much as may make satisfaction for the harm he has suffered.

§. 11. . . . That, he who has suffered the damage has a right to demand in his own name, and he alone can remit : the damnified person has this power of appropriating to himself the goods or service of the offender, *by right of self-preservation,* as every man has a power to punish the crime, to prevent its being committed again, *by the right he has of preserving all mankind,* and doing all reasonable things he can in order to that end : and thus it is, that every man, in the state of nature, has a power to kill a murderer, both *to deter* others from doing the like injury, which no reparation can compensate, by the example of the punishment that attends it from every body, and also to secure men from the attempts of a criminal, who having renounced reason, the common rule and measure God hath given to mankind, hath, by the unjust violence and slaughter he hath committed upon one, declared war against all mankind, and therefore may be destroyed as a *lion* or a *tyger,* one of those wild savage beasts, with whom men can have no society nor security : and upon this is grounded that great law of nature, *Whoso sheddeth man's blood, by man shall his blood be shed.* And *Cain* was so fully convinced, that every one had a right to destroy such a criminal, that after the murder of his brother, he cries out, *Every one that findeth me, shall slay me ;* so plain was it writ in the hearts of all mankind.

§. 12. By the same reason may a man in the state of nature *punish the lesser breaches of that law.* It will perhaps be demanded, with death? I answer, each transgression may be *punished* to that *degree,* and with so much *severity,* as will suffice to make it an ill bargain to the offender, give him cause to repent, and terrify others from doing the like. Every offence, that can be committed in the state of nature, may in the state of nature be also punished equally, and as far forth as it may, in a common-wealth : for though it would be besides my present purpose, to enter here into the particulars of the law of nature, or its *measures of punishment ;* yet, it is certain there is such a law, and that too, as intelligible and plain to a rational crea-ture, and a studier of that law, as the positive laws of common-wealths ; nay, possibly plainer ; as much as reason is easier to be understood, than the fancies and intricate contrivances of men, following contrary and hidden interests put into words ; for so truly are a great part of the *municipal laws* of countries, which are only so far right, as they are founded on the law of nature, by which they are to be regulated and interpreted.

§. 13. To this strange doctrine, viz., that *in the state of nature every one has the executive power* of the law of nature, I doubt not but it will be objected, that it is unreasonable for men to be judges in their own cases, that self-love will make men partial to themselves and their friends : and on the other side, that ill nature, passion and revenge will carry them too far in punishing others ; and hence nothing but confusion and disorder will follow, and that therefore God hath certainly appointed government to restrain the partiality and violence of men. I easily grant, that *civil government* is the proper remedy for the inconveniences of the state of nature, which must certainly be great, where men may be judges in their own case, since it is easy to be imagined, that he who was so unjust as to do his brother an injury, will scarce be so just as to condemn himself for it : but I shall desire those who make this objection, to remember, that *absolute monarchs* are but men ; and if government is to be the remedy of those evils, which necessarily follow from men's being judges in their own cases, and the state of nature is therefore not to be endured, I desire to know what kind of government that is, and how much better it is than the state of nature, where one man, commanding a multitude, has the liberty to be judge in his own case, and may do to all his subjects whatever he pleases, without the least liberty to any one to question or controul those who execute his pleasure ? . . .

§. 14. It is often asked as a mighty objection, *where are,* or ever were there any *men in such a state of nature ?* To which it may suffice as an answer at present, that since all princes and rulers of *independent* governments all through the world, are in a state of nature, it is plain the world never was, nor ever will be, without numbers of men in that state. I have named all governors of *independent communities,* whether they are, or are not, in league with others : for it is not every compact that puts an end to the state of nature between men, but only this one of agreeing together mutually to enter into one community, and make one body politic ; other promises, and compacts, men may make one with another, and yet still be in the state of nature. The promises and bargains for truck, etc., between the two men in the desert island, mentioned by *Garcilasso de la Vega,* in his history of *Peru ;* or between a *Swiss* and an *Indian,* in the woods of *America,* are binding to them, though they are perfectly in a state of nature, in reference to one another : for truth and keeping of faith belongs to men, as men, and not as members of society.

§. 15. To those that say, there were never any men in the state of nature, I will not only oppose the authority of the judicious *Hooker, Eccl. Pol. lib.* i. *sect.* 10. where he says, *The laws which have been hitherto mentioned, i.e.,* the laws of nature, *do bind men absolutely, even as they are men, although they have never any settled fellowship, never any solemn agreement amongst themselves what to do, or not to do : but forasmuch as we are not by ourselves sufficient to furnish ourselves with competent store of things, needful for such a life as our nature doth desire, a life fit for the dignity of man ; therefore to supply those defects and imperfections which are in us, as living single and solely by ourselves, we are naturally induced to seek communion and fellowship with others : this was the cause of men's uniting themselves at first in politic societies.* But I moreover affirm, that all men are naturally in that state, and remain so, till by their own consents they make themselves members of some politic society ; and I doubt not in the sequel of this discourse, to make it very clear.

Chapter 3: Of the State of War.

. . .

§. 19. And here we have the plain *difference between the state of nature and the state of war,* which however some men have confounded, are as far distant, as a state of peace, good will, mutual assistance and preservation, and a state of enmity, malice, violence and mutual destruction, are one from another. Men living together according to reason, without a common superior on earth, with authority to judge between them, is *properly the state of nature.* But force, or a declared design of force, upon the person of another, where there is no common superior on earth to appeal to for relief, *is the state of war :* and it is the want of such an appeal gives a man the right of war even against an *aggressor,* tho' he be in society and a fellow subject. Thus a *thief,* whom I cannot harm, but by appeal to the law, for having stolen all that I am worth, I may kill, when he sets on me to rob me but of my horse or coat ; because the law, which was made for my preservation, where it cannot interpose to secure my life from present force, which, if lost, is capable of no reparation, permits me my own defence, and the right of war, a liberty to kill the aggressor, because the aggressor allows not time to appeal to our common judge, nor the decision of the law, for remedy in a case where the mischief may be irreparable. Want of a common judge with authority, puts all men in a state of nature : force without right, upon a man's person, makes a state of war, both where there is, and is not, a common judge.

. . .

Chapter 4:   Of Slavery.   §. 22. The *natural liberty* of man is to be free from any superior power on earth, and not to be under the will or legislative authority of man, but to have only the law of nature for his rule. The *liberty of man,* in society, is to be under no other legislative power, but that established, by consent, in the common-wealth ; nor under the dominion of any will, or restraint of any law, but what that legislative shall enact, according to the trust put in it. Freedom then is not what Sir *Robert Filmer* tells us, *Observations, A. 55. a liberty for every one to do what he lists, to live as he pleases, and not to be tied by any laws :* but *freedom of men under government* is, to have a standing rule to live by, common to every one of that society, and made by the legislative power erected in it ; a liberty to follow my own will in all things, where the rule prescribes not ; and not to be subject to the inconstant, uncertain, unknown, arbitrary will of another man : as *freedom of nature* is, to be under no other restraint but the law of nature.

§. 23. This *freedom* from absolute, arbitrary power, is so necessary to, and closely joined with a man's preservation, that he cannot part with it, but by what forfeits his preservation and life together : for a man, not having the power of his own life, *cannot,* by compact, or his own consent, *enslave himself* to any one, nor put himself under the absolute, arbitrary power of another, to take away his life, when he pleases. No body can give more power than he has himself ; and he that cannot take away his own life, cannot give another power over it. . . .

.   .   .

Chapter 5:   Of Property.

.   .   .

§. 26. God, who hath given the world to men in common, hath also given them reason to make use of it to the best advantage of life, and convenience. The earth, and all that is therein, is given to men for the support and comfort of their being. And tho' all the fruits it naturally produces, and beasts it feeds, belong to mankind in common, as they are produced by the spontaneous hand of nature ; and no body has originally a private dominion, exclusive of the rest of mankind, in any of them, as they are thus in their natural state : yet being given for the use of men, there must of necessity be *a means to appropriate* them some way or other, before they can be of any use, or at all beneficial to any particular man. The fruit, or venison, which nourishes the wild *Indian,* who knows no inclosure, and is still a tenant in common, must be his, and so his, i.e., a part of him, that another can no longer have any right to it, before it can do him any good for the support of his life.

§. 27. Though the earth, and all inferior creatures, be common to all men, yet every man has a *property* in his own *person :* this no body has any right to but himself. The *labour* of his body, and the *work* of his hands, we may say, are properly his. Whatsoever then he removes out of the state that nature hath provided, and left it in, he hath mixed his *labour* with, and joined to it something that is his own, and thereby makes it his *property.* It being by him removed from the common state nature hath placed it in, it hath by this *labour* something annexed to it, that excludes the common right of other men : for this *labour* being the unquestionable property of the labourer, no man but he can have a right to what that is once joined to, at least where there is enough, and as good, left in common for others.

. . .

§. 31. It will perhaps be objected to this, that if gathering the acorns, or other fruits of the earth, etc., makes a right to them, then any one may *ingross* as much as he will. To which I answer, Not so. The same law of nature, that does by this means give us property, does also *bound* that *property* too. *God has given us all things richly,* I Tim. vi. 12. is the voice of reason confirmed by inspiration. But how far has he given it us ? *To enjoy.* As much as any one can make use of to any advantage of life before it spoils, so much he may by his labour fix a property in : whatever is beyond this, is more than his share, and belongs to others. Nothing was made by God for man to spoil or destroy. And thus, considering the plenty of natural provisions there was a long time in the world, and the few spenders ; and to how small a part of that provision the industry of one man could extend itself, and ingross it to the prejudice of others ; especially keeping within the *bounds,* set by reason, of what might serve for his *use ;* there could be then little room for quarrels or contentions about property so established.

. . .

§. 50. But since gold and silver, being little useful to the life of man in proportion to food, raiment, and carriage, has its *value* only from the consent of men, whereof *labour* yet *makes,* in great part, *the measure,* it is plain, that men have agreed to a disproportionate and unequal *possession of the earth,* they having, by a tacit and voluntary consent, found out a way how a man may fairly possess more land than he himself can use the product of, by receiving in exchange for the overplus gold and silver, which may be hoarded up without injury to any one; these metals not spoiling or decaying in the hands of the possessor. This partage of things in an inequality of private possessions, men have made practicable out of the bounds of society, and without compact, only by putting a value on gold and silver, and tacitly agreeing in the use of money : for in governments, the laws regulate the right of property, and the possession of land is determined by positive constitutions.

. . .

Chapter 6: Of Paternal Power.

. . .

§. 57. . . . *law,* in its true notion, *is* not so much the limitation as *the direction of a free and intelligent agent* to his proper interest, and prescribes no farther than is for the general good of those under that law : could they be happier without it, the *law,* as an useless thing, would of itself vanish ; and that ill deserves the name of confinement which hedges us in only from bogs and precipices. So that, however it may be mistaken, *the end of law is* not to abolish or restrain, but *to preserve and enlarge freedom :* for in all the states of created beings capable of laws, *where there is no law, there is no freedom :* for *liberty* is, to be free from restraint and violence from others ; which cannot be, where there is no law : but freedom is not, as we are told, *a liberty for every man to do what he lists :* (for who could be free, when every other man's humour might domineer over him ?) but a *liberty* to dispose, and order as he lists, his person, actions, possessions, and his whole property, within the allowance of those laws under which he is, and therein not to be subject to the arbitrary will of another, but freely follow his own. . . .

. . .

Chapter 8: Of the Beginning of Political Societies. §. 95. Men being, as has been said, by nature, all free, equal, and independent, no one can be put out of this estate, and subjected to the political power of another, without his own consent. The only way whereby any one divests himself of his natural liberty, and puts on the *bonds of civil society,* is by agreeing with other men to join and unite into a community, for their comfortable, safe, and peaceable living one amongst another, in a secure enjoyment of their properties, and a greater security against any, that are not of it. This any number of men may do, because it injures not the freedom of the rest ; they are left as they were in the liberty of the state of nature. When any number of men have so *consented to make one community or government,* they are thereby presently incorporated, and make *one body politic,* wherein the *majority* have a right to act and conclude the rest.

§. 96.   For when any number of men have, by the consent of every individual, made a *community,* they have thereby made that *community* one body, with a power to act as one body, which is only by the will and determination of the *majority :* for that which acts any community, being only the consent of the individuals of it, and it being necessary to that which is one body to move one way ; it is necessary the body should move that way whither the greater force carries it, which is the *consent of the majority :* or else it is impossible it should act or continue one body, *one community,* which the consent of every individual that united into it, agreed that it should ; and so every one is bound by that consent to be concluded by the *majority.* And therefore we see, that in assemblies, impowered to act by positive laws, where no number is set by that positive law which impowers them, the *act of the majority* passes for the act of the whole, and of course determines, as having, by the law of nature and reason, the power of the whole.

§. 97.   And thus every man, by consenting with others to make one body politic under one government, puts himself under an obligation, to every one of that society, to submit to the determination of the *majority,* and to be concluded by it ; or else this *original compact,* whereby he with others incorporates into *one society,* would signify nothing. . . .

§. 98.   For if *the consent of the majority* shall not, in reason, be received as *the act of the whole,* and conclude every individual ; nothing but the consent of every individual can make any thing to be the act of the whole. . . . Such a constitution as this would make the mighty *Leviathan* of a shorter duration, than the feeblest creatures, and not let it outlast the day it was born in : which cannot be supposed, till we can think, that rational creatures should desire and constitute societies only to be dissolved : for where the *majority* cannot conclude the rest, there they cannot act as one body, and consequently will be immediately dissolved again.

§. 99. Whosoever therefore out of a state of nature unite into a *community,* must be understood to give up all the power, necessary to the ends for which they unite into society, to the *majority* of the community, unless they expresly agreed in any number greater than the majority. And this is done by barely agreeing to *unite into one political society,* which is *all the compact* that is, or needs be, between the individuals, that enter into, or make up a *common-wealth.* And thus that, which begins and actually *constitutes any political society,* is nothing but the consent of any number of freemen capable of a majority to unite and incorporate into such a society. And this is that, and that only, which did, or could give beginning to any *lawful government* in the world.

§. 100. To this I find two objections made.

First, *that there are no instances to be found in story, of a company of men independent, and equal one amongst another, that met together, and in this way began and set up a government.*

. . .

§. 101. To the first there is this to answer. That it is not at all to be wondered, that *history* gives us but a very little account of *men, that lived together in the state of nature.* The inconveniences of that condition, and the love and want of society, no sooner brought any number of them together, but they presently united and incorporated, if they designed to continue together. And if we may not suppose *men* ever to have been *in the state of nature,* because we hear not much of them in such a state, we may as well suppose the armies of *Salmanasser* or *Xerxes* were never children, because we hear little of them, till they were men, and imbodied in armies. Government is every where antecedent to records. . . .

. . .

§. 112. . . . as far as we have any light from history, we have reason to conclude, that all peaceful beginnings of *govern-*

ment have been *laid in the consent of the people.* I say *peaceful,* because I shall have occasion in another place to speak of conquest, which some esteem a way of beginning of governments.

The other objection I find urged against the beginning of polities, in the way I have mentioned, is this, viz.,

§. 113. *That all men being born under government, some or other, it is impossible any of them should ever be free, and at liberty to unite together, and begin a new one, or ever be able to erect a lawful government.*

. . .

§. 115. For there are no examples so frequent in history, both sacred and profane, as those of men withdrawing themselves, and their obedience, from the jurisdiction they were born under, and the family or community they were bred up in, and *setting up new governments* in other places. . . .

§. 116. This has been the practice of the world from its first beginning to this day ; nor is it now any more hindrance to the freedom of mankind, that they are *born under constituted and ancient polities,* that have established laws, and set forms of government, than if they were born in the woods, amongst the unconfined inhabitants, that run loose in them. . . .

§. 117. And this has generally given the occasion to mistake in this matter ; because common-wealths not permitting any part of their dominions to be dismembered, nor to be enjoyed by any but those of their community, the son cannot ordinarily enjoy the possessions of his father, but under the same terms his father did, by becoming a member of the society ; whereby he puts himself presently under the government he finds there established, as much as any other subject of that common-wealth. And thus *the consent of freemen, born under government,* which only *makes them members of it,* being given separately in their turns, as each comes to be of age, and not in a multitude together ; people take no notice of it, and thinking it not done at all, or not necessary, conclude they are naturally subjects as they are men.

. . .

§. 119. *Every man* being, as has been shewed, *naturally free,* and nothing being able to put him into subjection to any earthly power, but only his own *consent ;* it is to be considered, what shall be understood to be a *sufficient declaration* of a man's *consent, to make him subject* to the laws of any government. There is a common distinction of an express and a tacit consent, which will concern our present case. No body doubts but an express *consent,* of any man entering into any society, makes him a perfect member of that society, a subject of that government. The difficulty is, what ought to be looked upon as a *tacit consent,* and how far it binds, i.e., how far any one shall be looked on to have consented, and thereby submitted to any government, where he has made no expressions of it at all. And to this I say, that every man, that hath any possessions, or enjoyment, of any part of the dominions of any government, doth thereby give his *tacit consent,* and is as far forth obliged to obedience to the laws of that government, during such enjoyment, as any one under it ; whether this his possession be of land, to him and his heirs for ever, or a lodging only for a week ; or whether it be barely travelling freely on the highway ; and in effect, it reaches as far as the very being of any one within the territories of that government.

§. 120. . . . Whoever therefore, from thenceforth, by inheritance, purchase, permission, or otherways, *enjoys any part of the land,* so annexed to, and under the government *of that common-wealth, must take it with the condition* it is under ; that is, *of submitting to the government of the common-wealth,* under whose jurisdiction it is, as far forth as any subject of it.

§. 121. But since the government has a direct jurisdiction only over the land, and reaches the possessor of it, (before he has actually incorporated himself in the society) only as he dwells upon, and enjoys that ; the obligation any one is under, by virtue of such enjoyment, to *submit to the government, begins and ends with the enjoyment ;* so that whenever the owner, who has given nothing but such a *tacit consent* to the government, will, by donation, sale, or otherwise, quit the said possession, he is at liberty to go and incorporate himself into any other common-wealth ; to agree with others to begin a new one, *in vacuis locis,* in any part of the world, they can find free and unpossessed : whereas he, that has once, by actual agreement, and any *express* declaration, given his *consent* to be of any common-wealth, is perpetually and indispensibly obliged to be, and remain unalterably a subject to it, and can never be again in the liberty of the state of nature ; unless, by any calamity, the government he was under comes to be dissolved ; or else by some public act cuts him off from being any longer a member of it.

§. 122. But submitting to the laws of any country, living quietly, and enjoying privileges and protection under them, *makes not a man a member of that society :* this is only a local protection and homage due to and from all those, who, not being in a state of war, come within the territories belonging to any government, to all parts whereof the force of its laws extends. But this no more *makes a man a member of that society,* a perpetual subject of that common-wealth, than it would make a man a subject to another, in whose family he found it convenient to abide for some time ; though, whilst he continued in it, he were obliged to comply with the laws, and submit to the government he found there. And thus we see, that *foreigners,* by living all their lives under another government, and enjoying the privileges and protection of it, though they are bound, even in conscience, to submit to its administration, as far forth as any denison ; yet do not thereby come to be *subjects or members of that common-wealth.* Nothing can make any man so, but his actually entering into it by positive engagement, and express promise and compact. This is that, which I think, concerning the beginning of political societies, and that *consent which makes any one a member* of any common-wealth.

Chapter 9: Of the Ends of Political Society and Government.
§. 123. If man in the state of nature be so free, as has been said ; if he be absolute lord of his own person and possessions, equal to the greatest, and subject to no body, why will he part with his freedom ? why will he give up this empire, and subject himself to the dominion and controul of any other power ? To which it is obvious to answer, that though in the state of nature he hath such a right, yet the enjoyment of it is very uncertain, and constantly exposed to the invasion of others : for all being kings as much as he, every man his equal, and the greater part no strict observers of equity and justice, the

enjoyment of the property he has in this state is very unsafe, very unsecure. This makes him willing to quit a condition, which, however free, is full of fears and continual dangers : and it is not without reason, that he seeks out, and is willing to join in society with others, who are already united, or have a mind to unite, for the mutual *preservation* of their lives, liberties and estates, which I call by the general name, *property*.

§. 124. The great and *chief end,* therefore, of men's uniting into common-wealths, and putting themselves under government, *is the preservation of their property.* To which in the state of nature there are many things wanting.

First, there wants an *established,* settled, known *law,* received and allowed by common consent to be the standard of right and wrong, and the common measure to decide all controversies between them : for though the law of nature be plain and intelligible to all rational creatures ; yet men being biassed by their interest, as well as ignorant for want of study of it, are not apt to allow of it as a law binding to them in the application of it to their particular cases.

§. 125. *Secondly,* in the state of nature there wants *a known and indifferent judge,* with authority to determine all differences according to the established law : for every one in that state being both judge and executioner of the law of nature, men being partial to themselves, passion and revenge is very apt to carry them too far, and with too much heat, in their own cases ; as well as negligence, and unconcernedness, to make them too remiss in other men's.

§. 126. *Thirdly,* in the state of nature there often wants *power* to back and support the sentence when right, and to *give* it due *execution.* They who by any injustice offended, will seldom fail, where they are able, by force to make good their injustice ; such resistance many times makes the punishment dangerous, and frequently destructive, to those who attempt it.

§. 127. Thus mankind, notwithstanding all the privileges of the state of nature, being but in an ill condition, while they remain in it, are quickly driven into society. Hence it comes to pass, that we seldom find any number of men live any time together in this state. The inconveniencies that they are therein exposed to, by the irregular and uncertain exercise of the power every man has of punishing the transgressions of others, make them take sanctuary under the established laws of government, and therein seek *the preservation of their property*. It is this makes them so willingly give up every one his single power of punishing, to be exercised by such alone, as shall be appointed to it amongst them ; and by such rules as the community, or those authorized by them to that purpose, shall agree on. And in this we have the original *right and rise of both the legislative and executive power,* as well as of the governments and societies themselves.

§. 128. For in the state of nature, to omit the liberty he has of innocent delights, a man has two powers.

The first is to do whatsoever he thinks fit for the preservation of himself, and others within the permission of the *law of nature :* by which law, common to them all, he and all the rest of *mankind are one community,* make up one society, distinct from all other creatures. And were it not for the corruption and vitiousness of degenerate men, there would be no need of any other ; no necessity that men should separate from this great and natural community, and by positive agreements combine into smaller and divided associations.

The other power a man has in the state of nature, is the *power to punish the crimes* committed against that law. Both these he gives up, when he joins in a private, if I may so call it, or particular politic society, and incorporates into any common-wealth, separate from the rest of mankind.

§. 129. The first *power, viz., of doing whatsoever he thought for the preservation of himself,* and the rest of mankind, *he gives up* to be regulated by laws made by the society, so far forth as the preservation of himself, and the rest of that society shall require ; which laws of the society in many things confine the liberty he had by the law of nature.

§. 130. *Secondly,* the *power of punishing he wholly gives up,* and engages his natural force, (which he might before employ in the execution of the law of nature, by his own single authority, as he thought fit) to assist the executive power of the society, as the law thereof shall require : for being now in a new state, wherein he is to enjoy many conveniencies, from the labour, assistance, and society of others in the same community, as well as protection from its whole strength ; he is to part also with as much of his natural liberty, in providing for himself, as the good, prosperity, and safety of the society shall require ; which is not only necessary, but just, since the other members of the society do the like.

§. 131. But though men, when they enter into society, give up the equality, liberty, and executive power they had in the state of nature, into the hands of the society, to be so far disposed of by the legislative, as the good of the society shall require ; yet it being only with an intention in every one the better to preserve himself, his liberty and property ; (for no rational creature can be supposed to change his condition with an intention to be worse) the power of the society, or *legislative* constituted by them, can *never be supposed to extend farther, than the common good ;* but is obliged to secure every one's property, by providing against those three defects above mentioned, that made the state of nature so unsafe and uneasy. And so whoever has the legislative or supreme power of any common-wealth, is bound to govern by established *standing laws,* promulgated and known to the people, and not by extemporary decrees ; by *indifferent* and upright *judges,* who are to decide controversies by those laws ; and to employ the force of the community at home, *only in the execution of such laws,* or abroad to prevent or redress foreign injuries, and secure the community from inroads and invasion. And all this to be directed to no other *end,* but the *peace, safety,* and *public good* of the people.

. . .

Chapter 11: Of the Extent of the Legislative Power. §. 134. The great end of men's entering into society, being the enjoyment of their properties in peace and safety, and the great instrument and means of that being the laws established in that society ; the *first and fundamental positive law* of all commonwealths *is the establishing of the legislative* power ; as the *first and fundamental natural law,* which is to govern even the legislative itself, *is the preservation of the society,* and (as far as will consist with the public good) of every person in it. This *legislative* is not only *the supreme power* of the commonwealth, but sacred and unalterable in the hands where the community have once placed it ; nor can any edict of any body else, in what form soever conceived, or by what power soever backed, have the force and obligation of a *law,* which has not its *sanction from* that *legislative* which the public has chosen and appointed : for without this the law could not have that, which is absolutely necessary to its being a *law,*[1] *the consent of the society,* over whom no body can have a power to make laws, but by their own consent, and by authority received from them ; and therefore all the *obedience,* which by the most solemn ties any one can be obliged *to* pay, ultimately terminates in this *supreme power,* and is directed by those laws which it enacts : nor can any oaths to any foreign power whatsoever, or any domestic subordinate power, discharge any member of the society from his *obedience to the legislative,* acting pursuant to their trust ; nor oblige him to any obedience contrary to the laws so enacted, or farther than they do allow ; it being ridiculous to imagine one can be tied ultimately to *obey* any *power* in the society, which is not the *supreme.*

§. 135. Though the *legislative,* whether placed in one or more, whether it be always in being, or only by intervals, though it be the *supreme* power in every common-wealth ; yet,

First, it is *not,* nor can possibly be absolutely *arbitrary* over the lives and fortunes of the people. . . .

. . .

§. 142. These are the *bounds* which the trust, that is put in them by the society, and the law of God and nature, have

---

[1] The lawful power of making laws to command whole politic societies of men, belonging so properly unto the same intire societies, that for any prince or potentate of what kind soever upon earth, to exercise the same of himself, and not by express commission immediately and personally received from God, or else by authority derived at the first from their consent, upon whose persons they impose laws, it is no better than mere tyranny. Laws they are not therefore which public approbation hath not made so. *Hooker's Eccl. Pol. I* i. *sect.* 10. Of this point therefore we are to note, that sith men naturally have no full and perfect power to command whole politic multitudes of men, therefore utterly without our consent, we could in such sort be at no man's commandment living. And to be commanded we do consent, when that society, whereof we be a part, hath at any time before consented, without revoking the same after by the like universal agreement.

Laws therefore human, of what kind so ever, are available by consent. *Ibid.*

set to the legislative power of every common-wealth, in all forms of government.

First, they are to govern by *promulgated established laws,* not to be varied in particular cases, but to have one rule for rich and poor, for the favourite at court, and the country man at plough.

Secondly, these *laws* also ought to be designed *for* no other end ultimately, but *the good of the people.*

Thirdly, they must *not raise taxes* on the *property of the people, without the consent of the people,* given by themselves, or their deputies. And this properly concerns only such governments where the *legislative* is always in being, or at least where the people have not reserved any part of the legislative to deputies, to be from time to time chosen by themselves.

Fourthly, the *legislative* neither must *nor can transfer the power of making laws* to any body else, or place it any where, but where the people have.

. . .

Chapter 18: Of Tyranny.   §. 199. As usurpation is the exercise of power, which another hath a right to ; so *tyranny is the exercise of power beyond right,* which no body can have a right to. And this is making use of the power any one has in his hands, not for the good of those who are under it, but for his own private separate advantage. . . .

. . .

§. 202. *Where-ever law ends, tyranny begins,* if the law be transgressed to another's harm ; and whosoever in authority exceeds the power given him by the law, and makes use of the force he has under his command, to compass that upon the subject, which the law allows not, ceases in that to be a magistrate ; and, acting without authority, may be opposed, as any other man, who by force invades the right of another. . . .

. . .

3 SELECTIONS FROM

A Treatise of Human Nature: Being an Attempt to Introduce the Experimental Method of Reasoning into Moral Subjects

DAVID HUME

David Hume was born in 1711, entered Edinburgh University at an early age, and was urged by his family to study the law. In 1729, however, having formed "an insurmountable aversion to everything but the pursuits of philosophy and general learning," he turned to "literature"—"the ruling passion" of his life. After several years of intense work and attacks of nerves, he went in 1734 to France where in three years he largely composed A Treatise of Human Nature. *This work "fell deadborn from the press" in 1739–1740; his* Essays, Moral and Political, *published in 1742, had a somewhat greater success. Rejected as professor at Edinburgh, at least partly because of suspicions of atheism aroused by the* Treatise, *he spent the years of 1746–1748 on the Continent.* Three Essays *appeared in 1748 along with* Enquiry Concerning Human Understanding, *a reworking of Book 1 of the* Treatise; *a new version of Book 3 appeared as* Enquiry Concerning the Principles of Morals *in 1751. A year later, after having been refused a professorship at Glasgow, he became keeper of the Advocates' Library in Edinburgh.* Political Discourses *(1752) was an immediate success at home and abroad, and when the* History of England *began to appear in 1754, his fame was finally secure. In 1763 he was appointed secretary of the Embassy at Paris, where he was much feted as "le bon David"; later in London he served as undersecretary of state. He returned to Edinburgh in 1769, revised his writings,*

The following selections are reprinted from an old college text, *Hume's Treatise of Morals: and Selections from the Treatise of the Passions* (Boston: Ginn & Company, 1893), edited by J. H. Hyslop. Apart from the lack of marginal headings, it is almost identical to the first edition of 1740.

but was restrained by friends from publishing his Dialogues
Concerning Natural Religion *until after his death in 1776.*

Book 3. Of Morals

Part 2: Of Justice and Injustice
Section 2: Of the origin of justice and property. We now
proceed to examine two questions, viz., *concerning the manner,
in which the rules of justice are establish'd by the artifice of men;
and concerning the reasons which determine us to attribute to
the observance or neglect of these rules a moral beauty and deformity.* These questions will appear afterwards to be distinct.
We shall begin with the former.

Of all the animals, with which this globe is peopled, there
is none towards whom nature seems, at first sight to have ex-
ercis'd more cruelty than towards man, in the numberless wants
and necessities, with which she has loaded him, and in the
slender means, which she affords to the relieving these necessities. In other creatures these two particulars generally compensate each other. If we consider the lion as a voracious and
carnivorous animal, we shall easily discover him to be very
necessitous ; but if we turn our eye to his make and temper, his
agility, his courage, his arms, and his force, we shall find, that
his advantages hold proportion with his wants. The sheep and
ox are depriv'd of all these advantages ; but their appetites are
moderate, and their food is of easy purchase. In man alone,
this unnatural conjunction of infirmity, and of necessity, may
be observ'd in its greatest perfection. Not only the food, which
is requir'd for his sustenance, flies his search and approach, or
at least requires his labour to be produc'd, but he must be
possess'd of cloaths and lodging, to defend him against the injuries of the weather ; tho' to consider him only in himself, he
is provided, neither with arms, nor force, nor other natural
abilities, which are in any degree answerable to so many necessities.

'Tis by society alone he is able to supply his defects, and
raise himself up to an equality with his fellow-creatures, and
even acquire a superiority above them. By society all his infirmities are compensated ; and tho' in that situation his wants

multiply every moment upon him, yet his abilities are still more augmented, and leave him in every respect more satisfied and happy, than 'tis possible for him, in his savage and solitary condition, ever to become. When every individual person labours a-part, and only for himself, his force is too small to execute any considerable work ; his labour being employ'd in supplying all his different necessities, he never attains a perfection in any particular art ; and as his force and success are not at all times equal, the least failure in either of these particulars must be attended with inevitable ruin and misery. Society provides a remedy for these *three* inconveniences. By the conjunction of forces, our power is augmented : By the partition of employments, our ability encreases : And by mutual succour we are less expos'd to fortune and accidents. 'Tis by this additional *force, ability,* and *security,* that society becomes advantageous.

But in order to form society, 'tis requisite not only that it be advantageous, but also that men be sensible of these advantages ; and 'tis impossible, in their wild uncultivated state, that by study and reflection alone, they should ever be able to attain this knowledge. Most fortunately, therefore, there is conjoin'd to those necessities, whose remedies are remote and obscure, another necessity, which having a present and more obvious remedy, may justly be regarded as the first and original principle of human society. This necessity is no other than that natural appetite betwixt the sexes, which unites them together, and preserves their union, till a new tye takes place in their concern for their common offspring. This new concern becomes also a principle of union betwixt the parents and offspring, and forms a more numerous society ; where the parents govern by the advantage of their superior strength and wisdom, and at the same time are restrain'd in the exercise of their authority by that natural affection, which they bear their children. In a little time, custom and habit operating on the tender minds of the children, makes them sensible of the advantages, which they may reap from society, as well as fashions them by degrees for it, by rubbing off those rough corners and untoward affections, which prevent their coalition.

For it must be confest, that however the circumstances of human nature may render an union necessary, and however those passions of lust and natural affection may seem to render it unavoidable ; yet there are other particulars in our *natural temper,* and in our *outward circumstances,* which are very incommodious, and are even contrary to the requisite conjunction. Among the former, we may justly esteem our *selfishness* to be the most considerable. I am sensible, that, generally speaking, the representations of this quality have been carried much too far ; and that the descriptions, which certain philosophers delight so much to form of mankind in this particular, are as wide of nature as any accounts of monsters, which we meet with in fables and romances. So far from thinking, that men have no affection for anything beyond themselves, I am of opinion, that tho' it be rare to meet with one, who loves any single person better than himself ; yet 'tis as rare to meet with one, in whom all the kind affections, taken together, do not over-balance all the selfish. Consult common experience : Do you not see, that tho' the whole expence of the family be generally under the direction of the master of it, yet there are few that do not bestow the largest part of their fortunes on the pleasures of their wives, and the education of their children, reserving the smallest portion for their own proper use and entertainment. This is what we may observe concerning such as have those endearing ties ; and may presume, that the case would be the same with others, were they plac'd in a like situation.

But tho' this generosity must be acknowledg'd to the honour of human nature, we may at the same time remark, that so noble an affection, instead of fitting men for large societies, is almost as contrary to them, as the most narrow selfishness. For while each person loves himself better than any other single person, and in his love to others bears the greatest affection to his relations and acquaintance, this must necessarily produce an opposition of passions, and a consequent opposition of actions ; which cannot but be dangerous to the new-establish'd union.

'Tis however worth while to remark, that this contrariety of passions wou'd be attended with but small danger, did it not concur with a peculiarity in our *outward circumstances,* which affords it an opportunity of exerting itself. There are three different species of goods, which we are possess'd of ; the internal satisfaction of our minds, the external advantages of our body, and the enjoyment of such possessions as we have acquir'd by our industry and good fortune. We are perfectly secure in the enjoyment of the first. The second may be ravish'd from us, but can be of no advantage to him who deprives us of them. The last only are both expos'd to the violence of others, and may be transferr'd without suffering any loss or alteration ; while at the same time, there is not a sufficient quantity of them to supply every one's desires and necessities. As the improvement, therefore, of these goods is the chief advantage of society, so the *instability* of their possession, along with their *scarcity*, is the chief impediment.

In vain shou'd we expect to find, in *uncultivated nature*, a remedy to this inconvenience ; or hope for any inartificial principle of the human mind, which might controul those partial affections, and make us overcome the temptations arising from our circumstances. . . . [Our] natural uncultivated ideas of morality, instead of providing a remedy for the partiality of our affections, do rather conform themselves to that partiality, and give it an additional force and influence.

The remedy, then, is not deriv'd from nature, but from *artifice ;* or more properly speaking, nature provides a remedy in the judgment and understanding, for what is irregular and incommodious in the affections. For when men, from their early education in society, have become sensible of the infinite advantages that result from it, and have besides acquir'd a new affection to company and conversation ; and when they have observ'd, that the principal disturbance in society arises from those goods, which we call external, and from their looseness and easy transition from one person to another ; they must seek for a remedy, by putting these goods, as far as possible, on the same footing with the fix'd and constant advantages of the mind and body. This can be done after no other manner, than by a convention enter'd into by all the members of the society to bestow stability on the possession of those external goods, and leave every one in the peaceable enjoyment of what he may acquire by his fortune and industry. By this means, every one knows what he may safely possess ; and the passions are restrain'd in their partial and contradictory motions. Nor is such a restraint contrary to these passions ; for if so, it cou'd never be entered into, nor maintain'd ; but it is only contrary to their heedless and impetuous movement. Instead of departing from our own interest, or from that of our nearest friends, by abstaining from the possessions of others, we cannot better consult both these interests, than by such a convention ; because it is by that means we maintain society, which is so necessary to their well-being and subsistence, as well as to our own.

This convention is not of the nature of a *promise* : For even promises themselves, as we shall see afterwards, arise from human conventions. It is only a general sense of common interest ; which sense all the members of the society express to one another, and which induces them to regulate their conduct by certain rules. I observe, that it will be for my interest to leave another in the possession of his goods, *provided* he will act in the same manner with regard to me. He is sensible of a like interest in the regulation of his conduct. When this common sense of interest is mutually express'd, and is known to both, it produces a suitable resolution and behaviour. And this may properly enough be call'd a convention or agreement betwixt us, tho' without the interposition of a promise ; since the actions of each of us have a reference to those of the other, and are perform'd upon the supposition, that something is to be perform'd on the other part. Two men, who pull the oars of a boat, do it by an agreement or convention, tho' they have never given promises to each other. Nor is the rule concerning the stability of possession the less deriv'd from human conventions, that it arises gradually, and acquires force by a slow progression, and by our repeated experience of the inconveniences of transgressing it. On the contrary, this experience assures us still more, that the sense of interest has become common to all our fellows, and gives us a confidence of the future regularity of their conduct : And 'tis only on the expectation of this, that our moderation and abstinence are founded. In like manner are languages gradually establish'd by human conventions without any promise. In like manner do gold and silver become the common measures of exchange, and are esteem'd sufficient payment for what is of a hundred times their value.

After this convention, concerning abstinence from the possessions of others, is enter'd into, and every one has acquir'd a stability in his possessions, there immediately arise the ideas of justice and injustice ; as also those of *property, right,* and *obligation.* The latter are altogether unintelligible without first understanding the former. Our property is nothing but those goods, whose constant possession is establish'd by the laws of society ; that is, by the laws of justice. Those, therefore, who make use of the words *property,* or *right,* or *obligation,* before they have explain'd the origin of justice, or even make use of them in that explication, are guilty of a very gross fallacy, and can never reason upon any solid foundation. A man's property is some object related to him. This relation is not natural, but moral, and founded on justice. 'Tis very preposterous, therefore, to imagine, that we can have any idea of property, without fully comprehending the nature of justice, and shewing its origin in the artifice and contrivance of men. The origin of justice explains that of property. The same artifice gives rise to both. As our first and most natural sentiment of morals is founded on the nature of our passions, and gives the preference to our-selves and friends, above strangers ; 'tis impossible there can be naturally any such thing as a fix'd right or property, while the opposite passions of men impel them in contrary directions, and are not restrain'd by any convention or agreement.

No one can doubt, that the convention for the distinction of property, and for the stability of possession, is of all circumstances the most necessary to the establishment of human society, and that after the agreement for the fixing and observing of this rule, there remains little or nothing to be done towards settling a perfect harmony and concord. All the other passions, beside this of interest, are either easily restrain'd, or are not of such pernicious consequence, when indulg'd. . . . This avidity alone, of acquiring goods and possessions for ourselves and our nearest friends, is insatiable, perpetual, universal, and directly destructive of society. . . .

'Tis certain, that no affection of the human mind has both a sufficient force, and a proper direction to counter-balance the love of gain, and render men fit members of society, by making them abstain from the possessions of others. Benevolence to strangers is too weak for this purpose ; and as to the other passions, they rather inflame this avidity, when we observe, that the larger our possessions are, the more ability we have of gratifying all our appetites. There is no passion, therefore, capable of controlling the interested affection, but the very affection itself, by an alteration of its direction. Now this alteration must necessarily take place upon the least reflection ; since 'tis evident, that the passion is much better satisfy'd by its restraint, than by its liberty, and that in preserving society, we make much greater advances in the acquiring possessions, than in the solitary and forlorn condition, which must follow upon violence and an universal licence. . . .

Now as 'tis by establishing the rule for the stability of possession, that this passion restrains itself ; if that rule be very abstruse, and of difficult invention ; society must be esteem'd, in a manner, accidental, and the effect of many ages. But if it be found, that nothing can be more simple and obvious than that rule ; that every parent, in order to preserve peace among his children, must establish it ; and that these first rudiments of justice must every day be improv'd, as the society enlarges : If all this appear evident, as it certainly must, we may conclude, that 'tis utterly impossible for men to remain any considerable time in that savage condition, which precedes society ; but that his very first state and situation may justly be esteem'd social. This, however, hinders not, but that philosophers may, if they please, extend their reasoning to the suppos'd *state of nature ;* provided they allow it to be a mere philosophical fiction, which never had, and never cou'd have any reality. . . .

. . .

. . . I have already observ'd, that justice takes its rise from human conventions ; and that these are intended as a remedy to some inconveniences, which proceed from the concurrence of certain *qualities* of the human mind with the *situation* of external objects. The qualities of the mind are *selfishness* and *limited generosity :* And the situation of external objects is their *easy change,* join'd to their *scarcity* in comparison of the wants and desires of men. But however philosophers may have been bewilder'd in those speculations, poets have been guided more infallibly, by a certain taste or common instinct, which in most kinds of reasoning goes farther than any of that art and philosophy, with which we have been yet acquainted. They easily perceiv'd, if every man had a tender regard for another, or if nature supplied abundantly all our wants and desires, that the jealousy of interest, which justice supposes, could no longer have place ; nor would there be any occasion for those distinctions and limits of property and possession, which at present are in use among mankind. Encrease to a sufficient degree the benevolence of men, or the bounty of nature, and you render justice useless. . . .

Nor need we have recourse to the fictions of poets to learn this ; but beside the reason of the thing, may discover the same truth by common exper ence and observation. 'Tis easy to remark, that a cordial affection renders all things common among friends ; and that married people in particular mutually lose their property, and are unacquainted with the *mine* and *thine,* which are so necessary, and yet cause such disturbance in human society. The same effect arises from any alteration in the circumstances of mankind ; as when there is such a plenty of anything as satisfies all the desires of men : In which case the distinction of property is entirely lost, and every thing remains in common. This we may observe with regard to air and water, tho' the most valuable of all external objects ; and may easily conclude, that if men were supplied with every thing in the same abundance, or if *every one* had the same affection and tender regard for *every one* as for himself ; justice and injustice would be equally unknown among mankind.

Here then is a proposition, which, I think, may be regarded as certain, *that 'tis only from the selfishness and confin'd generosity of men, along with the scanty provision nature has made for his wants, that justice derives its origin.* If we look backward we shall find, that this proposition bestows an additional force on some of those observations, which we have already made on this subject.

First, we may conclude from it, that a regard to public interest, or a strong extensive benevolence, is not our first and original motive for the observation of the rules of justice ; since 'tis allow'd, that if men were endow'd with such a benevolence, these rules would never have been dreamt of.

Secondly, we may conclude from the same principle, that the sense of justice is not founded in reason, or on the discovery of certain connexions and relations of ideas, which are eternal, immutable, and universally obligatory. For since it is confest, that such an alteration as that above-mention'd, in the temper and circumstances of mankind, wou'd entirely alter our duties and obligations, 'tis necessary upon the common system, *that the sense of virtue is deriv'd from reason,* to shew the change which this must produce in the relations and ideas. But 'tis evident, that the only cause, why the extensive generosity of man, and the perfect abundance of every thing, wou'd destroy the very idea of justice, is because they render it useless ; and that, on the other hand, his confin'd benevolence, and his necessitous condition, give rise to that virtue, only by making it requisite to the publick interest, and to that of every individual. 'Twas therefore a concern for our own, and the publick interest, which made us establish the laws of justice ; and nothing can be more certain, than that it is not any relation of ideas, which gives us this concern, but our impressions and sentiments, without which every thing in nature is perfectly indifferent to us, and can never in the least affect us. The sense of justice, therefore, is not founded on our ideas, but on our impressions.

Thirdly, we may farther confirm the foregoing proposition, *that those impressions, which give rise to this sense of justice, are not natural to the mind of man, but arise from artifice and human conventions.* For since any considerable alteration of temper and circumstances destroys equally justice and injustice ; and since such an alteration has an effect only by changing our own and the publick interest ; it follows, that the first establishment of the rules of justice depends on these different interests. But if men pursu'd the publick interest naturally, and with a hearty affection, they wou'd never have dream'd of restraining each other by these rules ; and if they pursu'd their own interest, without any precaution, they wou'd run head-long into every kind of injustice and violence. These rules, therefore, are artificial, and seek their end in an oblique and indirect manner ; nor is the interest, which gives rise to them, of a kind that cou'd be pursu'd by the natural and inartificial passions of men.

To make this more evident, consider, that tho' the rules of justice are establish'd merely by interest, their connexion with interest is somewhat singular, and is different from what may be observ'd on other occasions. A single act of justice is frequently contrary to *public interest ;* and were it to stand alone, without being follow'd by other acts, may, in itself, be very prejudicial to society. When a man of merit, of a beneficent disposition, restores a great fortune to a miser, or a seditious bigot, he has acted justly and laudably, but the public is a real sufferer. Nor is every single act of justice, consider'd apart, more conducive to private interest, than to public ; and 'tis easily conceiv'd how a man may impoverish himself by a signal instance of integrity, and have reason to wish, that with regard to that single act, the laws of justice were for a moment suspended in the universe. But however single acts of justice may be contrary, either to public or private interest, 'tis certain, that the whole plan or scheme is highly conducive, or indeed absolutely requisite, both to the support of society, and the well-being of every individual. 'Tis impossible to separate the good from the ill. Property must be stable, and must be fix'd by general rules. Tho' in one instance the public be a sufferer, this momentary ill is amply compensated by the steady prosecution of the rule, and by the peace and order, which it establishes in society. And even every individual person must find himself a gainer, on ballancing the account ; since, without justice, society must immediately dissolve, and every one must fall into that savage and solitary condition, which is infinitely worse than the worse situation that can possibly be suppos'd in society. When therefore men have had experience enough to observe, that whatever may be the consequence of any single act of justice, perform'd by a single person, yet the whole system of actions, concurr'd in by the whole society, is infinitely advantageous to the whole, and to every part ; it is not long before justice and property take place. Every member of society is sensible of this interest : Every one expresses this sense to his fellows, along with the resolution he has taken of squaring his actions by it, on condition that others will do the same. No more is requisite to induce any one of them to perform an act of justice, who has the first opportunity. This becomes an example to others. And thus justice establishes itself by a kind of convention or agreement ; that is, by a sense of interest, suppos'd to be common to all, and where every single act is perform'd in expectation that others are to perform the like. Without such a convention, no one wou'd ever have dream'd, that there was such a virtue as justice, or have been induced to conform his actions to it. Taking any single act, my justice may be pernicious in every respect ; and 'tis only upon the supposition, that others are to imitate my example, that I can be induc'd to embrace that virtue ; since nothing but this combination can render justice advantageous, or afford me any motives to conform myself to its rules.

We come now to the *second* question we propos'd, viz., *Why we annex the idea of virtue to justice, and of vice to injustice*. This question will not detain us long after the principles, which we have already establish'd. All we can say of it at present will be dispatch'd in a few words : And for farther satisfaction, the reader must wait till we come to the *third* part of this book. The *natural* obligation to justice, viz., interest, has been fully explain'd ; but as to the *moral* obligation, or the sentiment of right and wrong, 'twill first be requisite to examine the natural virtues, before we can give a full and satisfactory account of it.

After men have found by experience, that their selfishness and confin'd generosity, acting at their liberty, totally incapacitate them for society ; and at the same time have observ'd, that society is necessary to the satisfaction of those very passions, they are naturally induc'd to lay themselves under the restraint of such rules, as may render their commerce more safe and commodious. To the imposition then, and observance of these rules, both in general, and in every particular instance, they are at first induc'd only by a regard to interest ; and this motive, on the first formation of society, is sufficiently strong and forcible. But when society has become numerous, and has encreas'd to a tribe or nation, this interest is more remote ; nor do men so readily perceive, that disorder and confusion follow upon every breach of these rules, as in a more narrow and contracted society. But tho' in our own actions we may frequently lose sight of that interest, which we have in maintaining order, and may follow a lesser and more present interest, we never fail to observe the prejudice we receive, either mediately or immediately, from the injustice of others ; as not being in that case either blinded by passion, or byass'd by any contrary temptation. Nay when the injustice is so distant from us, as no way to affect our interest, it still displeases us ; because we consider it as prejudicial to human society, and pernicious to every one that approaches the person guilty of it. We partake of their uneasiness by *sympathy ;* and as every thing, which gives uneasiness in human actions, upon the general survey, is call'd Vice, and whatever produces satisfaction, in the same manner, is denominated Virtue ; this is the reason why the sense of moral good and evil follows upon justice and injustice. And tho' this sense, in the present case, be deriv'd only from contemplating the actions of others, yet we fail not to extend it even to our own actions. The *general rule* reaches beyond those instances, from which it arose ; while at the same time we naturally *sympathize* with others in the sentiments they entertain of us. *Thus self-interest is the original motive to the* establishment *of justice: but a* sympathy *with public interest is the source of the* moral approbation, *which attends that virtue.*

Tho' this progress of the sentiments be *natural,* and even necessary, 'tis certain, that it is here forwarded by the artifice of politicians, who, in order to govern men more easily, and preserve peace in human society, have endeavour'd to produce an esteem for justice, and an abhorrence of injustice. This, no doubt, must have its effect. . . . but 'tis impossible it should be the sole cause of the distinction we make betwixt vice and virtue. For if nature did not aid us in this particular, 'twou'd be in vain for politicians to talk of *honourable* or *dishonourable, praiseworthy* or *blameable.* . . . The utmost politicians can perform, is, to extend the natural sentiments beyond their original bounds ; but still nature must furnish the materials, and give us some notion of moral distinctions.

As publick praise and blame encrease our esteem for justice ; so private education and instruction contribute to the same effect. . . . By this means the sentiments of honour may take root in . . . tender minds, and acquire such firmness and solidity, that they may fall little short of those principles, which are the most essential to our natures, and the most deeply radicated in our internal constitution.

What farther contributes to encrease their solidity, is the interest of our reputation. . . . There is nothing, which touches us more nearly than our reputation, and nothing on which our reputation more depends than our conduct, with relation to the property of others. . . .

I shall make only one observation before I leave this subject, viz., that tho' I assert, that in the *state of nature,* or that imaginary state, which preceded society, there be neither justice nor injustice, yet I assert not, that it was allowable, in

 seno978

such a state, to violate the property of others. I only maintain, that there was no such thing as property ; and consequently cou'd be no such thing as justice or injustice. I shall have occasion to make a similar reflection with regard to *promises,* when I come to treat of them ; and I hope this reflection, when duly weigh'd, will suffice to remove all odium from the foregoing opinions, with regard to justice and injustice.

Section 3: Of the rules, which determine property. Tho' the establishment of the rule, concerning the stability of possession, be not only useful, but even absolutely necessary to human society, it can never serve to any purpose, while it remains in such general terms. Some method must be shewn, by which we may distinguish what particular goods are to be assign'd to each particular person, while the rest of mankind are excluded from their possession and enjoyment. Our next business, then, must be to discover the reasons which modify this general rule, and fit it to the common use and practice of the world.

'Tis obvious, that those reasons are not deriv'd from any utility or advantage, which either the *particular* person or the public may reap from his enjoyment of any *particular* goods, beyond what wou'd result from the possession of them by any other person. 'Twere better, no doubt, that every one were possess'd of what is most suitable to him, and proper for his use : But besides, that this relation of fitness may be common to several at once, 'tis liable to so many controversies, and men are so partial and passionate in judging of these controversies, that such a loose and uncertain rule would be absolutely incompatible with the peace of human society. The convention concerning the stability of possession is enter'd into, in order to cut off all occasions of discord and contention ; and this end wou'd never be attain'd, were we allowed to apply this rule differently in every particular case, according to every particular utility, which might be discover'd in such an application. Justice, in her decisions, never regards the fitness or unfitness of objects to particular persons, but conducts herself by more extensive views. Whether a man be generous, or a miser, he is equally well receiv'd by her, and obtains with the same facility a decision in his favour, even for what is entirely useless to him.

It follows, therefore, that the general rule, *that possession must be stable,* is not apply'd by particular judgments, but by other general rules, which must extend to the whole society, and be inflexible either by spite or favour. . . .[1]

.   .   .

Section 5: Of the obligation of promises.

.   .   .

. . . I venture to conclude, that promises are human inventions, founded on the necessities and interests of society.

In order to discover these necessities and interests, we must consider the same qualities of human nature, which we have already found to give rise to the preceding laws of society. Men being naturally selfish, or endow'd only with a confin'd generosity, they are not easily induc'd to perform any action for the interest of strangers, except with a view to some reciprocal advantage, which they have no hope of obtaining but by such a performance. Now as it frequently happens, that these mutual performances cannot be finish'd at the same instant, 'tis necessary, that one party be contented to remain in uncertainty. . . . Your corn is ripe to-day ; mine will be so to-morrow. 'Tis profitable for us both, that I shou'd labour with you to-day, and that you shou'd aid me to-morrow. I have no kindness for you, and know you have as little for me. . . .

---

[1] In the remainder of this section, Hume discusses several "circumstances" that may give rise to rules of property: "first possession," "long possession," "accession" (e.g., when one's animal has offspring), and "inheritance." In a note he adds, "There seldom is any very precise argument to fix our choice, and men must be contented to be guided by a kind of taste or fancy, arising from analogy, and a comparison of similar instances. Thus, in the present case, there are, no doubt, motives of public interest for most of the rules, which determine property; but still I suspect, that these rules are principally fix'd by the imagination, or the more frivolous properties of our thought and conception. . . ."

In Section 4: *Of the transference of property by consent,* Hume briefly discusses the utility of a convention under which a person is allowed to transfer property to another whenever he wishes to do so.—Ed.

. . . I learn to do a service to another, without bearing him any real kindness ; because I forsee, that he will return my service, in expectation of another of the same kind, and in order to maintain the same correspondence of good offices with me or with others. And accordingly, after I have serv'd him, and he is in possession of the advantage arising from my action, he is induc'd to perform his part, as forseeing the consequences of his refusal.

But tho' this self-interested commerce of men begins to take place, and to predominate in society, it does not entirely abolish the more generous and noble intercourse of friendship and good offices. I may still do services to such persons as I love, and am more particularly acquainted with, without any prospect of advantage ; and they make me a return in the same manner, without any view but that of recompensing my past services. In order, therefore, to distinguish those two different sorts of commerce, the interested and the disinterested, there is a *certain form of words* invented for the former, by which we bind ourselves to the performance of any action. This form of words constitutes what we call a *promise,* which is the sanction of the interested commerce of mankind. When a man says *he promises any thing,* he in effect expresses a *resolution* of performing it ; and along with that, by making use of this *form of words,* subjects himself to the penalty of never being trusted again in case of failure. . . .

Nor is that knowledge, which is requisite to make mankind sensible of this interest in the *institution* and *observance* of promises, to be esteem'd superior to the capacity of human nature, however savage and uncultivated. There needs but a very little practice of the world, to make us perceive all these consequences and advantages. The shortest experience of society discovers them to every mortal ; and when each individual perceives the same sense of interest in all his fellows, he immediately performs his part of any contract, as being assur'd, that they will not be wanting in theirs. All of them, by concert, enter into a scheme of actions, calculated for common benefit, and agree to be true to their word ; nor is there any thing requisite to form this concert or convention, but that every one have a sense of interest in the faithful fulfilling of engagements, and express that sense to other members of the society. This immediately causes that interest to operate upon them ; and interest is the *first* obligation to the performance of promises.

Afterwards a sentiment of morals concurs with interest, and becomes a new obligation upon mankind. This sentiment of morality, in the performance of promises, arises from the same principles as that in the abstinence from the property of others. *Public interest, education,* and *the artifices of politicians,* have the same effect in both cases. . . .

.   .   .

Section 6:   Some farther reflections concerning justice and injustice.   We have now run over the three fundamental laws of nature, *that of the stability of possession, of its transference by consent,* and *of the performance of promises.* 'Tis on the strict observance of those three laws, that the peace and security of human society entirely depend. . . . Nothing is more vigilant and inventive than our passions ; and nothing is more obvious, than the convention for the observance of these rules. Nature has, therefore, trusted this affair entirely to the conduct of men, and has not plac'd in the mind any peculiar original principles, to determine us to a set of actions, into which the other principles of our frame and constitution were sufficient to lead us. . . .

I. . . . Justice is commonly defin'd to be *a constant and perpetual will of giving every one his due.* In this definition 'tis supposed, that there are such things as right and property, independent of justice, and antecedent to it ; and that they wou'd have subsisted, tho' men had never dreamt of practicing such a virtue. I have already observ'd, in a cursory manner, the fallacy of this opinion. . . .

.   .   .

III. . . . Upon the whole, then, we are to consider this distinction betwixt justice and injustice, as having two different foundations, viz., that of *interest,* when men observe, that 'tis impossible to live in society without restraining themselves by certain rules ; and that of *morality,* when this interest is once observ'd, and men receive a pleasure from the view of such actions as tend to the peace of society, and an uneasiness from such as are contrary to it. 'Tis the voluntary convention and artifice of men, which makes the first interest take place ; and therefore those laws of justice are so far to be consider'd as *artificial.* After that interest is once establish'd and acknowledg'd, the sense of morality in the observance of these rules follows *naturally,* and of itself ; tho' 'tis certain, that it is also augmented by a new *artifice,* and that the public instructions of politicians, and the private education of parents, contribute to the giving us a sense of honour and duty in the strict regulation of our actions with regard to the properties of others.

Section 7: Of the origin of government.

. . .

It has been observ'd, in treating of the passions, that men are mightily govern'd by the imagination, and proportion their affections more to the light, under which any object appears to them, than to its real and intrinsic value. What strikes upon them with a strong and lively idea commonly prevails above what lies in a more obscure light ; and it must be a great superiority of value, that is able to compensate this advantage. Now as every thing, that is contiguous to us, either in space or time, strikes upon us with such an idea, it has a proportional effect on the will and passions, and commonly operates with more force than any object, that lies in a more distant and obscure light. Tho' we may be fully convinc'd, that the latter object excels the former, we are not able to regulate our actions by this judgment ; but yield to the sollicitations of our passions, which always plead in favour of whatever is near and contiguous.

This is the reason why men so often act in contradiction to their known interest ; and in particular why they prefer any trivial advantage, that is present, to the maintenance of order in society, which so much depends on the observance of justice. The consequences of every breach of equity seem to lie very remote, and are not able to counterballance any immediate advantage, that may be reap'd from it. They are, however, never the less real for being remote ; and as all men are, in some degree, subject to the same weakness, it necessarily happens, that the violations of equity must become very frequent in society, and the commerce of men, by that means, be render'd very dangerous and uncertain. . . .

This quality, therefore, of human nature, not only is very dangerous to society, but also seems, on a cursory view, to be incapable of any remedy. The remedy can only come from the consent of men ; and if men be incapable of themselves to prefer remote to contiguous, they will never consent to any thing, which wou'd oblige them to such a choice, and contradict, in so sensible a manner, their natural principles and propensities. . . .

. . .

The only difficulty, therefore, is to find out this expedient, by which men cure their natural weakness, and lay themselves under the necessity of observing the laws of justice and equity, notwithstanding their violent propension to prefer contiguous to remote. 'Tis evident such a remedy can never be effectual without correcting this propensity ; and as 'tis impossible to change or correct any thing material in our nature, the utmost we can do is to change our circumstances and situation, and render the observance of the laws of justice our nearest interest, and their violation our most remote. But this being impracticable with respect to all mankind, it can only take place with respect to a few, whom we thus immediately interest in the execution of justice. These are the persons, whom we call civil magistrates, kings and their ministers, our governors and rulers, who being indifferent persons to the greatest part of the state, have no interest, or but a remote one, in any act of injustice ; and being satisfied with their present condition, and with their part in society, have an immediate interest in every execution of justice, which is so necessary to the upholding of society. Here then is the origin of civil government and society. Men are not able radically to cure, either in themselves or others, that narrowness of soul, which makes them prefer the present to the remote. They cannot change their natures. All they can do is to change their situation, and render the observance of justice the immediate interest of some particular persons, and its violation their more remote. These persons, then, are not only induc'd to observe those rules in their own conduct, but also to constrain others to a like regularity, and inforce the dictates of equity thro' the whole society. And if it be necessary, they may also interest others more immediately in the execution of justice, and create a number of officers, civil and military, to assist them in their government.

But this execution of justice, tho' the principal, is not the only advantage of government. As violent passion hinders men from seeing distinctly the interest they have in an equitable behaviour towards others ; so it hinders them from seeing that equity itself, and gives them a remarkable partiality in their own favours. This inconvenience is corrected in the same manner as that above-mention'd. The same persons, who execute the laws of justice, will also decide all controversies concerning them ; and being indifferent to the greatest part of the society, will decide them more equitably than every one wou'd in his own case.

By means of these two advantages, in the *execution* and *decision* of justice, men acquire a security against each others weakness and passion, as well as against their own, and under the shelter of their governors, begin to taste at ease the sweets of society and mutual assistance. But government extends farther its beneficial influence ; and not contented to protect men in those conventions they make for their mutual interest, it often obliges them to make such conventions, and forces them to seek their own advantage, by a concurrence in some common end or purpose. There is no quality in human nature, which causes more fatal errors in our conduct, than that which leads us to prefer whatever is present to the distant and remote, and makes us desire objects more according to their situation than their intrinsic value. Two neighbours may agree to drain a meadow, which they possess in common ; because 'tis easy for them to know each others mind ; and each must perceive, that the immediate consequence of his failing in his part, is the abandoning the whole project. But 'tis very difficult, and indeed impossible, that a thousand persons shou'd agree in any such action ; it being difficult for them to concert so complicated a design, and

still more difficult for them to execute it ; while each seeks a
pretext to free himself of the trouble and expence, and wou'd
lay the whole burden on others. Political society easily remedies
both these inconveniences. Magistrates find an immediate interest in the interest of any considerable part of their subjects.
They need consult no body but themselves to form any scheme
for the promoting of that interest. And as the failure of any one
piece in the execution is connected, tho' not immediately, with
the failure of the whole, they prevent that failure, because they
find no interest in it, either immediate or remote. Thus bridges
are built ; harbours open'd ; ramparts rais'd ; canals form'd ;
fleets equip'd ; and armies disciplin'd ; every where, by the care
of government, which, tho' compos'd of men subject to all human infirmities, becomes, by one of the finest and most subtle
inventions imaginable, a composition, which is, in some measures
exempted from all these infirmities.

Section 8: Of the source of allegiance.   Though government
be an invention very advantageous, and even in some circumstances absolutely necessary to mankind ; it is not necessary in
all circumstances, nor is it impossible for men to preserve society
for some time, without having recourse to such an invention. . . .

·   ·   ·

But tho' it be possible for men to maintain a small uncultivated society without government, 'tis impossible they shou'd
maintain a society of any kind without justice, and the observance of those three fundamental laws concerning the stability of
possession, its translation by consent, and the performance of
promises. These are, therefore, antecedent to government, and
are suppos'd to impose an obligation before the duty of allegiance to civil magistrates has once been thought of. Nay, I shall
go farther, and assert, that government, *upon its first establishment,* wou'd naturally be supposed to derive its obligation from
those laws of nature, and, in particular, from that concerning
the performance of promises. When men have once perceiv'd
the necessity of government to maintain peace, and execute
justice, they wou'd naturally assemble together, wou'd chuse

magistrates, determine their power, and *promise* them obedience. As a promise is suppos'd to be a bond or security already in use, and attended with a moral obligation, 'tis to be consider'd as the original sanction of government, and as the source of the first obligation to obedience. This reasoning appears so natural, that it has become the foundation of our fashionable system of politics, and is in a manner the creed of a party amongst us, who pride themselves, with reason, on the soundness of their philosophy, and their liberty of thought. *All men,* say they, *are born free and equal : Government and superiority can only be establish'd by consent : The consent of men, in establishing government, imposes on them a new obligation, unknown to the laws of nature. Men, therefore, are bound to obey their magistrates, only because they promise it ; and if they had not given their word, either expressly or tacitly, to preserve allegiance, it would never have become a part of their moral duty.* This conclusion, however, when carried so far as to comprehend government in all its ages and situations, is entirely erroneous ; and I maintain, that tho' the duty of allegiance be at first grafted on the obligation of promises, and be for some time supported by that obligation, yet it quickly takes root of itself, and has an original obligation and authority, independent of all contracts. This is a principle of moment, which we must examine with care and attention, before we proceed any farther.

'Tis reasonable for those philosophers, who assert justice to be a natural virtue, and antecedent to human conventions, to resolve all civil allegiance into the obligation of a promise, and assert that 'tis our own consent alone, which binds us to any submission to magistracy. . . . But being once undeceiv'd in this particular, and having found that *natural,* as well as *civil* justice, derives its origin from human conventions, we shall quickly perceive, how fruitless it is to resolve the one into the other, and seek, in the laws of nature, a stronger foundation for our political duties than interest, and human conventions ; while these laws themselves are built on the very same foundation. On which ever side we turn this subject, we shall find, that these two kinds of duty are exactly on the same footing, and have the same source both of their *first invention* and *moral obligation.* They are contriv'd to remedy like inconveniences, and acquire their moral sanction in the same manner, from their remedying those inconveniences. These are two points, which we shall endeavour to prove as distinctly as possible.

We have already shewn, that men *invented* the three fundamental laws of nature, when they observ'd the necessity of society to their mutual subsistance, and found, that 'twas impossible to maintain any correspondence together, without some restraint on their natural appetites. The same self-love, therefore, which renders men so incommodious to each other, taking a new and more convenient direction, produces the rules of justice, and is the *first* motive of their observance. But when men have observ'd, that tho' the rules of justice be sufficient to maintain any society, yet 'tis impossible for them, of themselves, to observe those rules, in large and polish'd societies ; they establish government, as a new invention to attain their ends, and preserve the old, or procure new advantages, by a more strict execution of justice. So far, therefore, our *civil* duties are connected with our *natural,* that the former are invented chiefly for the sake of the latter ; and that the principal object of government is to constrain men to observe the laws of nature. In this respect, however, that law of nature, concerning the performance of promises, is only compriz'd along with the rest ; and its exact observance is to be consider'd as an effect of the institution of government, and not the obedience to government as an effect of the obligation of a promise. Tho' the object of our civil duties be the enforcing of our natural, yet the *first* [2] motive of the invention, as well as performance of both, is nothing but self-interest : And since there is a separate interest in the obedience to government, from that in the performance of promises, we must also allow of a separate obligation. To obey the civil magistrate is requisite to preserve order and concord in society. To perform promises is requisite to beget mutual trust and confidence in the common offices of life. The ends, as well as the means, are perfectly distinct ; nor is the one subordinate to the other.

. . .

But 'tis not only the *natural* obligations of interest, which are distinct in promises and allegiance ; but also the *moral* obli-

---

[2] First in time, not in dignity or force.

gations of honour and conscience : Nor does the merit or de-
merit of the one depend in the least upon that of the other. And
indeed, if we consider the close connexion there is betwixt the
natural and moral obligations, we shall find this conclusion to
be entirely unavoidable. Our interest is always engag'd on the
side of obedience to magistracy ; and there is nothing but a great
present advantage, that can lead us to rebellion, by making us
over-look the remote interest, which we have in the preserving
of peace and order in society. But tho' a present interest may
thus blind us with regard to our own actions, it takes not place
with regard to those of others ; nor hinders them from appearing
in their true colours, as highly prejudicial to public interest, and
to our own in particular. This naturally gives us an uneasiness,
in considering such seditious and disloyal actions, and makes us
attach to them the idea of vice and moral deformity. 'Tis the
same principle, which causes us to disapprove of all kinds of
private injustice, and in particular of the breach of promises. We
blame all treachery and breach of faith ; because we consider,
that the freedom and extent of human commerce depend entirely on a fidelity with regard to promises. We blame all dis-
loyalty to magistrates ; because we perceive, that the execution
of justice, in the stability of possession, its translation by consent, and the performance of promises, is impossible, without
submission to government. As there are here two interests entirely distinct from each other, they must give rise to two moral
obligations, equally separate and independant. Tho' there was
no such thing as a promise in the world, government wou'd still
be necessary in all large and civiliz'd societies ; and if promises
had only their own proper obligation, without the separate sanction of government, they wou'd have but little efficacy in such
societies. This separates the boundaries of our public and private
duties, and shews that the latter are more dependant on the
former, than the former on the latter. *Education* and *the artifice
of politicians,* concur to bestow a farther morality on loyalty,
and to brand all rebellion with a greater degree of guilt and in-
famy. Nor is it a wonder, that politicians shou'd be very indus-
trious in inculcating such notions, where their interest is so particularly concern'd.

We find, that magistrates are so far from deriving their authority, and the obligation to obedience in their subjects, from the foundation of a promise or original contract, that they conceal, as far as possible, from their people, especially from the vulgar, that they have their origin from thence. Were this the sanction of government, our rulers wou'd never receive it tacitly, which is the utmost that can be pretended ; since what is given tacitly and insensibly can never have such influence on mankind, as what is perform'd expressly and openly. A tacit promise is, where the will is signified by other more diffuse signs than those of speech ; but a will there must certainly be in the case, and that can never escape the person's notice, who exerted it, however silent or tacit. But were you to ask the far greatest part of the nation, whether they had ever consented to the authority of their rulers, or promis'd to obey them they wou'd be inclin'd to think very strangely of you ; and wou'd certainly reply, that the affair depended not on their consent, but that they were born to such an obedience. . . .

Section 9: Of the measures of allegiance. Those political writers, who have had recourse to a promise, or original contract, as the source of our allegiance to government, intended to establish a principle, which is perfectly just and reasonable ; tho' the reasoning, upon which they endeavour'd to establish it, was fallacious and sophistical. They wou'd prove, that our submission to government admits of exceptions, and that an egregious tyranny in the rulers is sufficient to free the subjects from all ties of allegiance. Since men enter into society, say they, and submit themselves to government, by their free and voluntary consent, they must have in view certain advantages, which they propose to reap from it, and for which they are contented to resign their native liberty. There is, therefore, something mutual engag'd on the part of the magistrate, viz., protection and security ; and 'tis only by the hopes he affords of these advantages, that he can ever persuade men to submit to him. But when instead of protection and security, they meet with tyranny and oppression, they are free'd from their promises, (as happens in all conditional contracts) and return to that state of liberty, which preceded the institution of government. Men wou'd never be so foolish as to enter into such engagements as shou'd turn entirely to the advantage of others, without any view of bettering their own condition. Whoever proposes to draw any profit from our submission, must engage himself, either expressly or tacitly, to make us reap some advantage from his authority ; nor ought he to expect, that without the performance of his part we will ever continue in obedience.

I repeat it : This conclusion is just, tho' the principles be erroneous ; and I flatter myself, that I can establish the same conclusion on more reasonable principles. I shall not take such a compass, in establishing our political duties, as to assert, that men perceive the advantages of government ; that they institute government with a view to those advantages ; that this institution requires a promise of obedience ; which imposes a moral obligation to a certain degree, but being conditional, ceases to be binding, whenever the other contracting party performs not his part of the engagement. I perceive, that a promise itself arises entirely from human conventions, and is invented with a view to a certain interest. I seek, therefore, some such interest more immediately connected with government, and which may be at once the original motive to its institution, and the source of our obedience to it. This interest I find to consist in the security and protection, which we enjoy in political society, and which we can never attain, when perfectly free and independent. As interest, therefore, is the immediate sanction of government, the one can have no longer being than the other ; and whenever the civil magistrate carries his oppression so far as to render his authority perfectly intolerable, we are no longer bound to submit to it. The cause ceases ; the effect must cease also.

. . .

. . . 'Tis certain, that all men . . . are sensible, that they owe obedience to government merely on account of the public interest ; and at the same time, that human nature is so subject to frailties and passions, as may easily pervert this institution, and change their governors into tyrants and public enemies. If the sense of common interest were not our original motive to obedience, I wou'd fain ask, what other principle is there in human nature capable of subduing the natural ambition of men, and forcing them to such a submission ? Imitation and custom are not sufficient. For the question still recurs, what motive first produces those instances of submission, which we imitate, and that train of actions, which produces the custom ? There evidently is no other principle than common interest ; and if interest first produces obedience to government, the obligation to obedience must cease, whenever the interest ceases, in any great degree, and in a considerable number of instances.

Section 10: Of the objects of allegiance. But tho', on some occasions, it may be justifiable, both in sound politics and morality, to resist supreme power, 'tis certain, that in the ordinary course of human affairs nothing can be more pernicious and criminal ; and that besides the convulsions, which always attend revolutions, such a practice tends directly to the subversion of all government, and the causing an universal anarchy and confusion among mankind. As numerous and civiliz'd societies cannot subsist without government, so government is entirely useless without an exact obedience. We ought always to weigh the advantages, which we reap from authority, against the disadvantages ; and by this means we shall become more scrupulous of putting in practice the doctrine of resistance. The common rule requires submission ; and 'tis only in cases of grievous tyranny and oppression, that the exception can take place.

Since then such a blind submission is commonly due to magistracy, the next question is, *to whom it is due, and whom we are to regard as our lawful magistrates ?* In order to answer this question, let us recollect what we have already establish'd concerning the origin of government and political society. When men have once experienc'd the impossibility of preserving any steady order in society, while every one is his own master, and violates or observes the laws of society, according to his present interest or pleasure, they naturally run into the invention of government, and put it out of their own power, as far as possible, to transgress the laws of society. Government, therefore, arises from the voluntary convention of men ; and 'tis evident, that the same convention, which establishes government, will also determine the persons who are to govern, and will remove all doubt and ambiguity in this particular. . . .

But when government has been establish'd on this footing for some considerable time, and the separate interest, which we

have in submission, has produc'd a separate sentiment of morality, the case is entirely alter'd, and a promise is no longer able
to determine the particular magistrate ; since it is no longer consider'd as the foundation of government. We naturally suppose
ourselves born to submission ; and imagine, that such particular
persons have a right to command, as we on our part are bound
to obey. These notions of right and obligation are deriv'd from
nothing but the *advantage* we reap from government, which
gives us a repugnance to practise resistance ourselves, and makes
us displeas'd with any instance of it in others. But here 'tis remarkable, that in this new state of affairs, the original sanction
of government, which is *interest,* is not admitted to determine the
persons, whom we are to obey, as the original sanction did at
first, when affairs were on the footing of a *promise.* A *promise*
fixes and determines the persons, without any uncertainty : But
'tis evident, that if men were to regulate their conduct in this
particular, by the view of a peculiar *interest,* either public or
private, they wou'd involve themselves in endless confusion, and
wou'd render all government, in a great measure, ineffectual.
The private interest of every one is different ; and tho' the public interest in itself be always one and the same, yet it becomes
the source of as great dissentions, by reason of the different
opinions of particular persons concerning it. The same interest,
therefore, which causes us to submit to magistracy, makes us
renounce itself in the choice of our magistrates, and binds us
down to a certain form of government, and to particular persons,
without allowing us to aspire to the utmost perfection in either.
The case is here the same as in that law of nature concerning
the stability of possession. 'Tis highly advantageous, and even
absolutely necessary to society, that possession shou'd be stable ;
and this leads us to the establishment of such a rule : But we
find, that were we to follow the same advantage, in assigning
particular possessions to particular persons, we shou'd disap-
point our end, and perpetuate the confusion, which that rule is
intended to prevent. We must, therefore, proceed by general
rules, and regulate ourselves by general interests, in modifying
the law of nature concerning the stability of possession. Nor
need we fear, that our attachment to this law will diminish upon
account of the seeming frivolousness of those interests, by which
it is determined. The impulse of the mind is deriv'd from a very

strong interest ; and those other more minute interests serve only to direct the motion, without adding any thing to it, or diminishing from it. 'Tis the same case with government. Nothing is more advantageous to society than such an invention ; and this interest is sufficient to make us embrace it with ardour and alacrity ; tho' we are oblig'd afterwards to regulate and direct our devotion to government by several considerations, which are not of the same importance, and to chuse our magistrates without having in view any particular advantage from the choice.

. . .

4 SELECTIONS FROM
The Social Contract, or Principles of Political Right

JEAN JACQUES ROUSSEAU

Jean Jacques Rousseau was born in 1712, the son of a watch-maker. His mother did not survive his birth and at the age of ten he was left in the care of an uncle. Six years later, after a haphazard youth, he was taken in by Mme. de Warens and lived with her off and on while his life exposed him to music, society, love, and religion. In 1742 he found his way to Paris with an opera, a system of musical notation, a play, and some poems. They did not bring him fame, but Diderot became his friend, and he came to write articles on music for the Encyclopedia. *His interest in politics was not awakened until about 1750, when his essay,* Discourse on the Sciences and Arts, *won a prize at the academy of Dijon. In 1755 he published the more substantial* Discourse on the Origin and Foundations of Inequality Among Men *and "Political Economy," an* Encyclopedia *article. Soon thereafter, following a disastrous love affair, he broke with his friends, including Diderot; but he continued writing and had several highly productive years. In 1761–1762,* Julie, or the New Heloise, The Social Contract, *and* Emile *appeared, so irritating the Church and government that he was forced to flee France. During this period of his life, he worked on many projects, including a constitution for Corsica and his* Letters Written from the Mountain, *a reply to Genevan condemnation. Controversies, however, continued to pursue him, and Hume's attempt to be-friend him in 1766 failed. Thereafter, in France, he published*

The following selections are from an eighteenth-century translation of *The Social Contract,* completely revised and edited by Charles Frankel (New York: Hafner Publishing Co., 1947). Unfortunately, many of Professor Frankel's helpful notes could not be included. The selections are reprinted with the permission of the publisher.

his Musical Dictionary, *married his servant mistress of the past twenty-three years, read his* Confessions *in Paris salons, wrote* On the Government of Poland *and* Reveries, *and, somewhat mad, died in 1778.*

Book 1

My design in this treatise is to enquire whether, taking men such as they are, and laws such as they may be made, it is not possible to establish some just and certain rule for the administration of the civil order. In the course of my research I shall endeavour to unite what right permits with what interest prescribes, that justice and utility may not be separated.

. . .

Chapter 1: Subject of the First Book. Man is born free, and yet we see him everywhere in chains. Those who believe themselves the masters of others cease not to be even greater slaves than the people they govern. How this happens I am ignorant; but, if I am asked what renders it justifiable, I believe it may be in my power to resolve the question.

If I were only to consider force, and the effects of it, I should say, "When a people is constrained to obey, and does obey, it does well; but as soon as it can throw off its yoke, and does throw it off, it does better: for a people may certainly use, for the recovery of their liberty, the same right that was employed to deprive them of it: it was either justifiably recovered, or unjustifiably torn from them." But the social order is a sacred right which serves for the basis of all others. Yet this right comes not from nature; it is therefore founded on conventions. The question is, what those conventions are. But, before I come to that point, I must establish the principles which I have just asserted.

Chapter 2: Of the First Societies. The earliest and the only natural societies are families: yet the children remain attached to the father no longer than they have need for his protection.

As soon as that need ceases, the bond of nature is dissolved. The child, exempt from the obedience he owed the father, and the father, from the duties he owed the child, return equally to independence. If they continue to remain together, it is not in consequence of a natural, but a voluntary union; and the family itself is maintained only by a convention.

This common liberty is a consequence of the nature of man. His first law is that of self-preservation, his first cares those which he owes to himself; and as soon as he has attained the age of reason, being the only judge of the means proper to preserve himself, he becomes at once his own master.

. . .

Grotius denies that all human power is established for the benefit of those who are governed; and he instances slavery in proof of his assertion. But his constant manner of reasoning is to establish right by fact.[1] A more satisfactory mode might be employed, but none more favourable to tyrants.

It is therefore doubtful, according to Grotius, whether the whole human race belongs to about one hundred men, or this hundred men to the human race; and he appears throughout his book to incline to the former opinion, which is also the idea of Hobbes: so that, according to them, mankind is divided into herds of cattle, each herd having its master who protects it in order to devour it.

. . .

Chapter 3: Of the Right of the Strongest. The strongest are still never sufficiently strong to ensure them continual mastership, unless they find means of transforming force into right, and obedience into duty. Hence the right of the strongest—a right which seems ironical in appearance, but is really established as a principle. But shall we never have an explanation of this term? Force is a physical power; I do not see what morality

---

[1] "Learned studies of public right are often only the history of past abuses; and it is foolish and stubborn to take the trouble to study them too deeply." (*Essay on the Interests of France in Relation to its Neighbours,* by the Marquis d'Argenson.) This is precisely what Grotius did.

can result from its effects. To yield to force is an act of necessity, not of inclination; or it is at best only an act of prudence. In what sense then can it be a duty?

Let us suppose for a moment the existence of this pretended right. I see nothing that can arise from it but inexplicable nonsense. For, if we admit that force constitutes right, the effect changes with the cause: all force which overcomes the first succeeds to its right. As soon as men can disobey with impunity, they can do so justifiably; and because the strongest is always in the right, strength is the only thing men should seek to acquire. But what sort of right is that which perishes with the force that gave it existence? If it is necessary to obey by force, there can be no occasion to obey from duty; and when force is no more, all obligation ceases with it. We see, therefore, that this word "right" adds nothing to force, but is indeed an unmeaning term.

. . .

We must grant, therefore, that force does not constitute right, and that obedience is only due to legitimate powers. Thus everything goes back to my first question.

Chapter 4: Of Slavery. Since no man has any natural authority over his fellows, and since force produces no right to any, all justifiable authority among men must be established on the basis of conventions.

If an individual, says Grotius, can alienate his liberty, and become the slave of a master, why may not a whole people alienate theirs, and become the subject of a king? There are some equivocal words in this sentence, which require an explanation; but I will confine myself to the word "alienate." To alienate is to give or sell. But a man who becomes the slave of another, cannot give but must sell himself, at least for a subsistence. But for what do a people sell themselves? A king, so far from furnishing his subjects with subsistence, draws his own from them; and, according to Rabelais, a king does not subsist upon a little. Do subjects therefore give their persons on condition that the prince will condescend to accept their property also? I see nothing, after such a gratuity, that there remains for them to preserve.

We are told that a despot ensures civil tranquillity for his subjects. Be it so; but what do his subjects gain if the wars which his ambition draws them into, if his insatiable avarice, and the vexations of his administration, desolate the country even more than civil dissensions? What do they gain if this very tranquillity is one of their miseries? We find tranquillity also in dungeons. . . .

To say that a man gives himself gratuitously is absurd and incomprehensible; such an act is unjustifiable and void, because the person who performed it is not in his proper senses. To say the same of a whole people is to suppose the people are all mad; and folly does not make it right.

. . .

To renounce our liberty is to renounce our quality of man, and with it all the rights and duties of humanity. No adequate compensation can possibly be made for a sacrifice so complete. Such a renunciation is incompatible with the nature of man; whose actions, when once he is deprived of his free will, must be destitute of all morality. Finally, a convention which stipulates absolute authority on one side, and unlimited obedience on the other, must be considered as vain and contradictory. Is it not clear that there can be no obligation to a person from whom everything may be justly required? And does not the single circumstance of there being no equivalence and no exchange also annul the act? For what right can my slave have against me, since everything that he has belongs to me, and, his right being mine, this right of mine against myself is absolute nonsense?

. . .

Thus, in whatever light we view things, the right of slavery is found to be null, not only because it is unjustifiable but because it is absurd and has no meaning. The terms "slavery" and "right" contradict and exclude each other. Be it from man to man, or from a man to a people, it would be equally nonsensical to say: I make a covenant with you entirely at your expense, and for my benefit; I will observe it as far as my inclination leads me, and you shall observe it as far as I please.

Chapter 5: That We Must Always Go Back to a First Convention. Had I granted all which I have refuted, the favourers of despotism would not have found their cause advanced by it. There will always be a great difference between subduing a multitude and governing a society. When unorganized men are successively subjugated by one individual, whatever number there may be of them, they appear to me only as a master and slaves ; I cannot regard them as a people and their chief ; they are, if you please, an *aggregation,* but they are not as yet an *association ;* for there is neither public property, nor a political body, among them. . . .

. . .

Chapter 6: Of the Social Compact. I will suppose that men in the state of nature are arrived at that crisis when the strength of each individual is insufficient to overcome the resistance of the obstacles to his preservation. This primitive state can therefore subsist no longer; and the human race would perish unless it changed its manner of life.

As men cannot create for themselves new forces, but merely unite and direct those which already exist, the only means they can employ for their preservation is to form by aggregation an assemblage of forces that may be able to overcome the resistance, to be put in motion as one body, and to act in concert.

This assemblage of forces must be produced by the concurrence of many; but as the force and the liberty of each man are the chief instruments of his preservation, how can he engage them elsewhere without danger to himself, and without neglecting the care which is due himself? This difficulty, which leads directly to my subject, may be expressed in these words:

"Where shall we find a form of association which will defend and protect with the whole common force the person and the property of each associate, and by which every person, while uniting himself with all, shall obey only himself and remain as free as before?" Such is the fundamental problem of which the Social Contract gives the solution.

The articles of this contract are so unalterably fixed by the nature of the act that the least modification renders them vain and of no effect; so that they are the same everywhere, and are everywhere tacitly understood and admitted, even though they may never have been formally announced; until, the social compact being violated, each individual is restored to his original rights, and resumes his native liberty, while losing the conventional liberty for which he renounced it.

The articles of the social contract will, when clearly understood, be found reducible to this single point: the total alienation of each associate, and all his rights, to the whole community; for, in the first place, as every individual gives himself up entirely, the condition of every person is alike; and being so, it would not be to the interest of any one to render that condition offensive to others.

Nay, more than this, the alienation being made without any reserve, the union is as complete as it can be, and no associate has any further claim to anything: for if any individual retained rights not enjoyed in general by all, as there would be no common superior to decide between him and the public, each person being in some points his own judge, would soon pretend to be so in everything; and thus would the state of nature be continued and the association necessarily become tyrannical or be annihilated.

Finally, each person gives himself to all, and so not to any one individual; and as there is no one associate over whom the same right is not acquired which is ceded to him by others, each gains an equivalent for what he loses, and finds his force increased for preserving that which he possesses.

If, therefore, we exclude from the social compact all that is not essential, we shall find it reduced to the following terms:

Each of us places in common his person and all his power under the supreme direction of the general will; and as one body we all receive each member as an indivisible part of the whole.

From that moment, instead of as many separate persons as there are contracting parties, this act of association produces a moral and collective body, composed of as many members as there are votes in the assembly, which from this act receives its unity, its common self, its life, and its will. This public person, which is thus formed by the union of all other persons, took formerly the name of "city," [2] and now takes that of "republic"

---

[2] The true sense of this word is almost entirely lost among the moderns: the name of "city" is now generally used to signify a town, and that of "citizen" applied to a burgess. Men do not seem to know that *houses* make a "town," but that *citizens* make a "city." . . .

or "body politic." It is called by its members "State" when it is passive, "Sovereign" when in activity, and, whenever it is compared with other bodies of a similar kind, it is denominated "power." The associates take collectively the name of "people," and separately, that of "citizens," as participating in the sovereign authority, and of "subjects," because they are subjected to the laws of the State. But these terms are frequently confounded and used one for the other; and it is enough that a man understands how to distinguish them when they are employed in all their precision.

Chapter 7: Of the Sovereign. It appears from this formula that the act of association contains a reciprocal engagement between the public and individuals, and that each individual, contracting, as it were, with himself, is engaged under a double character; that is, as a member of the Sovereign engaging with individuals, and as a member of the State engaged with the Sovereign. But we cannot apply here the maxim of civil right, that no person is bound by any engagement which he makes with himself; for there is a material difference between an obligation to oneself individually, and an obligation to a collective body of which oneself constitutes a part.

.   .   .

As soon as this multitude is united in one body, you cannot offend one of its members without attacking the body; much less can you offend the body without incurring the resentment of all the members. Thus duty and interest equally oblige the two contracting parties to lend aid to each other; and the same men must endeavour to unite under this double character all the advantages which attend it.

Further, the Sovereign, being formed only of the individuals who compose it, neither has, nor can have, any interest contrary to theirs; consequently, the sovereign power need give no guarantee to its subjects, because it is impossible that the body should seek to injure all its members; and we shall see presently that it can do no injury to any individual in particular. The Sovereign, by its nature, is always everything it ought to be.

But this is not so with the relation of subjects towards the

Sovereign, which, notwithstanding the common interest, has nothing to make them responsible for the performance of their engagements if some means is not found of ensuring their fidelity.

In fact, each individual may, as a man, have a private will,[3] dissimilar or contrary to the general will which he has as a citizen. His own private interest [4] may dictate to him very differently from the common interest; his absolute and naturally independent existence may make him regard what he owes to the common cause as a gratuitous contribution, the omission of which would be less injurious to others than the payment would be burdensome to himself; and considering the moral person which constitutes the State as a creature of the imagination, because it is not a man, he may wish to enjoy the rights of a citizen without being disposed to fulfil the duties of a subject. Such an injustice would in its progress cause the ruin of the body politic.

In order, therefore, to prevent the social compact from becoming an empty formula, it tacitly comprehends the engagement, which alone can give effect to the others—that whoever refuses to obey the general will shall be compelled to it by the whole body: this in fact only forces him to be free; for this is the condition which, by giving each citizen to his country, guarantees his absolute personal independence, a condition which gives motion and effect to the political machine. This alone renders all civil engagements justifiable, and without it they would be absurd, tyrannical, and subject to the most enormous abuses.

Chapter 8: Of the Civil State. The passing from the state of nature to the civil state produces in man a very remarkable change, by substituting justice for instinct in his conduct, and giving to his actions a moral character which they lacked before. It is then only that the voice of duty succeeds to physical impulse, and a sense of what is right, to the incitements of appetite. Man, who had till then regarded none but himself, perceives that he must act on other principles, and learns to consult his reason before he listens to his inclinations. Although he is de-

[3] [*volonté particulière.*]—C. F.
[4] [*intérêt particulier.*]—C. F.

prived in this new state of many advantages which he enjoyed from nature, he gains in return others so great, his faculties so unfold themselves by being exercised, his ideas are so extended, his sentiments so exalted, and his whole mind so enlarged and refined, that if, by abusing his new condition, he did not sometimes degrade it even below that from which he emerged, he ought to bless continually the happy moment that snatched him forever from it, and transformed him from a circumscribed and stupid animal to an intelligent being and a man.

In order to draw a balance between the advantages and disadvantages attending his new situation, let us state them in such a manner that they may be easily compared. Man loses by the social contract his *natural* liberty, and an unlimited right to all which tempts him, and which he can obtain; in return he acquires *civil* liberty, and proprietorship of all he possesses. That we may not be deceived in the value of these compensations, we must distinguish natural liberty, which knows no bounds but the power of the individual, from civil liberty, which is limited by the general will; and between possession, which is only the effect of force or of the right of the first occupant, from property, which must be founded on a positive title. In addition we might add to the other acquisitions of the civil state that of moral liberty, which alone renders a man master of himself; for it is *slavery* to be under the impulse of mere appetite, and *freedom* to obey a law which we prescribe for ourselves. But I have already said too much on this head, and the philosophical sense of the word "liberty" is not at present my subject.

Chapter 9: Of Real Property. Each member of the community, at the moment of its formation, gives himself up to it just as he is: himself and all his forces, of which his wealth forms a part. By this act, however, possession does not change in nature when it changes its master, and become property when it falls into the hands of the Sovereign; but as the forces of the city are infinitely greater than those of an individual, it is better secured when it becomes a public possession, without being more justifiable, at least with respect to foreigners. As to its members, the State is made master of all their wealth by the social contract, which within the State serves as the basis of all rights; but with regard to other powers, it claims only under the title of first occupancy, which it derives from individuals.

. . .

The singular circumstance attending this alienation is that, in accepting the property of individuals, the community is far from despoiling them, and only ensures them justifiable possession, changes usurpation into a true right, and enjoyment into property. By this means, the possessors being considered as depositaries of the public good, their rights are respected by all the members of the State, and protected with all their force against foreigners. So that by a resignation, advantageous to the public, and still more so to the resigners, they may be justly said to have acquired all that they gave up: a paradox which will be easily explained by distinguishing, as I shall do hereafter, between the rights which the Sovereign and the proprietors have in the same property.

It may also happen that men begin to associate before they have any possessions, and that, spreading afterwards over a country sufficient for them all, they may either enjoy it in common, or part it between them equally, or in such proportions as the Sovereign shall direct. In whatever manner the acquisition is made, the right which each individual has over his own property is always subordinate to the right which the community has over all; without which there would be no solidity in the social bond, nor any real force in the exercise of sovereignty.

I shall conclude this chapter and book with a remark which must serve for the basis of the whole social system: it is that, instead of destroying the natural equality of mankind, the fundamental compact substitutes, on the contrary, a moral and legal equality for that physical inequality which nature placed among men, and that, let men be ever so unequal in strength or in genius, they are all equalized by convention and legal right.[5]

[5] Under bad governments this equality is but an illusive appearance, which only serves to keep the poor in misery, and support the rich in their usurpations. In fact, laws are always useful to those who have abundance, and injurious to those who have nothing: from whence it follows that the social state is only advantageous to men when every individual has some property, and no one has too much.

Book 2

Chapter 1: That Sovereignty is Inalienable. The first and most important consequence of the principles already established is that the general will alone can direct the forces of the State agreeably to the end of its institution, which is the common good; for if the clashing of private interests has rendered the establishing of societies necessary, the agreement of the same interests has made such establishments possible. It is what is common in these different interests that forms the social bond; and if there was not some point in which they all unanimously centered, no society could exist. It is on the basis of this common interest alone that society must be governed.

I say, therefore, that sovereignty, being only the exercise of the general will, can never alienate itself, and that the Sovereign, which is only a collective being, cannot be represented but by itself: the *power* may well be transmitted but not the *will*.

Indeed, if it is not impossible that a private will should accord on some point with the general will, it is at least impossible that such agreement should be regular and lasting; for the private will is inclined by its nature to partiality, and the general will to impartiality.[6] It is even more impossible to guarantee the continuance of this agreement, even if we were to see it always exist; because that existence must be owing not to art but to chance. The Sovereign may indeed say: "My will at present actually agrees with the will of such and such a man, or at least with what he declares to be his will"; but it cannot say, "Our wills shall likewise agree tomorrow"; since it would be absurd for the will to bind itself for the future, and since it does not belong to any will to consent to what might be injurious to the being from whom the will proceeds. If, therefore, the people promise unconditionally to obey, the act of making such a promise dissolves their existence, and they lose their quality of a people; for at the moment that there is a master, there is no longer a Sovereign, and from that moment the body politic is destroyed.

I do not say that the commands of chiefs cannot pass for

---

[6] [*La volonté particulière tend, par sa nature, aux préférences, et la volonté générale à l'égalité.*]—C. F.

general wills, so long as the Sovereign, being free to oppose them, does not do so. In such cases we must presume from their silence that the people yield their consent. But I shall explain this more at large presently.

Chapter 2: That Sovereignty is Indivisible. For the same reason that sovereignty is inalienable, it is indivisible. For the will is general [7] or it is not; it is either the will of the whole body of the people, or only of a part. In the first case, this declared will is an act of sovereignty and constitutes law; in the second, it is but a private will or an act of magistracy, and is at most but a decree.

. . .

Chapter 3: Whether the General Will Can Err. It follows from what has been said that the general will is always right and tends always to the public advantage; but it does not follow that the deliberations of the people have always the same rectitude. Our will always seeks our own good, but we do not always perceive what it is. The people are never corrupted, but they are often deceived, and only then do they seem to will what is bad.

There is frequently much difference between the *will of all* and the *general will.* The latter regards only the common interest; the former regards private interest, and is indeed but a sum of private wills : [8] but remove from these same wills the pluses and minuses that cancel each other, and then the general will remains as the sum of the differences.[9]

If, when the people, sufficiently informed, deliberated, there was to be no communication among them, from the grand total of trifling differences the general will would always result, and

[7] To make the will general, it is not always necessary that it should be unanimous; but it is indispensably necessary that every vote should be counted: any formal exclusion destroys generality.

[8] [*volontés particulières.*]—C. F.

[9] "Each interest," says the Marquis d'A. [d'Argenson], "has its different principles. The agreement of two private interests is formed by opposition to a third." He might have added that the agreement of all interests is produced by opposition to that of each. If there were no different interests, we should scarcely perceive the common interest, which never finds any opposer; everything would go on regularly of itself, and politics be no longer an art.

their resolutions be always good. But when cabals and partial associations are formed at the expense of the great association, the will of each such association, though *general* with regard to its members, is *private* with regard to the State: it can then be said no longer that there are as many voters as men, but only as many as there are associations. By this means the differences being less numerous, they produce a result less general. Finally, when one of these associations becomes so large that it prevails over all the rest, you have no longer the sum of many opinions dissenting in a small degree from each other, but one great dictating dissentient; from that moment there is no longer a general will, and the predominating opinion is only an individual one.

It is therefore of the utmost importance for obtaining the expression of the general will, that no partial society should be formed in the State, and that every citizen should speak his opinion entirely from himself:[10] such was the unique and sublime system of the great Lycurgus. When there are partial societies, it is politic to multiply their number, that they may be all kept on an equality. This method was pursued by Solon, Numa, and Servius. These are the only precautions that can be taken to make the general will always intelligent, and prevent the people from being deceived.

Chapter 4:   Of the Limits of the Sovereign Power.   If the state or city is only a moral person, the existence of which consists in the union of its members, and if its most important care is that of preserving itself, there is a necessity for its possessing a universally compulsive power, for moving and disposing each part in the manner most convenient to the whole. As nature gives to every man absolute command over all his members, the social compact gives to the body politic absolute command over the members of which it is formed; and it is this power, when directed by the general will, that bears, as I have said before, the name of "sovereignty."

[10] "Divisions," says Machiavelli, "sometimes injure and sometimes serve a republic. The injury is done by cabals and factions, the service by a party which maintains itself without cabals or faction. Since, therefore, it is impossible for the founder of a republic to provide against enmities, he must make the best provision he can against factions." (*History of Florence*, Bk. VII.)

But, besides the public person, we have to consider the private persons who compose it, and whose lives and liberty are naturally independent of it. The point here is to distinguish properly between the respective rights of the citizens and the Sovereign,[11] and between the duties which the former have to fulfil in quality of subjects, and the natural rights which they ought to enjoy in quality of men.

It is granted that all which an individual alienates by the social compact is only that part of his power, his property, and his liberty, the use of which is important to the community; but we must also grant that the Sovereign is the only judge of what is important to the community.

All the services which a citizen can render to the State ought to be rendered as soon as the Sovereign demands them; but the Sovereign cannot, on its side, impose any burden on the subject useless to the community; it cannot even have the inclination to do so; for, under the law of reason, nothing is done without a cause, any more than under the law of nature.

The engagements which bind us to the social body are only obligatory because they are mutual; and their nature is such that in fulfilling them we cannot labour for others without labouring at the same time for ourselves. Wherefore is the general will always right, and wherefore do all the wills invariably seek the happiness of every individual among them, if it is not that there is no person who does not appropriate the word "each" to himself, and who does not think of himself when he is voting for all? This proves that the equality of right, and the idea of justice which it inspires, is derived from the preference which each gives to himself, and consequently from the nature of man; that the general will, to be truly such, ought to be so in its object, as well as its essence: that it ought to come from all, if we are to apply it to all; and that it loses its natural rectitude when it tends towards any one individual and determinate object, because then, judging of what is external to us, we have no true principle of equity to guide us.

. . .

[11] Attentive readers, be not too hasty, I beg of you, to accuse me of contradicting myself. I could not avoid doing so terminologically, on account of the poverty of the language; but have patience until I explain my meaning.

We should perceive by this that the generality of the will depends less on the number of voters than on the common interest which unites them; for, in this institution, each necessarily submits to the conditions which he imposes on others—an admirable union of interest and justice, which gives to the common deliberations a character of equity that vanishes in the discussion of all private affairs for want of a common interest to combine and identify the ruling of the judge with that of the party.

By whatever path we return to our principle, we always arrive at the same conclusion—that is, that the social compact establishes among citizens such an equality that they are all engaged under the same conditions, and should all enjoy the same rights. Thus, by the nature of the compact all acts of sovereignty, that is to say, all authentic acts of the general will, oblige or favour all citizens alike in such a manner as evinces that the Sovereign knows no person but the body of the nation, and does not make any distinction among the individuals who compose it. What, therefore, is properly an act of sovereignty? It is not a convention between a superior and an inferior, but a convention of the body with each of its members—a justifiable convention because it has the social contract for its basis; equitable, because it is common to all; beneficial, because it can have no other object but the general good; and solid, because it is guaranteed by the public force and the supreme power. While subjects are under the governance of such conventions only, they obey no one but only their own will: and to enquire how far the respective rights of the Sovereign and citizens extend is to ask how far the citizens can engage with themselves, each towards all, and all towards each.

We see by this that the sovereign power, all absolute, all sacred, all inviolable as it is, neither will, nor can, exceed the bounds of general conventions, and that every man may fully dispose of what is left to him of his property and his liberty by these conventions; so that the Sovereign never has any right to lay a greater charge on one subject than on another, because then the affair would become personal,[12] and in such cases the power of the Sovereign is no longer competent.

[12] [*l'affaire devenant particulière.*]—C. F.

These distinctions once admitted, it is evidently false that individuals have made any real renunciation by the social contract. On the contrary, they find their situation, by the effect of that contract, really rendered preferable to what it was before. Instead of making any alienation they have only made an advantageous transition from a mode of living unsettled and precarious to one better and more secure, from a state of natural independence to one of liberty, from possessing the power of injuring others to security for themselves, and from their strength, which others might, by the employment of theirs, overcome, to a right which social union renders invincible. Even their lives, which they have devoted to the State, are continually protected by it; and when they are exposed in its defence, what is it but restoring that which they have received from it? What do they do but what they would do more frequently, and with more danger, in the state of nature, when, living in continual and unavoidable conflicts, they would have to defend at the peril of their lives what was necessary to the preservation of life? All, it is true, must fight for their country when their service is requisite; but then no person has occasion to fight for himself as an individual. And is it not gaining a great advantage to be obliged, for the protection of that to which we owe our security, to incur occasionally only a part of that danger to which we must be again exposed as individuals as soon as we were deprived of it?

.   .   .

Chapter 6:   Of the Law.   By the social compact we have given existence and life to the body politic; it now remains to give it motion and will by legislation. For the original act by which the body is formed and united determines none of the measures that ought to be taken for its preservation.

.   .   .

But what, in fine, is a law? While men content themselves with affixing none but metaphysical ideas to this word, they must continue to reason without understanding one another; and when they have said what a law of nature is, they will still be no less ignorant of what a law of the State is.

I have already said that there can be no general will directed towards a private object. That private object is either in the State, or outside the State. If it is outside the State, a will which is alien to it cannot be general with regard to it; and if it is in the State, it makes a part of it, and between the whole and its part there is a relation which proves the existence of two separate beings; of which the said part makes one, and the whole—less that same part—makes the other. But the whole less a part is not the whole; and while this relation subsists, there is no whole, but two unequal parts: from whence it follows that the will of one part cannot in any way be general with respect to the other.

But when the whole people determines for the whole people, it considers only itself; and if a relation is then formed it is only a relation of the whole object from one point of view to the whole object from another point of view, and the whole itself is not divided. Then the affair on which they enact is general, as is the will that enacts. It is this act that I call a "law."

. . .

Under this idea, we perceive at once how unnecessary it would be to enquire to whom the function of making laws belongs, because the laws are but the acts of the general will; neither need we ask whether the prince is above the laws, since he is a member of the State; nor whether the law can be unjust, as no one is unjust towards himself; nor how we can be free while subjected to the laws, since they are but the registers of our own wills.

We see also that, since the law unites universality of will with universality of object, whatever is ordered of his own accord by any man, whoever he may be, is not law; nay, even that which the Sovereign orders relative to a private object is not a law but a decree; neither is it an act of sovereignty but of magistracy.

I therefore denominate every State a "republic" which is governed by laws, under whatever form of administration it may be; for then only the public interest governs, and the affairs of the public obtain a due regard.[13] All justifiable governments are republican,[14] and I will hereafter explain what government is.

The laws are properly but the conditions of civil association. The people submit themselves to the laws, and ought to enjoy the right of making them; it pertains only to those who associate to regulate the terms of the society. But how do they regulate them? Is it by a common agreement, by a sudden inspiration? Has the body politic an organ for declaring its will? Who gives to that body the necessary foresight to form these acts and publish them beforehand? Or how are they declared at the moment of need? How can an unenlightened multitude, which often does not know what it wants, since it so seldom knows what is good for it, execute, of itself, so great, so difficult an enterprise as a system of legislation? Of themselves the people always will the good, but of themselves they do not always see in what it consists. The general will is always right, but the judgment that guides it is not always enlightened. It is therefore necessary to make the people see things as they are, and sometimes as they ought to appear, to point out to them the right path which they are seeking, to guard them from the seducing voice of private wills, and, helping them to see how times and places are connected, to induce them to balance the attraction of immediate and sensible advantage against the apprehension of unknown and distant evil. Individuals see the good they reject; the public wills the good it does not see. All have equally need for guidance. Some must have their wills made conformable to their reason, and others must be taught what it is they will. From this increase of public knowledge would result the union of judgment and will in the social body; from that union comes the harmony of the parties and the

[13] [*Car alors seulement . . . la chose publique est quelque chose.*] —C. F.

[14] I do not by the word "republic" mean an aristocracy or democracy only, but in general all governments guided by the general will, which is the law. To be justifiable, the government should not be confounded with the Sovereign, but be considered as its administrator. Then monarchy itself would be a republic. This will be further explained in the following book.

highest power of the whole. From thence is born the necessity of a legislator.

Chapter 7: Of the Legislator.   To discover those happy rules of government which would agree with every nation could only be the work of some superior intelligence, acquainted with all the passions of men, but liable to none of them; who, without bearing any affinity to our nature, knew it perfectly; whose happiness was independent of ours, but who still condescended to make us the object of his care; and who having persevered through a long course of years in the pursuit of distant glory, could enjoy in other ages the reward of his unwearied zeal.[15] In short, gods would be required to give laws to mankind.

. . .

He who compiles the laws, therefore, has not, nor ought he to have, any right to legislate, and the people cannot, even if they should be inclined, deprive themselves of that incommunicable right, because, according to the fundamental compact, it is only the general will that can compel individuals, and it can never be known whether a private will is conformable to the general will until it has been submitted to the free vote of the people. I have affirmed this already, but a repetition may not be useless.

Thus we find at the same time in the work of legislation two things which seem incompatible with each other: an enterprise exceeding human power, executed by an authority which is not an authority.

. . .

This sublime reason, so far above the comprehension of vulgar men, is that whose decisions legislators put in the mouth of the immortals, that those might be led along under the sanction of divine authority, whom it might be impossible for

---

[15] A people do not become celebrated until their legislation begins to decline. We do not know during how many ages the Lacedemonians lived happily under the laws of Lycurgus before there was any account made of them by the rest of Greece.

human prudence to conduct without it.[16] But it belongs not to all men to make the gods speak, nor to gain belief if they pretend to be the interpreters of the divine will. The magnanimous spirit of the legislator is the sole miracle which must prove his mission.

. . .

Book 3

Before I speak of the different forms of government, I shall endeavour to fix the precise sense of this word, which has not hitherto been very well explained.

Chapter 1: Of Government in General. I warn the reader that this chapter requires to be read very seriously, and that I am unacquainted with any art which can make the subject clear to those who will not bestow on it their serious attention.

Every free act must be produced by the concurrence of two causes: the one moral, that is to say, the will which must resolve upon the act, the other physical, that is to say, the power which must execute it. When I go towards an object, it is necessary, in the first place, that I should will to go; and, secondly, that my feet should bear me. If a paralytic person should will to go, and an active man should not will, both would remain where they were. The body politic has the same moving forces: and we find equally in it, as in the natural body, both force and will; the latter distinguished by the name of "legislative power," and the former by that of "executive power." Nothing is or should be done without their concurrence.

We have seen that the legislative power belongs to the people, and can belong to that body only. It is easy to see, on the contrary, by the principles already established, that the

---

[16] "It is true," says Machiavelli, "there never was, in any country, a promulgator of extraordinary laws who had not recourse to God; because otherwise his system would not have been received; a wise man may know many useful truths, though they are not so self-evident as to carry conviction to the minds of others." (*Discourses on Livy*, Bk. V, chap. II).

executive power cannot belong to the generality as legislator or Sovereign, because that power consists only in individual acts, which are not to be performed by the law, and consequently neither by the Sovereign, all whose acts must be laws.

It is therefore necessary that the public force should have an agent of its own which shall unite and apply that force according to the direction of the general will, to serve as the means of communication between the State and the Sovereign, and to form a sort of public person, in which, as in a man, the union of mind and body should be found. This is the reason why the government in a State is generally, and very improperly, confounded with the Sovereign, of which it is but the minister.

What then is that government? An intermediate body established between the subjects and the Sovereign, for their mutual correspondence, charged with the execution of the laws, and the maintenance of both civil and political liberty.

The members of this body are denominated "magistrates" or "kings," that is to say, "governors"; and the body collectively takes the name of "prince." [17] Thus those who think that the act by which a people submit themselves to their chiefs is not a contract have good foundation for their opinion. That act is certainly no more than a commission, an employment, under which, simply as officers of the Sovereign, the members of government exercise in the name of the Sovereign the power delegated to them, and which may be limited, modified, or recalled at the pleasure of the Sovereign, the alienation of such a right being incompatible with the nature of the social body, and contrary to the end of association.

I therefore give the name of "government" or "supreme administration" to the justifiable exercise of the executive power; and "prince" or "magistrate" to the man or body charged with that administration.

It is in government that those intermediate powers are found whose connections constitute that of the whole with the whole, or of the Sovereign with the State.

. . .

[17] At Venice they apply to the College [of government] the title of "Most Serene Prince," even when the Doge is not present.

There is this essential difference between the State and the government: the former is self-existent, and the existence of the latter depends entirely on the Sovereign. Thus the ruling will of the prince neither is nor ought to be anything more than the general will or the law; his force is only the public force concentrated in his hands: if he attempts to execute on his own authority any absolute and independent act, the chain which combines the whole relaxes immediately. And if at last the private will of the prince is more active than the will of the Sovereign, and the public force in his hands is employed to enforce obedience to this private will, so that there are in effect two sovereigns, the one by right, and the other in fact, at that moment the social union ceases, and the body politic is dissolved.

It is, however, necessary that the government should so far have a real existence and life as to be distinguishable from the body of the State; in order that all its members should be able to act in concert and work for the end for which it was instituted, it must have a particular *self,* a sensibility common to its members, and a force and will sufficient for its preservation. This distinct existence supposes assemblies and councils, a power to deliberate and resolve, rights, titles, and privileges which belong to the prince alone, and which render the situation of a magistrate more honourable in proportion as it is more laborious. The great difficulty of forming a body of government lies in ordering this subaltern whole within the whole in such a manner that the general constitution may not be altered by giving too much strength to this part; that the particular force necessary for preserving itself may be kept distinct from the public force which is necessary to preserve the State; and, in fine, that on every occasion the government may be sacrificed to the people, and not the people to the government.

.   .   .

Book 4

Chapter 1: That the General Will Cannot Be Destroyed. So long as several men unite and consider themselves as one body, they have but one will, which is to promote the common safety and general well-being. While this union continues, all the springs of the State will be vigorous and simple, the maxims by which they are regulated will be clear and comprehensible; and there will be no jarring, opposing interests; the common good will then be everywhere evident, and nothing will be necessary but a sound understanding to perceive it. For peace, union, and equality are enemies of political subtleties. Men of integrity and simplicity are difficult to deceive because of their very simplicity: lures and refined pretexts do not impose upon them, and they have not even cunning enough to be dupes. When we see, among the happiest people in the world, groups of peasants directing affairs of State under an oak, and always acting wisely, can we help but despise the refinements of those nations which render themselves illustrious and miserable by so much art and mystery?

A State thus governed requires but very few laws; and whenever it becomes necessary to promulgate new ones, the necessity is perceived universally. He who proposes them only says what all have already felt, and neither faction nor eloquence is required to obtain the passage of a measure which each person has already resolved to adopt, as soon as he is sure that the others will act with him.

What leads our reasoners astray on this point is that they consider only those States which have been ill-constructed originally, and suppose, because it would be impossible to pursue in them the system of simple policy I recommend, that it must be equally impossible everywhere. They make great game of the fact that in London or Paris an artful impostor or a man of insinuating eloquence can persuade the people to believe the most ridiculous absurdities. They do not know that Cromwell would be hooted at by the people of Berne, and the Duke of Beaufort would experience at the hands of the Genevese a discipline he might not greatly admire.

But when the social bond once begins to relax and the State to grow weak, when private interests begin to take the lead, and smaller societies have an influence on the greater, the common interest changes and finds many opposers: there is no longer unanimity of opinion; the general will is no longer the will of all; everything is contested; and the best advice is never adopted without much dispute and opposition.

Finally, when a State upon the brink of ruin supports only a vain illusory form and the social bond no longer unites the hearts of the people, and when the sacred name of public good is made use of to cover the basest interest, then the general will is silenced; and every one, being directed by secret motives, no more gives an opinion as a citizen than if the State had never existed; decrees which have no other object but private interest are then passed, to which the name of laws is falsely given.

But does it follow that the general will is annihilated or corrupted? No: it will remain always constant, unalterable, and pure; but it is rendered subordinate to other wills, which domineer over it. In this state of affairs, though each individual detaches his interest from the common interest, yet he finds it impossible to separate them entirely; but his part of the common ill appears trifling to him when balanced against some private advantage which he has in view. This particular object only excepted, he is in every point as solicitous as any other member to promote the general welfare on his own account. Even by selling his vote for money he does not destroy his own general will, he only eludes it. The fault which such a man commits is that of changing the state of the question, and answering something else than what he was asked: instead of saying by his vote, "It is advantageous to the State," he says, "It is advantageous to such a man, or to such a party, that such a motion should pass." Thus the law for regulating public assemblies is not so much intended to maintain there the general will as to enforce the full and clear repetition of the question on which that will is to determine.

I could make many reflections on the simple right of voting in all acts of sovereignty—a right which nothing can deprive the citizens of; and also upon that of stating opinions, proposing, dividing and discussing, which government is always particularly careful to confine solely to the members of its own body; but this important subject requires a separate treatise, as it cannot be comprehended in that I am now writing.

Chapter 2: Of Suffrage. It is evident from what has been said in the preceding chapter that the manner of conducting general affairs is the best criterion by which to judge of the morality and health of the body politic. In proportion to the degree of concord which reigns in the assemblies, that is, the nearer opinion approaches unanimity, the more the general will predominates; while tumults, dissensions, and long debates declare the ascendancy of private interests and the declining situation of the State.

. . .

From these various considerations, maxims may be drawn for regulating the manner of counting the votes and determining the opinion of a public assembly, which must vary according as the general will is more or less easy to ascertain and the State more or less in decline.

There is one law only which, by its nature, requires unanimous consent; I mean the social compact: for civil association is the most voluntary of all acts; every man being born free and master of himself, no person can under any pretense whatever subject him without his consent. To affirm that the son of a slave is born a slave is to pronounce that he is not born a man.

Should there be any men who oppose the social compact, their opposition will not invalidate it, but only hinder their being included: they are foreigners among citizens. When the State is instituted, residence constitutes consent; to inhabit a territory is to submit to the sovereignty.[18]

Except in this original contract, a majority of votes is sufficient to bind all the others. This is a consequence of the contract itself. But it may be asked how a man can be free and yet forced to conform to the will of others. How are the opposers free when they are in submission to laws to which they have never consented?

I answer that the question is not fairly stated. The citizen consents to all the laws, to those which are passed in spite of

[18] This must always be understood of a man in a free State; because elsewhere his family, his property, or the want of an asylum to fly to, and also necessity or force, may detain an inhabitant against his will; and then his sojourn does not suppose his consent, either to the contract or to the violation of the contract.

his opposition, and even to those which sentence him to punishment if he violates any one of them. The constant will of all the members of the State is the general will; it is by that they are citizens and free.[19] When any law is proposed in the assembly of the people, the question is not precisely to enquire whether they approve the proposition or reject it, but if it is conformable or not to the general will, which is their will. Each citizen, in giving his suffrage, states his mind on that question; and the general will is found by counting the votes. When, therefore, the motion which I opposed carries, it only proves to me that I was mistaken, and that what I believed to be the general will was not so. If my particular opinion had prevailed, I should have done what I was not willing to do, and, consequently, I should not have been in a state of freedom.

This is indeed supposing that all the characteristics which mark the general will still reside in the most votes: when that ceases to be the case, whatever measures may be adopted, it means the end of liberty.

In showing heretofore how private wills are often substituted for the general will in public deliberations, I have shown the most practicable means of preventing that abuse; and I shall speak again upon the subject later on. With regard to the proportional number of votes necessary to declare this will, I have also laid down the principles on which it should be determined. I have now to add that, though the difference of one single vote will destroy equality, and one opposing voice prevent unanimity, yet there are several grades of unequal division between equality and unanimity, and in each of them the number may be fixed according to the situation and occasions of the body politic.

Two general rules may suffice for regulating these proportions: one is that the more serious and important the deliberations are, the nearer the number of votes which pass them should approach unanimity; the other is that the greater necessity there is for expediting the affair, the smaller may be the

[19] At Genoa we see inscribed over the gates of their prisons and on the chains affixed to their galley slaves the word "Libertas." This application of it is noble as well as just. In fact, it is only the bad people in every State that hinder the citizens from being free. Any country where all such men were chained to the oar would be the seat of perfect liberty.

majority: and on motions which require to be determined on the spot, a majority of one may be deemed sufficient. The first of these maxims seems most applicable to laws, and the second to practical business. Be that as it may, it is by combining these two rules that the number of voices proper to form the majority on different occasions must be established.

.   .   .

Justice and the Common Good

Some Interpretations of Justice

Although classical political philosophy, ancient and modern, has much to say about justice and the common good,[1] it has neither left us settled interpretations of them nor clearly distinguished the one from the other. The most common characterization of justice was that which Plato attributed to the revered poet Simonides; later enshrined in the formula of the Roman jurist Ulpian, it read: "Justice is the constant and perpetual will of rendering to everyone his due." This formula was frequently cited and became traditional.[2] Use of the formula, however, often masked disagreement and the formula itself had only limited utility because it left open the questions what is "one's due" and by what standard this is to be determined.

Plato wrote the *Republic* in order to answer these questions. He believed that "a person's due" is "his good" and that, consequently, in order to say what is due a person, it is essential to give an outline account of a well-ordered society and the well-ordered, or "virtuous," individuals who are its citizens. But if justice is interpreted in this way, then either it is the whole of virtue, as Aristotle remarked,[3] or else it is that happy

---

[1] Or "the public good," "the public interest," "the common interest," etc. The choice of one of these expressions over the others by the classical philosophers does not appear significant.

[2] Plato, *Republic*, I (conversation of Socrates and Polemarchus); Cicero, *De Officiis*, I, 5; Ulpian, *Digest of Justinian*, I, 1, 10; Justinian, *Institutes*, I, 1; Saint Augustine, *City of God*, XIX, 21; Saint Thomas, *Summa Theologiae*, II, II, Q58, 1; Hobbes, *Leviathan*, XV; etc.

[3] Aristotle, *Nicomachean Ethics*, V, 1. See also the passages from Plato's *Republic* included in Part I of this book.

condition in which each has his due and the "common interest" is attained. Aristotle himself sometimes used the term *justice* (*dikaiosyne*) in this broad sense. He distinguished "right" or "just" constitutions from "perverted" ones on the ground that the former are in the common interest while the latter are in the ruler's interest; and at one point he said that justice is "the good in the sphere of politics," the end of the art and science of politics, thus equating justice and the common interest.[4]

In contrast to this broad view of justice we also find stricter interpretations based on much more limited views of a person's due. Hobbes, for example, took the commands of the sovereign, with very little limitation, as the effective measure of that due; he defined "injustice" as "non-performance of covenant." On somewhat the same pattern, Hume interpreted justice as the virtue of living by the elementary conventions that, being required for the existence of society, are a necessary *means* for securing both the public or common interest and private or self-interest as well. For both of them, justice consisted essentially in the observance of "useful" laws or conventions that afford security and promote individual interests, or, alternatively, in the respect of rights that arise from such laws or conventions.

Locke and Rousseau took a middle course. Locke referred to the public good, along with peace and safety, as the end of political society, but he mentioned justice infrequently in the *Two Treatises;* when he did, it was most often in connection with law or a system of justice. Although this suggests a view similar to that of Hobbes, the law which constituted Locke's basic standard of justice was natural law, not the law or convention of Hobbes or Hume; from Locke's standpoint, one's due, at least primarily, was the set of his "natural rights." The contemporary view, that justice consists primarily in respecting a person's basic rights, owes very much to this doctrine. Locke, however, was not single-minded: The famous quotation "the well-being of the people shall be the supreme law" suggests the broad interpretation,[5] one that lived on. James Madison, for example, spoke of justice and the common good together and

---

[4] Aristotle, *Politics*, III, 6–7, 12.
[5] Locke, *Second Treatise*, § 158; the source is probably Cicero, *De Legibus*, III, 3 (8).

proclaimed justice to be the end of government and civil society.[6]

Rousseau, it will be recalled, proposed a new interpretation of justice. He regarded justice and utility as the twin goals of society, justice and the common good as joint derivatives of "the general will." For him, the starkest injustice was coercion, the violation of moral autonomy; what was most one's due was the moral right to live under laws that one legislates for oneself. This moral right accounts for the necessity of "the general will"; its object, "the common good," could be attained, and justice made secure, only if persons lived under such a will.

In the philosophies so far considered, we thus find a broad interpretation, which takes justice to lie in every person's attaining his good, and a narrow interpretation, according to which justice consists in the acceptance of laws and conventions. Somewhere between them are interpretations that take justice primarily to require respect for natural rights (Locke) and moral autonomy (Rousseau). Each theory proposes its own view of one's due.

Notwithstanding the variety, one theme runs through all these theories. In all of them "the common good" is taken in opposition to a special interest (whether it be Aristotle's "interest of the rulers," or Locke's "private good," or Hume's and Madison's "interested factions," or Rousseau's "particular wills"). The common good, moreover, is said to be the proper end of government. From this point of view any government that serves a special interest is naturally regarded as perverted and unjust; to promote the common good is to promote "the just ends of government" and not to become a tool of some persons at the expense of others. Some modern authors have gone so far as to interpret the statement that government should promote the common good simply as an alternative way of saying that government should be impartial, and in this sense "just." [7]

There is wide agreement that justice requires impartiality. No one should be exempted from the rule of law and law should

---

[6] A. Hamilton, J. Jay, and J. Madison, *The Federalist Papers,* Numbers 10, 51 (written by Madison).

[7] See S. Benn and R. Peters, *Principles of Political Thought* (New York: The Free Press, 1965), pp. 318 ff.

be regularly and impartially administered. More generally, all should be treated alike when there are no relevant differences—in the name of justice, no one should be favored and no one should be discriminated against. Impartiality, characterized in one or another of these ways, is a common requirement of almost all theories and, as a consequence, it has sometimes been called "formal justice." [8]

When one speaks of impartiality as formal justice, however, one generally assumes a background of reasonably just laws and institutions. The undeviating administration of highly unjust laws, or the consistent use of such laws to specify "legitimate differences" between persons, is dubiously called "just" in *any* sense of the term. To recognize this is not to deny that the institution of "the rule of law" is a great social achievement. But it is to acknowledge that the idea of "impartiality," when abstracted from the conditions in which it is applied, is not as helpful as one might think. As a characterization of justice, impartiality, broadly interpreted, is too much like "giving each his due"; it is only a starting point. And unless it is interpreted broadly, it is not equivalent either to justice or the common good as these were traditionally conceived.

Particular Justice: Distributive and Commutative

Aristotle tried to introduce clarity by distinguishing the aforementioned broad sense of justice from "particular" justice, which he divided into "distributive" and "rectificatory." Distributive justice was said to be concerned with distributions of honor, wealth, etc., to members of the community. By the time of the *Politics,* however, if not before, it was clear to Aristotle that the most important problem of distribution was that of "offices" in the *polis,* and especially "citizenship." The basic

[8] *Ibid.,* pp. 126–129. Also see C. Perelman, *The Idea of Justice and the Problem of Argument* (London: Routledge & Kegan Paul Ltd., 1963), Essay 1; and D. Lyons, "On Formal Justice," *Cornell Law Review,* 58, No. 5 (June 1973).

problem of distributive justice (although not the only one) was the problem of rightly framing a constitution.

Rectificatory or "commutative" [9] justice, on the other hand, was said to be concerned with transactions between one person and another, both voluntary, such as buying and selling, and involuntary, such as theft and assault. Its object was to rectify "wrong treatment" and produce just treatment of one person by another. This kind of justice was distinguished from other kinds primarily in virtue of the fact that it regards all as equal: What is due a person in his transactions is determined by laws that treat all persons, or all in a society, equally (a thief is, however noble or ignoble in other respects, a thief). Distributive justice, on the other hand, is not bound to equality; ideally it allocates in proportion to one's worth or merit.

Aristotle's distinction helps one to understand how Hobbes and Hume, both of whom were impressed by the necessity of human beings living under common laws, could have looked at justice as the performance of covenant or the following of convention: As Hobbes noted, the main thrust of such a view is to limit justice to commutative justice. He argued that giving a person his due directly depends on the establishment of civil power, for without the Commonwealth no one could even be said to have a due. Hume argued the same point, but substituted commonly accepted general rules, or conventions, for civil power. Both of them gave distributive justice short shrift: Hobbes rejected it explicitly; Hume, if not wholly unmindful of it, emphasized the impracticability of distribution on the basis of either merit or equality in arguing for the necessity of general rules to fix expectations.[10] Hobbes and Hume were interested in the bare essentials that must be required of people in order both to have a society and to preserve one torn by virulent self-interested factions. They were not much concerned with problems of distribution, or, as we speak of it, "the problem of attaining a just society."

[9] "Commutative" was the medieval name, from *commutationes* (transactions). See Saint Thomas Aquinas, *Summa Theologiae*, II, II, Q58, Q61.

[10] See Hobbes' *Leviathan*, XV, in a passage omitted above; and Hume's *Enquiry Concerning the Principles of Morals*, III, 2. Also see Hume's *Treatise*, III, 2, 2–6. On justice as keeping faith, see Cicero's *De Officiis*, I, vii.

The historical tendency to interpret justice on the model of Aristotle's commutative justice is naturally regarded as essentially conservative, especially if one associates this tendency with contemporary cries for law and order. However, if people, rightly concerned with problems of distribution, no longer even think of theft, promise-breaking, and the like as injustices, then they are apt to overlook a fundamental unfairness, a taking advantage of another, which these acts commonly involve. Commutative justice is re-emphasized, moreover, whenever society is threatened. For both reasons, commutative justice must have a place in any relatively complete theory of justice. It is worth noting that J. S. Mill, in giving his own account of justice in *Utilitarianism,* said: "Justice is a name for certain classes of moral rules which concern the essentials of human well-being more nearly, and are therefore of more absolute obligation, than any other rules for the guidance of life. . . ." These moral requirements "regarded collectively, stand higher in the scale of social utility . . . than any others. . . ." The "interest involved" in enforcing rules of justice is "that of security."

Political philosophy in the nineteenth century, however, became increasingly concerned with problems of distributive justice, especially when this is taken to include the problem of rightly framing the constitution of society. With the extension of the industrial revolution, the great increase in wealth, and the unfairness of the traditional system of land ownership, the gross inequalities in society became both more brutal and more apparent. The recommended theoretical corrections took very different forms and the requirements of justice were shaped accordingly. Some thought that the only way to accomplish reform was by concentrating power in the state; the state would check the demon of self-interest. Others thought that self-interest was ineradicable, the only solution being to extend civil, political, and economic liberties so that every self-interested voice could be heard. Both of these extreme positions were concerned with securing a "more rational" organization of the state and society, one that would promote the interests of all. Since both positions were critical of existing institutions, Hobbes' and Hume's conception of justice as conforming to society's laws or conventions, or as respecting legal and conventional rights, came to appear more and more conservative and antiquated. (There is, perhaps, no clearer example of a practical concept being reshaped by the practical problems which people face.)

In order to understand the character of these new conceptions of justice and the common good, we shall very briefly consider two extreme philosophies which became prominent at the beginning of the nineteenth century. One of them is commonly referred to as "the organic view," the other as "utilitarianism." After considering them, and the movements toward revolution and reform which they generated, we shall turn our attention to T. H. Green, who tried to combine the virtues of both these philosophies. Finally, we shall consider Professor John Rawls' new attempt at synthesis, based partly on the contract theory of Rousseau, but including both more ancient and more modern conceptions of justice and the common good.

The Organic Theories of Hegel and Marx

The political philosophies of seventeenth- and eighteenth-century Britain, as we saw in Part II, had several distinctive characteristics. For one thing, unlike their ancient and medieval forebears, they assigned the state quite limited goals and functions; its goal was no longer taken, even in theory, to be the all-inclusive or self-sufficient good, or even secular good, of the citizens. Second, the goods that people most want were taken to be such things as security and pleasure, not participation in forms of life constituted by social and political institutions; thus the state was regarded as a useful and necessary means, not as helping to shape human ends. Third, the specialized and instrumental function of the state was conceived negatively: Government is primarily needed in order to conserve something—life, natural rights, or conventions—against the destructive tendencies of self-interested human nature. Hume said that it is "a just political maxim, that every man must be supposed a knave," and several American constitutionalists agreed with him that the essential political problem is to devise institutions to neutralize self-interest, especially self-interested factions.[11] Very much in evidence in these views is the underlying individualism: Political society was conceived as a collection of individuals joined together for security, the protection of individual rights, and the promotion of individual interests.

In the late eighteenth and early nineteenth centuries the so-called "organic" theory of society developed in opposition to this individualism. Influenced by Rousseau but quickly proceeding far beyond him, this new theory regarded individualist political philosophy, including the doctrine of natural law and natural rights, not as the truth, but as a kind of abstraction from the course of history. Individualist philosophy was thought to be a mere manifestation in theory of a stage of economic development in which private property was extolled and self-interest was rampant. The inexorable flow of history, however, was seen as rational and progressive, with the anarchy of fragmented interests inevitably leading to a reassertion of centralized authority and the development of social forms essential to individual well-being. The state or nation, conceived not as a collection of individuals but as a natural organism that receives life from and gives life to its members, was viewed as the culmination of this rational process. The state was an objective embodiment of reason that manifested itself not in a static natural law but in the "dialectic" of opposed social forces and their resolution in history.

The most influential of the early "organicists" was G. W. F. Hegel (1770–1831), who, somewhat in the tradition of ancient philosophers, undertook to formulate a comprehensive view of the basic nature of all things and the whole of history. Rejecting limitations that Kant before him had placed on human reason, Hegel concluded that a human being can become self-consciously united with the Mind or Spirit of the world. His fundamental political interest was in the state and its development as an objectification of the World Mind. Much of Hegel's political philosophy, nevertheless, was quite independent of this metaphysics.

In the preface to *The Philosophy of Right*, Hegel an-

[11] See his essay, "Of the Independency of Parliament," first published in *Essays Moral and Political*. See also Hamilton, Jay, and Madison, *The Federalist Papers*, Number 10.

nounced: "After all, the truth about Right, Ethics, and the state is as old as its public recognition and formulation in the law of the land, in the morality of everyday life, and in religion." [12] This "truth," however, on Hegel's view, needed to be made explicit; a "system of reason," embodied in laws and institutions, integrated the institutions of the social order into an organic whole and determined their historical development.

The individualist philosophers, Hegel thought, failed to understand this basic fact about society. They failed to see that the state and other institutions are "inherently rational," and they consequently misunderstood the potentialities that a human being has as a rational being. Human nature cannot be discovered simply by examining natural needs, impulses, and the like. Each individual's life is shaped by the laws and institutions of the social order, and he has the natural capacity to unite himself with "the universal system of reason" that these laws and institutions embody. This capacity derives from his rational "essence," his distinctive character as mind or spirit. When not united with "the universal," an individual is "not himself," and his ends are capricious, insignificant, and even worthless (Introduction and §§ 123–124, 130).

On the other hand, for Hegel, individuality is not lost in "universality." Each human being, considered as a "subject," has "individuality of consciousness and will" (§ 264), and, as Rousseau observed, an individual would be neither moral nor human if he lacked the capacity to direct his own life. Welfare or happiness, moreover, is an essential end of a human being as a subject (§§ 123, 130); and the happiness of the citizens can even be said to be the end of the state (§ 265A). The individualists thus had a point, but they completely overlooked the fact that welfare or happiness depends for its content on the laws and institutions of the social order. It is a blunder to think that individuals can somehow stand apart from their institutions and judge them in terms of how much pleasure or happiness they afford, or how well they satisfy desire; pleasure and the desire for pleasure are, for the most part, reflections of institutions and

[12] Hegel, *Philosophy of Right,* trans. T. M. Knox (London: Oxford University Press, 1952), p. 3. This and the following quotations from this book are by permission of The Clarendon Press, Oxford. (A = Addition)

thus constitute no independent criterion. The worth of institutions is to be determined in quite a different way, by their contribution to freedom.

On Hegel's view, each individual lives most of his life in the roles and stations that laws and institutions make available to him; his potentialities are both relative to and actualized in different forms of institutional life. The individual realizes *himself* as the individual he is by acting as a family member, a worker, a citizen, and the like—these roles and stations of the social order embody modes of rationality. The laws and institutions of the ethical order are thus not alien to the subject: "His spirit bears witness to them as to its own essence, the essence in which he has a feeling of his selfhood, and in which he lives as in his own element which is not distinguished from himself" (§ 147). By self-consciously conforming to the system of reason which rational institutions embody, a human being actualizes his potentialities and becomes most himself. He determines himself in accordance with both reason and his own essential nature; he is rationally self-determined, and in this sense he is free. The laws and institutions that make ethical life possible are to be judged by their contribution to freedom, the "absolute end and aim of the world" (§ 129).[13]

Hegel undertook to explain how different stages of the ethical order contribute to freedom. The ethical order itself is the dialectical synthesis of two "abstract moments"; it synthesizes the contributions to freedom made, on the one hand, by external rights to property under mutually recognized law, and, on the other, by conscience and free will. It preserves within itself both of these dimensions of freedom. The most elementary of the three stages of the ethical order is the family, whose members, united by love, lose their personal independence in a "common sharing of their entire existence as individuals" (§ 163). When its members begin to think of their own individual ends, as children inevitably do, the family naturally dissolves. This marks the transition to the second stage of the ethical order, which Hegel called "civil society."

[13] For a helpful essay on this obscure and important notion, see R. Schacht, "Hegel on Freedom," in *Hegel: A Collection of Critical Essays*, A. MacIntyre (Ed.) (Garden City, N.Y.: Doubleday & Company, Inc., 1972).

Hegel's description of civil society was, with some modifications, very much like the individualists' account of political society. Civil society is basically concerned with the satisfaction of individual interests. Its primary mark is that "each member is his own end, everything else is nothing to him" (§ 182A). However, since each person's welfare is tied to the welfare of others, cooperative institutions develop; in theory each person, by pursuing his own interests, contributes to the welfare of all. The end of civil society is the protection of property and personal freedom (§§ 208, 258); its institutions include an economic system, the rule of law and administration of justice, the police, and "corporations" or "families" of persons with similar economic interests. The creation of these institutions was, for Hegel, an "achievement of the modern world," but one to which the individualist philosophers were captive. Civil society contains negative elements that make it fundamentally unstable. Its division of property is often accidental and capricious, like needs, desires, and the natural allocation of talents. A class of paupers, lacking even self-respect, is created. Civil society then "affords a spectacle of extravagance and want as well as of the physical and ethical degeneration common to them both" (§§ 185, 200, 243–244, 253). Since there is no institutionalized guardian of the common good, particular interests tend to destroy themselves.

Freedom achieves full objectification only in the third stage, the state or nation. The state, through its sovereign power, frees the institutions of civil society from domination by private interests and provides for individual welfare. It is able to do this because it is "the actuality of the ethical Idea" (§ 257), the self-sufficient social organism, which unites the lower institutions of the ethical order in a more perfect whole. The modern state has a "prodigious strength and depth" because it unites "the universal end of the whole . . . with the complete freedom of its particular members and with private well-being" (§§ 260, 260A). In its most perfect form it is a constitutional monarchy, but its constitution could not possibly have been made by "an agglomeration of atomic individuals" (§ 273). The state is "Mind on earth," the building of reason into the world in the course of history (§ 270). Each sovereign state, however, is inevitably opposed by other sovereign states and war is the natural consequence. In this case, "harangues are silenced by the solemn cycles of history" (§ 324A). "The one and only absolute judge . . . is the absolute mind which manifests itself in the history of the world" (§ 259A). This may help explain Hegel's conclusion that individuals can be most closely unified with the World Mind through art, religion, and philosophy.

Hegel often wrote with a terrible obscurity, and he was unduly enthusiastic—to say the least—about many of his ideas. Perhaps his two most important contributions to political philosophy were (a) his critique of individualism, combined with his attempt to integrate a veneration for individual choice with an organic conception of society, and (b) his claim that in order to evaluate one institution, it is necessary (at least for a time) to assume the validity of others. His influence, which extended in many directions, from National Socialism to American pragmatism, has been immense.

Karl Marx (1818–1883) was among those deeply influenced by Hegel. The thesis that a human being is dependent on society for his nature and potentialities was quite fundamental in Marx' thought, and he was especially impressed by Hegel's analyses of civil society, labor, and property. On Marx' view, however, constitutional monarchy obviously does not and cannot control the disruptive elements of civil society; the idea that the state is the final objectification of the World Mind is an example of Hegel's turning things upside down and interpreting the facts to fit his idealist metaphysics. If one is to get things straight, it is necessary to leave off philosophizing and attend to social and historical realities.

When Marx began his own analysis, he borrowed from Hegel's account of labor and property. For Hegel, the appropriation of objects was a basic step in the development of the individual. Labor was an "externalization of consciousness," and property was the external embodiment of personality. Consequently, when one disposes of his property, he "alienates" his personality to some extent. In civil society, with its capricious and accidental distribution of property, this alienation often becomes an extreme "alienation of oneself."

Marx' doctrine of "alienated labor," exemplifying his early humanism, developed this Hegelian view. On Marx' economic analysis, in the conditions of capitalist society the worker becomes a commodity. The more he produces, the more capital is used against him. He becomes alienated both from the product of his labor, which does not belong to him, and from his labor itself, which is foreign and unfulfilling. Only when not working, or when engaged in the most physical activities, is he "at home with himself." His labor is not a means of personal development; his being is sacrificed to his mere existence; and he becomes further alienated from himself and his humanity. Finally, given the egoism and greed of civil society, he is alienated from other persons, fellow workers included. And those persons to whom he is servile are little better off as human beings; life-producing activity is also alien to them.

Thus, it seemed to Marx that the division of labor under capitalism is not a form of cooperative *human* activity. Notwithstanding the wealth it produces, the division of labor is debasing and inhumane, and even the capitalists themselves are degraded. The real culprit, that which produces and is produced by alienated labor, is the capitalist system of private property. Consequently, the essence of communism is the abolition of "bourgeois property," especially private ownership of the means of production.

Marx believed, as Hegel had before him, that "negative elements" in civil society will inevitably produce its fall. For Marx, the instrument of this fall would be the growing number of workers who have no reason to espouse bourgeois ideals of liberty and individuality. The revolution of the proletariat was not only a necessary means to ending human degradation, but a necessary consequence of historical social forces. Marx' convictions on both points led him to disagree vehemently with both the aims and the tactics of other revolutionaries. To him, a revolution that had to be fomented was doomed from the start. And one that aimed at an equitable redistribution of wealth was a victim of bourgeois ideals of justice. In order to achieve the "socialization of man" and true human individuality, a fundamental restructuring of society would have to be accomplished, one in which both the capitalist division of labor and the state would be superseded and transformed. Just what form the social organization would take is unclear, but suffrage would be universal and all would participate. Each person through his work would be able both to contribute to society maximally and to develop his potentialities fully. The needs of all would then be met. As Marx said in his *Critique of the Gotha Program,* only when this ideal is attained can society "inscribe on its banners 'From each according to his ability, to each according to his needs.' " Public power will then "lose its political character." These points, and others as well, are succinctly stated in the selection from the *Manifesto* which is reprinted below.

There was no objective, unchanging standard of justice, on Marx' view, and when justice was conceived in terms of the Enlightenment's "rights of man" or the socialist ideal of "a fair share of the proceeds of labor," he heaped scorn on appeals to it; for him, the equitable distribution of rights and wealth was a superficial goal. These points can be made against those who have regarded Marx as basically protesting against the *injustice* of capitalist society.[14] Marx, nevertheless, was fundamentally interested in the "constitution of society" and thus in distributive justice in the broad sense given it in Aristotle's *Politics,* that which equates justice and the common good. He was scornful of bourgeois justice only because he thought a more radical restructuring of society was needed. He often seems to have been moved primarily by the vision of a society that would fully realize human capacities; much of his criticism of industrial society attacks it for debasing humanity. Regarded in this way, Marx was first of all a humanist and visionary, and in this respect not wholly unlike the Greeks. This is one of several interpretations that help explain the character of his contribution and his enormous influence. But there is also the other side to consider: His moral ideas, those that shaped his own moral ideal— as well as his ideas of rights and justice—are undeveloped; his idyllic solutions are problematical; and his claim, like Hegel's, to a special understanding of the forces of history, in his case including the future of communism, is very dubious.

---

[14] See R. C. Tucker, *Philosophy and Myth in Karl Marx* (Cambridge, England: The University Press, 1961), Introduction and Chapter 15; also his "Marx and Distributive Justice" in *Nomos VI: Justice,* C. J. Friedrich and J. W. Chapman (Eds.) (New York: Atherton Press, 1963).

Utilitarianism: Bentham and J. S. Mill

Even while Hegel was developing his philosophical idealism in Germany, Jeremy Bentham (1748–1832) was attempting a rational reform of English law and institutions. Both men appealed to reason, but their views were diametrically opposed; to Bentham, society was the individuals who compose it, and institutions were habits of those individuals. By and large, he saw these habits as an embodiment not of reason, but of unreason; what seemed to him most needed was the subjection of habit and institutions to reason, which is the best instrument a person has for directing his acts. And just as the most rational action for one individual is the action that is most efficient in promoting his goals, so the most rational action for a society is the one that most efficiently promotes the goals of all the individuals who compose it. On these lines, Bentham undertook a sweeping and detailed criticism of English law; the great liberal reforms of the nineteenth century owe much to him. The "utilitarian principle" that he adopted as the foundation of enlightened jurisprudence had wide applications.

At the beginning of *An Introduction to the Principles of Morals and Legislation,* Bentham said: "Nature has placed mankind under the governance of two sovereign masters, *pain* and *pleasure*. It is for them alone to point out what we ought to do, as well as to determine what we shall do. On the one hand the standard of right and wrong, on the other the chain of causes and effects, are fastened to their throne." Much later, in the preface to his ideally rational *Constitutional Code,* he wrote: "In the here proposed code, of every proposed arrangement, from first to last, without any one exception, the end in view is the greatest happiness of the greatest number." This end is "the right and proper end of government in every political community"; and every impartial legislator will have "the same regard for the happiness of every member of the community in question, as for that of every other." [15] Thus Bentham made "the

---

[15] J. Bentham, *Works,* J. Bowring (Ed.) (Edinburgh: William Tait, 1838–1843), Vol. 9, pp. 2, 5–6.

greatest happiness principle," which he found in Hume, the fundamental criterion of both the morality and the efficiency, the justice and the utility, of all institutions of government.

The basic problem of good government derives from the nature of the end in combination with the "psychological fact" that self-interest "is predominant over all other interests put together"; the problem is to institute the form of government in which each person, pursuing his own interest, will bring about the greatest happiness of all. This wonderful harmony can only be produced in a representative democracy with the people sovereign; for when there is such a democracy, and government is in the hands of all—

. . . the natural effect of the principle of self-preference is— not as in the case where it is in the hands of one, or of a few, the sacrifice of the interest of all, to the interest of that one or those few ; but the sacrifice of all interests that are opposed to the happiness of all. In so far as his aim is, to sacrifice all interests to his own,—the interests of others, to that which is peculiar to himself, no man finds any effective number of hands disposed to join with his: in so far as his aim is, to serve such of his interests alone, as are theirs as well as his, he finds all hands disposed to join with his : and these common interests correspond to the immediately subordinate right and proper ends of government, maximization of subsistence, abundance, security, and equality. In so far as by the principle of self-preference, he is led to promote his own happiness, by augmenting theirs at the same time, or even without diminishing it, so far he finds himself capable of acting without obstruction : but no sooner does he attempt to promote his own happiness, by means by which theirs is diminished, than he finds obstruction thrown in his way, by all whose happiness is, by this his enterprise, already more or less diminished, and by all who, in case of his success, are apprehensive of suffering the like diminution. Thus, then, the principle of self-preference, has for its regulator in the breast of each, the consciousness of the existence and power of the same principle in the breasts of all the rest : and thus it is that the whole mechanism is at all times kept in a state of perfect

order, and at all times performs to admiration everything that is desired of it, everything it was made for.[16]

Since the "greatest happiness" is simply the sum of the pleasures, minus the pains, of the individuals concerned, and since, generally speaking, each man is the best final judge of his own happiness, the most effective way of clarifying and articulating the end of government is to institute a representative democracy. The people, having a "greater aptitude," can be counted on, more than any other authority that could be proposed, to secure the happiness of all.[17] Bentham considered the checks and balances that Hume and Madison thought essential for controlling factions, as well as many "technicalities" of law, to be so many irrational, antiquated devices for retaining political power. Majority tyranny would somehow not be a problem if the suffrage were extended; with a simple (and perhaps simple-minded) faith, Bentham thought that the effective guarantee of good government is to have each person speak for himself.

Although utilitarianism was associated initially with the doctrine of laissez-faire, there is nothing in the logic of the position, certainly as regards the end of government, that requires this kind of individualism. Bentham, and even more the utilitarians who followed him, sometimes in alliance with a new breed of humanitarian, increasingly supported social legislation designed to improve the lot of the working class and afford educational opportunities to all. This modification and extension of the utilitarian program was a distinctive feature of English utilitarianism in the nineteenth century. Although for Bentham government was still an instrument, and still rather negatively conceived, the utilitarian end of government was later to become more and more the object of positive social legislation.

The changed conception of utilitarianism is especially evident in the writings of John Stuart Mill (1806–1873). In his essay *Utilitarianism*, Mill in effect rejected Bentham's "scientific hedonism": According to Mill, pleasures differ qualitatively as

16 *Ibid.* p. 63. Bentham is commenting on the government of the United States!
17 *Ibid.* pp. 96–98.

well as quantitatively, and man through his sense of dignity prefers the nobler; moreover, happiness is a concrete whole of which virtue can be a part. In *Representative Government,* Mill acknowledged that government is a means; but the end, far from being a sum of pleasures, is "the virtue and intelligence of the people themselves." Representative democracy is the best form of government, not, as Bentham said, because it produces a simple harmony of interests (which it cannot do), but because it leads every citizen "to take an actual part in the government, by the personal discharge of some public function." It leads its citizens to exert "their energies for the good of themselves and of the community" and enables them to participate in the "benefits of freedom." In his *On Liberty,* Mill explicitly rejected the idea that if only government is put into the hands of the people, all will be well and no limitations on government will be needed. "Self-government," he wrote, is often "not the government of each by himself, but of each by all the rest": Moreover, there is not only a great danger of governmental majority tyranny, but an equally great danger of an oppressive social majority stifling all ideas, tastes, convictions, and ways of living that do not conform to what is customary.[18] And in both his *Principles of Political Economy* and his *Autobiography,* Mill showed an increasing sympathy with socialism. He did not think that modes of distribution are fixed by economic laws of nature: "The economic generalizations which depend, not on the necessities of nature but on those combined with the existing arrangements of society, [the *Principles of Political Economy*] deals with only as provisional, and as liable to be much altered by the progress of social improvement." [19]

Mill thus rejected much of Bentham's rationalistic method and many of his substantive views, while continuing to associate himself with utilitarianism. As a social philosopher, he was an eclectic, trying to fit a great variety of highly significant ideas into an inherited utilitarian frame, and he often failed in his attempts to provide systematic clarification. Nevertheless, Mill's work was highly important. The utilitarian criterion of government and social institutions, suggested indirectly by Hobbes, greatly developed by Hume, and both simplified and made into

[18] J. S. Mill, *On Liberty,* Chapter 1. See the reading below.
[19] J. S. Mill, *Autobiography,* Chapter 7.

an effective instrument of reform by Bentham, has been one of the most persistently attractive principles of social philosophy. In order to be made cogent, however, it needed to be further developed and pruned of the simple absurdities that had become attached to it. At almost every point at which Mill proposed modification, modification was needed; he was extraordinarily perceptive and sensitive. The development of utilitarian social philosophy and its present attractiveness owe much to him.

It should be stressed that this new utilitarianism is very different from older forms. Sometimes it is more like an adaptation of the political philosophy of the Greeks to the modern state than like anything in Bentham. Mill had much in common with T. H. Green who was a strong critic of classical utilitarianism: Neither of them thought of social institutions as simply a means to an end. Neither conceived of humanity as naturally self-interested in Bentham's sense; the degree to which persons are self-interested depends largely on their social institutions. Both Mill and Green were strong defenders of freedom, but both advocated more positive and extensive governmental action to correct injustice and promote the common good. Both were highly sensitive not only to political oppression, but to oppression within the new industrial system, and both believed that if people were not to become slaves to machines and to the owners of machines, then government must to some extent stand free of the system and change it for the better. There was opposition to this conclusion: The old individualism lived on (and continues, even after reaching a kind of apotheosis in the Social Darwinism of men like Herbert Spencer and William Graham Sumner). With increasing governmental intervention into the economy, however, a broader conception of the functions of government began to develop, and a new emphasis came to be put on "welfare," in an extended sense, as the proper object of government.

At the same time, especially in America and Western Europe, as part of the legacy of the long period of individualism, there was woven into this new conception of the functions of government a kind of reverence for individual freedoms, particularly the freedom "to pursue one's own good in one's own way." Mill's classic defense of these freedoms is found in his essay *On Liberty,* selections from which are found below.

Moral Equality: Green and Rawls

Utilitarianism in its simplest form requires a person to act in the way that will promote the greatest happiness of the greatest number. In order to determine "the right thing to do," one must both estimate the effect of each possible act on the happiness of every person and, in calculating total happiness, weigh each person's happiness equally with that of every other, at least within a domain. Utilitarianism thus assumes that at least rough calculations of total happiness in a society can, as Bentham and others believed, be intelligibly made. Let us suppose, however, that Bentham's rational legislator, after giving equal consideration (of the kind indicated) to all persons, concludes that the total happiness will be greatest if some persons in his society are made subservient to—even slaves of—other persons; in other words, let us assume that a situation might arise such that the loss in happiness of those who would be made "inferiors" is more than compensated by the gain of the potential "superiors." In such a case the subservience of some to others apparently would be not only permissible but morally required.

This consequence conflicts with many persons' intuitive ideas of justice, and it is often cited as a fatal objection to utilitarianism. In reply, it is argued that utilitarianism would never justify subservience, because the gain of some would not *in fact* compensate for the loss to others. But this reply usually fails to satisfy. The critics say that justice requires equal rights, or an equal treatment that goes beyond equal consideration of the kind indicated; and since this requirement is a "matter of moral principle," it cannot depend on the alleged fact that increments of happiness of some persons compensate for the loss of happiness of others. Who, the critics ask, would even dream of trying to make such a calculation before subscribing to equal rights?

This fundamental objection to utilitarianism presupposes that all persons are in some sense equal from the point of view of morality. But how is one to clarify the sense of the assertion that all persons are "moral equals"—persons surely are not equally moral—and what are the grounds for making such a claim? When, for example, Mill claimed that each person should be given the freedom to pursue his own good in his own way, how should this freedom be interpreted and defended? If the utilitarian line of defense is inadequate—it is doubtful that Mill was a utilitarian when he emphasized this freedom—how can the equal right to freedom, or any other equal moral right of all persons, be established? Hobbes and Hume did not offer any help directly, and Locke's theory of natural rights, which tried to offer help, is itself indefensible. Both Hegel and Marx were at times suggestive—each in his own way insisted on the rational development of each individual—but neither offered a clear line of defense for equal moral rights.

The challenge to clarify and defend "the moral equality of all persons," which so much of our common talk about justice seems to presuppose, and to show how it can serve as a ground for a theory of distributive justice, poses one (or a set) of the most central problems of modern political philosophy. The selections below will allow the reader to taste two theoretical attempts to meet the challenge. T. H. Green's theory is now almost a hundred years old. The other, John Rawls', is very recent. Both of these proposals make rather fundamental use of the political philosophy of Rousseau, who emphasized, more than any other philosopher before him, both the moral autonomy of each individual and the dependence of each individual on society.

T. H. Green (1836–1882) is sometimes referred to as one of the "English Hegelians." His Hegelianism is evident in his emphasis on the common good, his view of "freedom" as a goal, his talk of reason as "inner" (in thought) and "outer" (in institutions), his view that an individual's consciousness depends on social institutions (as thought depends on language), and his firm opposition to Lockean natural rights. But Green was also much affected by British individualism and Christian views of the inviolability of the person. When Green asserts that consciousness of a common good is essential to morality, this good, we soon discover, is a good of each and every individual. To be sure, Green thought that a moral conscience springs from a person's recognition that limited institutions, such as his own family, ideally serve the good of a *class* of persons, its members. But the "growth of the just man's conscience" depends on the person's further recognition that the argument that these institutions should serve all members of a class can be turned into an argument, by analogy, for developing a system of institutions to serve all persons regardless of class. The basic argument in both cases is that individual development itself depends on a person's participation in the life of the institutions of his society, and its fullest, and thus its most rational, development depends on institutions that serve the good of all.

For Green, moral rights and a moral community are constituted together when the members of a community acknowledge institutions and freely accept their rules for the good of all. Moral rights arise only from mutual recognition of institutions as for the common good; there are no Lockean natural rights. Nevertheless, some of these moral rights can properly be called natural "in the same sense in which according to Aristotle the state is natural"; these are basic moral rights that are "directly necessary" for human development. By insisting on the self-conscious acceptance of institutions as for the common good, however, Green, for all his Hegelianism, and notwithstanding his appeal to Aristotle, brought himself very close to Rousseau's doctrine that a moral community is possible only under the conditions of the social contract.

Since moral rights are generated only by the mutual recognition of institutions as for the common good, moral rights depend on the mutual recognition that each person has a due and is thus worthy of respect. Green cited Ulpian's definition of justice (as transmitted in Justinian's *Institutes*) with approval; this definition, by requiring the just person to recognize every other person as having a due, constituted Green's first principle of justice. However, a principle of this kind, like any other such principle, needs a content—in this case, a concrete doctrine of what is due a person—and this can be developed only by applying the principle in particular cases. Its applications both give it concrete meaning and confirm it as a principle of justice.

Thus, Green thought that an argument for moral rights could have no effect on an institutionless "man in a state of nature," even if there could be, contrary to fact, so inhuman a person. Any argument for subscribing to justice, and thus for acknowledging that all persons have moral rights, must proceed from at least a partial and concrete recognition that one's own good is bound up with other persons' goods, and that right-granting institutions that serve oneself also serve others. The argument proceeds from a person's seeing that there must be institutions (his family, his job, his state) that enable others to become "what they have it in themselves to become," in order for him to become "what he has it in himself to become." For example, only if a person participates in an institution-alized community of the best scientists can he himself become the best scientist he is capable of becoming. Similarily, for Green, a person can become most fully realized as the person he is only by living in a community whose institutions promote the good of all. The common good, of course, is an ideal end; it is equivalent to freedom conceived as a goal to be achieved.

John Rawls undertakes to develop his theory of justice by making a more direct appeal than Green to classical contract theories, especially to those of Rousseau and Kant. Rawls ac-cepts at the outset the intuitive assumption that all persons are in some sense equal from the moral point of view. And if our common moral sentiments can be relied on, then surely it is unjust to impose sacrifices on some persons for the sake of a greater good for others. Rawls' theory of justice takes such sentiments and intuitive ideas as its starting point; its initial aim is to discover the principles that underlie them. There are undoubtedly conflicts, confusions, and lacunae in our intuitive everyday judgments, but a developed theory of justice should lead both to a more coherent and systematically refined sense of justice and to a more articulate view of what the initially assumed moral equality of persons requires.

To Rawls, principles of justice are principles for assign-ing basic rights and duties and for determining a proper dis-tribution of the benefits and burdens of social cooperation. This is their role. The primary subject to which these principles need to be applied is the basic political, economic, and social structure of a society, because this structure has such profound and extensive effects on individuals. Rawls undertakes to de-velop his theory by looking at the principles of justice as those principles, designed to exercise justice's primary role, that free, equal, and rational persons, concerned with furthering their own interests, would agree to under conditions that guarantee a *fair* agreement between them. This method of determining the principles of justice is the guiding idea of his theory, and accounts for his calling his conception of justice "Justice as Fairness." His method constitutes a distinctive use of contract theory.

The idea behind Rawls' technique for developing his theory is fairly simple. Let us think of persons in an initial—or hypothetical—choice situation, attempting to decide on the principles under which they shall live. If we are to generate any principles in this way, and if we are to be able to regard them reasonably as principles of justice, then we must give these principles, these persons, and the "initial choice situation" itself certain well-defined characteristics. These characteristics are taken at first from our intuitive ideas about moral principles, the role of justice, a "fair bargain," and the like. In order for us to be able to regard these principles reasonably as moral principles, let us lay it down that the principles to be agreed to must be general in form, and that they must be able to be publicly recognized both as applying to all and as a final court of appeal—in the case of justice, for ordering conflicting claims. In order for the principles to have their proper adjudicative or allocative role, let us characterize persons in the "initial situation" as willing to live under the principles agreed to, and yet as equally interested and rational in advancing their interests. And in order to guarantee that the agreement on principles shall be fair (and that it shall therefore secure to each person a fair share of rights and benefits), let us put these persons behind a "veil of ignorance" that denies them any knowledge of how they may be advantaged or disadvantaged by social or natural contingencies. (Thus each must bargain from an equal place.) Conditions such as these—there are others as well—are designed to guarantee that the principles agreed to will have the character of principles of justice, according to our intuitive or everyday notions of what we expect principles of justice to be like; these conditions, in other words, constitute an interpretation of the initial situation that is "most favorable" for generating principles of justice. Rawls calls the initial choice situation so interpreted the "original position." This position corresponds to the state of nature in traditional contract theory, but in Rawls' theory, as in Kant's, it is purely hypothetical. It may be thought of either as an expository device or as an encapsulation of our intuitive notions of justice.

One should guard against taking Rawls' characterization of persons in the original position to express his view of the character of actual persons. He does not think that persons in the real world are mutually disinterested in one another in the way persons in the original position are. To interpret him as saying this would be to misconstrue the analytical function of the original position. Moreover, one should bear in mind that, on Rawls' view, the ultimate justification of the theory of justice does not derive *simply* from showing that persons in the original position would choose its principles; it also derives from a certain "reflective equilibrium," an adjustment of our principles, on the one hand, and "our considered judgments" of what is just, on the other, to fit one another. The test of the theory, in other words, depends on whether the principles of justice proposed by the theory order, illuminate, and reveal an inner logic in our considered judgments of what is just and unjust.

The readings below will introduce one to Rawls' approach and give his first statement of his two principles of justice. Although in this book it is impossible to present the formal development of the theory, the selections below attempt to capture some of the theory's intuitive appeal. Part of the intuitive argument for the first principle, that which requires an equal right to maximum basic liberty, Rawls finds in Mill's essay *On Liberty*. The highly original interpretation that Rawls puts on justice's demand for an equality of benefits, as presented in his discussion of the second principle, and the intuitive arguments for it, are briefly outlined in the readings. The second principle, under the interpretation called "Democratic Equality" that Rawls gives it, is certainly the most novel element in his theory. It constitutes a highly significant (and controversial) interpretation of what our common ideas of moral equality ultimately require of us. In the final chapter of his book (readings from which, unfortunately, could not be included below), especially in a section entitled "The Idea of Social Union," Rawls also gives an illuminating interpretation of the common good, some themes of which go back through both Marx and the idealists, finally, to the Greeks.

Bibliography

On justice and the common good:

Barry, B., *Political Argument*. London: Routledge & Kegan Paul Ltd., 1965.

Benn, S. I., and R. S. Peters, *Principles of Political Thought,* especially Ch. 5–6, 12. New York: The Free Press, 1965.

Blackstone, W. T. (Ed.), *The Concept of Equality*. Minneapolis: Burgess Publishing Co., 1969.

Brandt, R. B., *Ethical Theory: The Problems of Normative and Critical Ethics,* Ch. 15–19. Englewood Cliffs, N.J.: Prentice-Hall, Inc., 1959.

Brandt, R. B. (Ed.), *Social Justice*. Englewood Cliffs, N.J.: Prentice-Hall, Inc., 1962.

Feinberg, J., *Social Philosophy*. Englewood Cliffs, N.J.: Prentice-Hall, Inc., 1973.

Flathman, R. E., *The Public Interest*. New York: John Wiley & Sons, Inc., 1966.

Frankena, W. K., *Some Beliefs About Justice*. The Lindley Lecture, University of Kansas, 1966.

Friedrich, C. J., and J. W. Chapman (Eds.), *Nomos VI: Justice*. New York: Atherton Press, Inc., 1963.

Held, V., *The Public Interest and Individual Interests*. New York: Basic Books, Inc., Publishers, 1970.

Melden, A. I. (Ed.), *Human Rights,* especially the papers by H. L. A. Hart and M. Macdonald. Belmont, Calif.: Wadsworth Publishing Co., Inc., 1970.

Pennock, J. R., and J. W. Chapman (Eds.), *Nomos IX: Equality*. New York: Atherton Press, Inc., 1967.

Resher, N., *Distributive Justice: A Constructive Critique of the Utilitarian Theory of Distribution*. Indianapolis: The Bobbs-Merrill Co., Inc., 1966.

Ritchie, D. G., *Natural Rights: A Criticism of Some Political and Ethical Conceptions*. London: George Allen & Unwin Ltd., 1894.

On Hegelianism, Marxism, utilitarianism, and English idealism:

Avineri, S., *The Social and Political Thought of Karl Marx*. Cambridge, England: The University Press, 1968.

Berlin, I., *Four Essays on Liberty*. London: Oxford University Press, 1969.

Marcuse, H., *Reason and Revolution: Hegel and the Rise of Social Theory*, 2nd ed. New York: Humanities Press, Inc., 1954.

Milne, A. J. M., *The Social Philosophy of English Idealism*. London: George Allen & Unwin Ltd., 1962.

Plamenatz, J., *Consent, Freedom and Political Obligation*, 2nd ed. London: Oxford University Press, 1968.

Plamenatz, J., *The English Utilitarians* 2nd ed. Oxford: Basil Blackwell & Mott Ltd., 1966.

Popper, K., *The Open Society and Its Enemies*, Vol. 2, 5th ed. Princeton, N. J.: Princeton University Press, 1966.

Sabine, G. H., *A History of Political Theory*, 3rd ed., Part III, Ch. 30–35. New York: Holt, Rinehart & Winston, Inc., 1961.

Stephen, L., *The English Utilitarians*. London: Gerald Duckworth & Co. Ltd., 1900.

KARL MARX
AND FRIEDRICH ENGELS

*Karl Marx was born in 1818, entered the University of Bonn
at 17, soon transferred to the University of Berlin, and, after
concentrating on law and then philosophy, received his Ph.D.
in 1841 from the University of Jena for a dissertation on Democ-
ritus and Epicurus. Unable to obtain a teaching position, he
turned to journalism and in 1843 moved to Paris to edit a
radical journal. While there, he developed the main features of
his "historical materialism" and wrote many essays, including*
Critique of Hegel's Philosophy of Right *and* Economic-Philo-
sophical Manuscripts. *At this time, he also began his long and
fruitful collaboration with Friedrich Engels. In 1845, however,
Marx was expelled from France and sought refuge in Brussels
where, for three years, he taught economics to workingmen and
wrote* The German Ideology, The Poverty of Philosophy (a
reply to Proudhon's Philosophy of Poverty), *and, with Engels'
draft before him,* The Communist Manifesto. *The collapse of
the European revolutions of 1848 forced several moves on him;
a year later he settled permanently in London. Although he
lived out his life in extreme poverty and suffered the deaths of
three of his children, with his wife's and Engels' help he worked
in patient anticipation of proletarian revolution. His* Critique
of Political Economy *appeared in 1859; the first volume of*
Capital, *his classic, in 1867. From 1864 to 1872, he helped
found and lead the International Workingmen's Association,
the famous "First International." He condemned German socialist tactics in* Critique of the Gotha Programme *(1875); the*

The following selections are reprinted from Samuel Moore's translation of *The Communist Manifesto,* as revised and edited by Engels,
published in 1888.

second and third volumes of Capital, *compiled from his extensive notes and manuscripts by the faithful Engels, were not
published until after his death in 1883.*

*Friedrich Engels was born in 1820, the son of a wealthy
cotton manufacturer, and at an early age became an apprentice
in his father's business. He found scholarship more to his liking,
however, read widely, and, while working for a textile firm in
Manchester, wrote* The Condition of the Working Classes in
England, *published in 1845. Unlike Bakunin, Proudhon, and
other revolutionaries who elicited Marx' scorn, Engels became
Marx' faithful friend and devoted follower—from the time
their collaboration began in Paris. In 1849, partly in order to
contribute to Marx' support, Engels returned to his father's
factory in Manchester, where in the next twenty years he was
successively a clerk, partner, and director. He published* Anti-
Dühring: Socialism, Utopian and Scientific *in 1878. Among his
many other writings, published after his death in 1895, are*
The Origin of the Family, Private Property and the State;
Dialectics of Nature; *and* The Peasant War in Germany.

The Communist Manifesto

A specter is haunting Europe—the specter of Communism.
All the powers of old Europe have entered into a holy alliance
to exorcise this specter; Pope and Czar, Metternich and Guizot,
French radicals and German police spies.

Where is the party in opposition that has not been decried
as Communistic by its opponents in power? Where the opposition that has not hurled back the branding reproach of Communism, against the more advanced opposition parties, as well
as against its reactionary adversaries?

Two things result from this fact.

I. Communism is already acknowledged by all European
powers to be in itself a power.

II. It is high time that Communists should openly, in the
face of the whole world, publish their views, their aims, their
tendencies, and meet this nursery tale of the Specter of Communism with a Manifesto of the party itself.

To this end the Communists of various nationalities have

assembled in London, and sketched the following manifesto to be published in the English, French, German, Italian, Flemish and Danish languages.

. . .

2. *Proletarians and Communists.*   In what relation do the Communists stand to the proletarians as a whole?

The Communists do not form a separate party opposed to other working class parties.

They have no interests separate and apart from those of the proletariat as a whole.

They do not set up any sectarian principles of their own by which to shape and mould the proletarian movement.

The Communists are distinguished from the other working class parties by this only: 1. In the national struggles of the proletarians of the different countries, they point out and bring to the front the common interests of the entire proletariat, independently of all nationality. 2. In the various stages of development which the struggle of the working class against the bourgeoisie has to pass through, they always and everywhere represent the interests of the movement as a whole.

The Communists, therefore, are on the one hand, practically, the most advanced and resolute section of the working class parties of every country, that section which pushes forward all others; on the other hand, theoretically, they have over the great mass of the proletariat the advantage of clearly understanding the line of march, the conditions, and the ultimate general results of the proletarian movement.

The immediate aim of the Communists is the same as that of all the other proletarian parties: formation of the proletariat into a class, overthrow of the bourgeois supremacy, conquest of political power by the proletariat.

The theoretical conclusions of the Communists are in no way based on ideas or principles that have been invented, or discovered, by this or that would-be universal reformer.

They merely express, in general terms, actual relations springing from an existing class struggle, from a historical movement going on under our very eyes. The abolition of existing property relations is not at all a distinctive feature of Communism.

All property relations in the past have continually been subject to historical change, consequent upon the change in historical conditions.

The French revolution, for example, abolished feudal property in favor of bourgeois property.

The distinguishing feature of Communism is not the abolition of property generally, but the abolition of bourgeois property. But modern bourgeois private property is the final and most complete expression of the system of producing and appropriating products, that is based on class antagonisms, on the exploitation of the many by the few.

In this sense the theory of the Communists may be summed up in the single sentence: Abolition of private property.

We Communists have been reproached with the desire of abolishing the right of personally acquiring property as the fruit of a man's own labor, which property is alleged to be the ground work of all personal freedom, activity and independence.

Hard-won, self-acquired, self-earned property! Do you mean the property of the petty artisan and of the small peasant, a form of property that preceded the bourgeois form? There is no need to abolish that; the development of industry has to a great extent already destroyed it, and is still destroying it daily.

Or do you mean modern bourgeois private property?

But does wage labor create any property for the laborer? Not a bit. It creates capital, i.e., that kind of property which exploits wage-labor, and which cannot increase except upon condition of begetting a new supply of wage-labor for fresh exploitation. Property, in its present form, is based on the antagonism of capital and wage labor. Let us examine both sides of this antagonism.

To be a capitalist, is to have not only a purely personal, but a social *status* in production. Capital is a collective product, and only by the united action of many members, nay, in the last resort, only by the united action of all members of society, can it be set in motion.

Capital is therefore not a personal, it is a social power.

When, therefore, capital is converted into common property, into the property of all members of society, personal property is not thereby transformed into social property. It is only the social character of the property that is changed. It loses its class character.

Let us now take wage-labor.

The average price of wage-labor is the minimum wage, i.e., that quantum of the means of subsistence, which is absolutely requisite to keep the laborer in bare existence as a laborer. What, therefore, the wage-laborer appropriates by means of his labor, merely suffices to prolong and reproduce a bare existence. We by no means intend to abolish this personal appropriation of the products of labor, an appropriation that is made for the maintenance and reproduction of human life, and that leaves no surplus wherewith to command the labor of others. All that we want to do away with, is the miserable character of this appropriation, under which the laborer lives merely to increase capital, and is allowed to live only in so far as the interest of the ruling class requires it.

In bourgeois society living labor is but a means to increase accumulated labor. In Communist society accumulated labor is but a means to widen, to enrich, to promote the existence of the laborer.

In bourgeois society, therefore, the past dominates the present; in Communist society, the present dominates the past. In bourgeois society capital is independent and has individuality, while the living person is dependent and has no individuality.

And the abolition of this state of things is called by the bourgeois: abolition of individuality and freedom! And rightly so. The abolition of bourgeois individuality, bourgeois independence, and bourgeois freedom is undoubtedly aimed at.

By freedom is meant, under the present bourgeois conditions of production, free trade, free selling and buying.

But if selling and buying disappears, free selling and buying disappears also. This talk about free selling and buying, and all the other "brave words" of our bourgeoisie about freedom in general, have a meaning, if any, only in contrast with restricted selling and buying, with the fettered traders of the middle ages, but have no meaning when opposed to the Communistic abolition of buying and selling, of the bourgeois conditions of production, and of the bourgeoisie itself.

You are horrified at our intending to do away with private property. But in your existing society private property is already done away with for nine-tenths of the population; its existence for the few is solely due to its non-existence in the hands of those nine-tenths. You reproach us, therefore, with intending to do away with a form of property, the necessary condition for whose existence is the non-existence of any property for the immense majority of society.

In one word, you reproach us with intending to do away with your property. Precisely so: that is just what we intend.

From the moment when labor can no longer be converted into capital, money, or rent, into a social power capable of being monopolized, i.e., from the moment when individual property can no longer be transformed into bourgeois property, into capital, from that moment, you say, individuality vanishes!

You must, therefore, confess that by "individual" you mean no other person than the bourgeois, than the middle class owner of property. This person must, indeed, be swept out of the way, and made impossible.

Communism deprives no man of the power to appropriate the products of society: all that it does is to deprive him of the power to subjugate the labor of others by means of such appropriation.

It has been objected, that upon the abolition of private property all work will cease, and universal laziness will overtake us.

According to this, bourgeois society ought long ago to have gone to the dogs through sheer idleness; for those of its members who work, acquire nothing, and those who acquire anything, do not work. The whole of this objection is but another expression of tautology, that there can no longer be any wage-labor when there is no longer any capital.

All objections against the Communistic mode of producing and appropriating material products, have, in the same way, been urged against the Communistic modes of producing and appropriating intellectual products. Just as, to the bourgeois the disappearance of class property is the disappearance of production itself, so the disappearance of class culture is to him identical with the disappearance of all culture.

That culture, the loss of which he laments, is, for the enormous majority, a mere training to act as a machine.

But don't wrangle with us so long as you apply to our intended abolition of bourgeois property, the standard of your bourgeois notions of freedom, culture, law, etc. Your very ideas are but the outgrowth of the conditions of your bourgeois production and bourgeois property, just as your jurisprudence is but the will of your class made into a law for all, a will, whose essential character and direction are determined by the economical conditions of existence of your class.

The selfish misconception that induces you to transform into eternal laws of nature and of reason, the social forms springing from your present mode of production and form of property—historical relations that rise and disappear in the progress of production—the misconception you share with every ruling class that has preceded you. What you see clearly in the case of ancient property, what you admit in the case of feudal property, you are of course forbidden to admit in the case of your own bourgeois form of property.

Abolition of the family! Even the most radical flare up at this infamous proposal of the Communists.

On what foundation is the present family, the bourgeois family, based? On capital, on private gain. In its completely developed form this family exists only among the bourgeoisie. But this state of things finds its complement in the practical absence of the family among the proletarians, and in public prostitution.

The bourgeois family will vanish as a matter of course when its complement vanishes, and both will vanish with the vanishing of capital.

Do you charge us with wanting to stop the exploitation of children by their parents? To this crime we plead guilty.

But, you will say, we destroy the most hallowed of relations, when we replace home education by social.

And your education! Is not that also social, and determined by the social conditions under which you educate, by the intervention, direct or indirect, of society by means of schools, etc.? The Communists have not invented the intervention of society in education; they do but seek to alter the character of that intervention, and to rescue education from the influence of the ruling class.

The bourgeois clap-trap about the family and education, about the hallowed co-relation of parent and child become all the more disgusting, as, by the action of modern industry, all family ties among the proletarians are torn asunder, and their children transformed into simple articles of commerce and instruments of labor.

But you Communists would introduce community of women, screams the whole bourgeoisie in chorus.

The bourgeois sees in his wife a mere instrument of production. He hears that the instruments of production are to be exploited in common, and, naturally, can come to no other conclusion than that the lot of being common to all will likewise fall to the women.

He has not even a suspicion that the real point aimed at is to do away with the status of women as mere instruments of production.

For the rest nothing is more ridiculous than the virtuous indignation of our bourgeois at the community of women which, they pretend, is to be openly and officially established by the Communists. The Communists have no need to introduce community of women; it has existed almost from time immemorial.

Our bourgeois, not content with having the wives and daughters of their proletarians at their disposal, not to speak of common prostitutes, take the greatest pleasure in seducing each other's wives.

Bourgeois marriage is in reality a system of wives in common, and thus, at the most, what the Communists might possibly be reproached with, is that they desire to introduce, in substitution for a hypocritically concealed, an openly legalized community of women. For the rest it is self-evident that the abolition of the present system of production must bring with it the abolition of the community of women springing from that system, i.e., of prostitution both public and private.

The Communists are further reproached with desiring to abolish countries and nationality.

The workingmen have no country. We cannot take from them what they have not got. Since the proletariat must first of all acquire political supremacy, must rise to be the leading class of the nation, must constitute itself *the* nation, it is, so far, itself national, though not in the bourgeois sense of the word.

National differences and antagonisms between peoples are daily more and more vanishing, owing to the development of the bourgeoisie, to freedom of commerce, to the world's market, to uniformity in the mode of production and in the conditions of life corresponding thereto.

The supremacy of the proletariat will cause them to vanish still faster. United action, of the leading civilized countries at least, is one of the first conditions for the emancipation of the proletariat.

In proportion as the exploitation of one individual by another is put an end to, the exploitation of one nation by another will also be put an end to. In proportion as the antagonism between classes within the nation vanishes, the hostility of one nation to another will come to an end.

The charges against Communism made from a religious, a philosophical, and, generally, from an ideological standpoint are not deserving of serious examination.

Does it require deep intuition to comprehend that man's ideas, views, and conceptions, in one word, man's consciousness changes with every change in the conditions of his material existence, in his social relations and in his social life?

What else does the history of ideas prove, than that intellectual production changes its character in proportion as material production is changed? The ruling ideas of each age have ever been the ideas of its ruling class.

When people speak of ideas that revolutionize society they do but express the fact that within the old society the elements of a new one have been created, and that the dissolution of the old ideas keeps even pace with the dissolution of the old conditions of existence.

When the ancient world was in its last throes the ancient religions were overcome by Christianity. When Christian ideas succumbed in the eighteenth century to rationalist ideas, feudal society fought its death battle with the then revolutionary bourgeoisie. The ideas of religious liberty and freedom of conscience merely gave expression to the sway of free competition within the domain of knowledge.

"Undoubtedly," it will be said, "religious, moral, philosophical and juridical ideas have been modified in the course of historical development. But religion, morality, philosophy, political science, and law, constantly survived this change.

"There are besides, eternal truths, such as Freedom, Justice, etc., that are common to all states of society. But Communism abolishes eternal truths, it abolishes all religion and all morality, instead of constituting them on a new basis; it therefore acts in contradiction to all past historical experience."

What does this accusation reduce itself to? The history of all past society has consisted in the development of class antagonisms, antagonisms that assumed different forms at different epochs.

But whatever form they may have taken, one fact is common to all past ages, viz., the exploitation of one part of society by the other. No wonder, then, that the social consciousness of past ages, despite all the multiplicity and variety it displays, moves within certain common forms, or general ideas, which cannot completely vanish except with the total disappearance of class antagonisms.

The Communist revolution is the most radical rupture with traditional property relations; no wonder that its development involves the most radical rupture with traditional ideas.

But let us have done with the bourgeois objections to Communism.

We have seen above that the first step in the revolution by the working class is to raise the proletariat to the position of the ruling class; to win the battle of democracy.

The proletariat will use its political supremacy to wrest, by degrees, all capital from the bourgeoisie; to centralize all instruments of production in the hands of the State, i.e., of the proletariat organized as the ruling class; and to increase the total of productive forces as rapidly as possible.

Of course, in the beginning this cannot be effected except by means of despotic inroads on the rights of property and on the conditions of bourgeois production; by means of measures, therefore, which appear economically insufficient and untenable, but which, in the course of the movement, outstrip themselves, necessitate further inroads upon the old social order and are unavoidable as a means of entirely revolutionizing the mode of production.

These measures will, of course, be different in different countries.

Nevertheless in the most advanced countries the following will be pretty generally applicable:

1. Abolition of property in land and application of all rents of land to public purposes.

2. A heavy progressive or graduated income tax.

3. Abolition of all right of inheritance.

4. Confiscation of the property of all emigrants and rebels.

5. Centralization of credit in the hands of the State, by means of a national bank with State capital and an exclusive monopoly.

6. Centralization of the means of communication and transport in the hands of the State.

7. Extension of factories and instruments of production owned by the State; the bringing into cultivation of waste lands, and the improvement of the soil generally in accordance with a common plan.

8. Equal liability of all to labor. Establishment of industrial armies, especially for agriculture.

9. Combination of agriculture with manufacturing industries: gradual abolition of the distinction between town and country, by a more equable distribution of the population over the country.

10. Free education for all children in public schools. Abolition of children's factory labor in its present form. Combination of education with industrial production, etc., etc.

When, in the course of development, class distinctions have disappeared and all production has been concentrated in the hands of a vast association of the whole nation, the public power will lose its political character. Political power, properly so called, is merely the organized power of one class for oppressing another. If the proletariat during its contest with the bourgeoisie is compelled, by the force of circumstances, to organize itself as a class, if, by means of a revolution, it makes itself the ruling class, and, as such, sweeps away by force the old conditions of production then it will, along with these conditions, have swept away the conditions for the existence of class antagonisms, and of classes generally, and will thereby have abolished its own supremacy as a class.

In place of the old bourgeois society with its classes and class antagonisms we shall have an association in which the free development of each is the condition for the free development of all.

. . .

4. *Position of the Communists in Relation to the Various Existing Opposition Parties.* Section 2 has made clear the relations of the Communists to the existing working class parties, such as the Chartists in England and the Agrarian Reformers in America.

The Communists fight for the attainment of the immediate aims, for the enforcement of the momentary interests of the working class; but in the movement of the present, they also represent and take care of the future of that movement. In France the Communists ally themselves with the Social-Democrats (a), against the conservative and radical bourgeoisie, reserving, however, the right to take up a critical position in regard to phrases and illusions traditionally handed down from the great Revolution.

In Switzerland they support the Radicals, without losing sight of the fact that this party consists of antagonistic elements, partly of Democratic Socialists, in the French sense, partly of radical bourgeois.

In Poland they support the party that insists on an agrarian revolution, as the prime condition for national emancipation, that party which fomented the insurrection of Cracow in 1846.

In Germany they fight with the bourgeoisie whenever it acts in a revolutionary way against the absolute monarchy, the feudal squirearchy, and the petty bourgeoisie.

(a) The party then represented in parliament by Ledru-Rollin, in literature by Louis Blanc, in the daily press by the Reforme. The name of Social-Democracy signified, with these its inventors, a section of the Democratic or Republican party more or less tinged with Socialism.—F.E.

But they never cease, for a single instant, to instil into the working class the clearest possible recognition of the hostile antagonism between bourgeoisie and proletariat, in order that the German workers may straightway use, as so many weapons against the bourgeoisie, the social and political conditions that the bourgeoisie must necessarily introduce along with its supremacy, and in order that, after the fall of the reactionary classes in Germany, the fight against the bourgeoisie itself may immediately begin.

The Communists turn their attention chiefly to Germany because that country is on the eve of a bourgeois revolution that is bound to be carried out under more advanced conditions of European civilization, and with a much more developed proletariat, than that of England was in the seventeenth, and of France in the eighteenth century, and because the bourgeois revolution in Germany will be but the prelude to an immediately following proletarian revolution.

In short, the Communists everywhere support every revolutionary movement against the existing social and political order of things.

In all these movements they bring to the front, as the leading question in each, the property question, no matter what its degree of development at the time.

Finally, they labor everywhere for the union and agreement of the democratic parties of all countries.

The Communists disdain to conceal their views and aims. They openly declare that their ends can be attained only by the forcible overthrow of all existing social conditions. Let the ruling classes tremble at a Communistic revolution. The proletarians have nothing to lose but their chains. They have a world to win.

Workingmen of all countries unite!

JOHN STUART MILL

*John Stuart Mill was born in 1806 and given a rigorous educa-
tion by his father, James Mill, himself a close friend of Bentham
and author of* Elements of Political Economy, *an influential*
Essay on Government, *and other works. By the age of 17, John
Stuart had studied the Greek and Latin classics, history, mathematics, political economy, philosophy, psychology, and law
(under John Austin), had spent a year in France, and had
begun his long career with the East India Company. An early
period of disillusionment with his father's and Bentham's utilitarianism, of which he had been a devotee, opened him to the
influences of Wordsworth, Coleridge, Carlyle, Saint-Simon, and
others. At 25 he met Harriet Taylor, who not only had an
enormous influence on him, but, after the death of her first
husband in 1851, became his wife for the last seven years of her
own life. During his East India Company employment, Mill
wrote extensively, debated, edited, and published his* System of
Logic *(1843) and* Principles of Political Economy—*with Some
of Their Applications to Social Philosophy (1848)—both
standard works in their fields.* On Liberty, *most prized by himself, appeared in 1859. This and his periodic essays were followed by* Considerations on Representative Government *(1861)*,
Utilitarianism *(1861)*, An Examination of Sir Wm. Hamilton's
Philosophy *(1865)*, Auguste Comte and Positivism *(1865)*, The
Subjection of Women *(1869)*, and* Autobiography *(1873, the
year of his death). He was also a member of Parliament from
1865 to 1868.*

The selections from *On Liberty* are from the 1859 edition (London:
John W. Parker and Son).

Chapter 1: Introductory

The subject of this Essay is not the so-called Liberty of the Will, so unfortunately opposed to the misnamed doctrine of Philosophical Necessity; but Civil, or Social Liberty: the nature and limits of the power which can be legitimately exercised by society over the individual. A question seldom stated, and hardly ever discussed, in general terms, but which profoundly influences the practical controversies of the age by its latent presence, and is likely soon to make itself recognised as the vital question of the future. It is so far from being new, that in a certain sense, it has divided mankind, almost from the remotest ages; but in the stage of progress into which the more civilized portions of the species have now entered, it presents itself under new conditions, and requires a different and more fundamental treatment.

The struggle between Liberty and Authority is the most conspicuous feature in the portions of history with which we are earliest familiar, particularly in that of Greece, Rome, and England. But in old times this contest was between subjects, or some classes of subjects, and the government. By liberty, was meant protection against the tyranny of the political rulers. The rulers were conceived (except in some of the popular governments of Greece) as in a necessarily antagonistic position to the people whom they ruled. They consisted of a governing One, or a governing tribe or caste, who derived their authority from inheritance or conquest, who, at all events, did not hold it at the pleasure of the governed, and whose supremacy men did not venture, perhaps did not desire, to contest, whatever precautions might be taken against its oppressive exercise. Their power was regarded as necessary, but also as highly dangerous; as a weapon which they would attempt to use against their subjects, no less than against external enemies. To prevent the weaker members of the community from being preyed upon by innumerable vultures, it was needful that there should be an animal of prey stronger than the rest, commissioned to keep them down. But as the king of the vultures would be no less bent upon preying on the flock, than any of the minor harpies, it was indispensable to be in a perpetual attitude of defence against his beak and claws. The aim, therefore, of patriots, was to set limits to the power which the ruler should be suffered to exercise over the community; and this limitation was what they meant by liberty. It was attempted in two ways. First, by obtaining a recognition of certain immunities, called political liberties or rights, which it was to be regarded as a breach of duty in the ruler to infringe, and which if he did infringe, specific resistance, or general rebellion, was held to be justifiable. A second, and generally a later expedient, was the establishment of constitutional checks; by which the consent of the community, or of a body of some sort, supposed to represent its interests, was made a necessary condition to some of the more important acts of the governing power. To the first of these modes of limitation, the ruling power, in most European countries, was compelled, more or less, to submit. It was not so with the second; and to attain this, or when already in some degree possessed, to attain it more completely, became everywhere the principal object of the lovers of liberty. And so long as mankind were content to combat one enemy by another, and to be ruled by a master, on condition of being guaranteed more or less efficaciously against his tyranny, they did not carry their aspirations beyond this point.

A time, however, came, in the progress of human affairs, when men ceased to think it a necessity of nature that their governors should be an independent power, opposed in interest to themselves. It appeared to them much better that the various magistrates of the State should be their tenants or delegates, revocable at their pleasure. In that way alone, it seemed, could they have complete security that the powers of government would never be abused to their disadvantage. By degrees, this new demand for elective and temporary rulers became the prominent object of the exertions of the popular party, wherever any such party existed; and superseded, to a considerable extent, the previous efforts to limit the power of rulers. As the struggle proceeded for making the ruling power emanate from the periodical choice of the ruled, some persons began to think that too much importance had been attached to the limitation of the power itself. *That* (it might seem) was a resource against rulers whose interests were habitually opposed to those of the people. What was now wanted was, that the rulers should be identified with the people; that their interest and will should be the interest and will of the nation. The nation did not need to be protected against its own will. There was no fear of its tyrannizing over itself. Let the rulers be effectually responsible to it, promptly removable by it, and it could afford to trust them with power of which it could itself dictate the use to be made. Their power was but the nation's own power, concentrated, and in a form convenient for exercise. This mode of thought, or rather perhaps of feeling, was common among the last generation of European liberalism, in the Continental section of which, it still apparently predominates. Those who admit any limit to what a government may do, except in the case of such governments as they think ought not to exist, stand out as brilliant exceptions among the political thinkers of the Continent. A similar tone of sentiment might by this time have been prevalent in our own country, if the circumstances which for a time encouraged it, had continued unaltered.

But, in political and philosophical theories, as well as in persons, success discloses faults and infirmities which failure might have concealed from observation. The notion, that the people have no need to limit their power over themselves, might seem axiomatic, when popular government was a thing only dreamed about, or read of as having existed at some distant period of the past. Neither was that notion necessarily disturbed by such temporary aberrations as those of the French Revolution, the worst of which were the work of an usurping few, and which, in any case, belonged, not to the permanent working of popular institutions, but to a sudden and convulsive outbreak against monarchical and aristocratic despotism. In time, however, a democratic republic came to occupy a large portion of the earth's surface, and made itself felt as one of the most powerful members of the community of nations; and elective and responsible government became subject to the observations and criticisms which wait upon a great existing fact. It was now perceived that such phrases as "self-government," and "the power of the people over themselves," do not express the true state of the case. The "people" who exercise the power, are not always the same people with those over whom it is exercised; and the "self-government" spoken of, is not the government of each by himself, but of each by all the rest. The will of the people, moreover, practically means, the will of the most numerous or the most active *part* of the people; the majority, or those who succeed in making themselves accepted as the majority: the people, consequently, *may* desire to oppress a part of their number; and precautions are as much needed against this, as against any other abuse of power. The limitation, therefore, of the power of government over individuals, loses none of its importance when the holders of power are regularly accountable to the community, that is, to the strongest party therein. This view of things, recommending itself equally to the intelligence of thinkers and to the inclination of those important classes in European society to whose real or supposed interests democracy is adverse, has had no difficulty in establishing itself; and in political speculations "the tyranny of the majority" is now generally included among the evils against which society requires to be on its guard.

Like other tyrannies, the tyranny of the majority was at first, and is still vulgarly, held in dread, chiefly as operating through the acts of the public authorities. But reflecting persons perceived that when society is itself the tyrant—society collectively, over the separate individuals who compose it—its means of tyrannizing are not restricted to the acts which it may do by the hands of its political functionaries. Society can and does execute its own mandates: and if it issues wrong mandates instead of right, or any mandates at all in things with which it ought not to meddle, it practises a social tyranny more formidable than many kinds of political oppression, since, though not usually upheld by such extreme penalties, it leaves fewer means of escape, penetrating much more deeply into the details of life, and enslaving the soul itself. Protection, therefore, against the tyranny of the magistrate is not enough: there needs protection also against the tyranny of the prevailing opinion and feeling; against the tendency of society to impose, by other means than civil penalties, its own ideas and practices as rules of conduct on those who dissent from them; to fetter the development, and, if possible, prevent the formation, of any individuality not in harmony with its ways, and compel all characters to fashion themselves upon the model of its own. There is a limit to the legitimate interference of collective opinion with individual independence: and to find that limit, and maintain it against encroachment, is as indispensable to a good condition of human affairs, as protection against political despotism.

. . .

The object of this Essay is to assert one very simple principle, as entitled to govern absolutely the dealings of society with the individual in the way of compulsion and control, whether the means used be physical force in the form of legal penalties, or the moral coercion of public opinion. That principle is, that the sole end for which mankind are warranted, individually or collectively, in interfering with the liberty of action of any of their number, is self-protection. That the only purpose for which power can be rightfully exercised over any member of a civilized community, against his will, is to prevent harm to others. His own good, either physical or moral, is not a sufficient warrant. He cannot rightfully be compelled to do or forbear because it will be better for him to do so, because it will make him happier, because, in the opinions of others, to do so would be wise, or even right. These are good reasons for remonstrating with him, or reasoning with him, or persuading him, or entreating him, but not for compelling him, or visiting him with any evil in case he do otherwise. To justify that, the conduct from which it is desired to deter him, must be calculated to produce evil to some one else. The only part of the conduct of any one, for which he is amenable to society, is that which concerns others. In the part which merely concerns himself, his independence is, of right, absolute. Over himself, over his own body and mind, the individual is sovereign.

It is, perhaps, hardly necessary to say that this doctrine is meant to apply only to human beings in the maturity of their faculties. We are not speaking of children, or of young persons below the age which the law may fix as that of manhood or womanhood. Those who are still in a state to require being taken care of by others, must be protected against their own actions as well as against external injury. For the same reason, we may leave out of consideration those backward states of society in which the race itself may be considered as in its nonage. The early difficulties in the way of spontaneous progress are so great, that there is seldom any choice of means for overcoming them; and a ruler full of the spirit of improvement is warranted in the use of any expedients that will attain an end, perhaps otherwise unattainable. Despotism is a legitimate mode of government in dealing with barbarians, provided the end be their improvement, and the means justified by actually effecting that end. Liberty, as a principle, has no application to any state of things anterior to the time when mankind have become capable of being improved by free and equal discussion. Until then, there is nothing for them but implicit obedience to an Akbar or a Charlemagne, if they are so fortunate as to find one. But as soon as mankind have attained the capacity of being guided to their own improvement by conviction or persuasion (a period long since reached in all nations with whom we need here concern ourselves), compulsion, either in the direct form or in that of pains and penalties for non-compliance, is no longer admissible as a means to their own good, and justifiable only for the security of others.

It is proper to state that I forego any advantage which could be derived to my argument from the idea of abstract right, as a thing independent of utility. I regard utility as the ultimate appeal on all ethical questions; but it must be utility in the largest sense, grounded on the permanent interests of man as a progressive being. Those interests, I contend, authorize the subjection of individual spontaneity to external control, only in respect to those actions of each, which concern the interest of other people. If any one does an act hurtful to others, there is a *primâ facie* case for punishing him, by law, or, where legal penalties are not safely applicable, by general disapprobation. There are also many positive acts for the benefit of others, which he may rightfully be compelled to perform; such as, to give evidence in a court of justice; to bear his fair share in the common defence, or in any other joint work necessary to the interest of the society of which he enjoys the protection; and to perform certain acts of individual beneficence, such as saving a fellow-creature's life, or interposing to protect the defenceless against ill-usage, things which whenever it is obviously a man's duty to do, he may rightfully be made responsible to society for not doing. A person may cause evil to others not only by his actions but by his inaction, and in either case he is justly accountable to them for the injury. The latter case, it is true, requires a much more cautious exercise of compulsion than the former. To make any one answerable for doing evil to others, is the rule; to make him answerable for not preventing evil, is, comparatively speaking, the exception. Yet there are many cases clear enough and grave enough to justify that exception. In all things which regard the external relations of the individual, he is *de jure* amenable to those whose interests are concerned, and if need be, to society as their protector. There are often good reasons for not holding him to the responsibility; but these reasons must arise from the special expediencies of the case: either because it is a kind of case in which he is on the whole likely to act better, when left to his own discretion, than when controlled in any way in which society have it in their power to control him; or because the attempt to exercise control would produce other evils, greater than those which it would prevent. When such reasons as these preclude the enforcement of responsibility, the conscience of the agent himself should step into the vacant judgment seat, and protect those interests of others which have no external protection; judging himself all the more rigidly, because the case does not admit of his being made accountable to the judgment of his fellow-creatures.

But there is a sphere of action in which society, as distinguished from the individual, has, if any, only an indirect interest; comprehending all that portion of a person's life and conduct which affects only himself, or if it also affects others, only with their free, voluntary, and undeceived consent and participation. When I say only himself, I mean directly, and in the first instance: for whatever affects himself, may affect others *through* himself; and the objection which may be grounded on this contingency, will receive consideration in the sequel. This, then, is the appropriate region of human liberty. It comprises, first, the inward domain of consciousness; demanding liberty of conscience, in the most comprehensive sense; liberty of thought and feeling; absolute freedom of opinion and sentiment on all subjects, practical or speculative, scientific, moral, or theological. The liberty of expressing and publishing opinions may seem to fall under a different principle, since it belongs to that part of the conduct of an individual which concerns other people; but, being almost of as much importance as the liberty of thought itself, and resting in great part on the same reasons, is practically inseparable from it. Secondly, the principle requires liberty of tastes and pursuits; of framing the plan of our life to suit our own character; of doing as we like, subject to such consequences as may follow: without impediment from our fellow-creatures, so long as what we do does not harm them, even though they should think our conduct foolish, perverse, or wrong. Thirdly, from this liberty of each individual, follows the liberty, within the same limits, of combination among individuals; freedom to unite, for any purpose not involving harm to others: the persons combining being supposed to be of full age, and not forced or deceived.

No society in which these liberties are not, on the whole, respected, is free, whatever may be its form of government; and none is completely free in which they do not exist absolute and unqualified. The only freedom which deserves the name, is that of pursuing our own good in our own way, so long as we do not attempt to deprive others of theirs, or impede their efforts to obtain it. Each is the proper guardian of his own health, whether bodily, or mental and spiritual. Mankind are greater gainers by suffering each other to live as seems good to themselves, than by compelling each to live as seems good to the rest.

. . .

Chapter 2: Of the Liberty of Thought and Discussion

. . . Let us suppose . . . that the government is entirely at one with the people, and never thinks of exerting any power of coercion unless in agreement with what it conceives to be their voice. But I deny the right of the people to exercise such coercion, either by themselves or by their government. The power itself is illegitimate. The best government has no more title to it than the worst. It is as noxious, or more noxious, when exerted in accordance with public opinion, than when in opposition to it. If all mankind minus one, were of one opinion, and only one person were of the contrary opinion, mankind would be no more justified in silencing that one person, than he, if he had the power, would be justified in silencing mankind. Were an opinion a personal possession of no value except to the owner; if to be obstructed in the enjoyment of it were simply a private injury, it would make some difference whether the injury was inflicted only on a few persons or on many. But the peculiar evil of silencing the expression of an opinion is, that it is robbing the human race; posterity as well as the existing generation; those who dissent from the opinion, still more than those who hold it. If the opinion is right, they are deprived of the opportunity of exchanging error for truth: if wrong, they lose, what is almost as great a benefit, the clearer perception and livelier impression of truth, produced by its collision with error.

. . .

We have now recognised the necessity to the mental well-being of mankind (on which all their other well-being depends) of freedom of opinion, and freedom of the expression of opinion, on four distinct grounds; which we will now briefly recapitulate.

First, if any opinion is compelled to silence, that opinion may, for aught we can certainly know, be true. To deny this is to assume our own infallibility.

Secondly, though the silenced opinion be an error, it may, and very commonly does, contain a portion of truth; and since the general or prevailing opinion on any subject is rarely or never the whole truth, it is only by the collision of adverse opinions that the remainder of the truth has any chance of being supplied.

Thirdly, even if the received opinion be not only true, but the whole truth; unless it is suffered to be, and actually is, vigorously and earnestly contested, it will, by most of those who receive it, be held in the manner of a prejudice, with little comprehension or feeling of its rational grounds. And not only this, but, fourthly, the meaning of the doctrine itself will be in danger of being lost, or enfeebled, and deprived of its vital effect on the character and conduct: the dogma becoming a mere formal profession, inefficacious for good, but cumbering the ground, and preventing the growth of any real and heartfelt conviction, from reason or personal experience.

Chapter 3: Of Individuality, as One of the Elements of Well-Being

. . . As it is useful that while mankind are imperfect there should be different opinions, so is it that there should be different experiments of living; that free scope should be given to varieties of character, short of injury to others; and that the worth of different modes of life should be proved practically, when any one thinks fit to try them. It is desirable, in short, that in things which do not primarily concern others, individuality should assert itself. Where, not the person's own character, but the traditions or customs of other people are the rule of conduct, there is wanting one of the principal ingredients of human happiness, and quite the chief ingredient of individual and social progress.

In maintaining this principle, the greatest difficulty to be encountered does not lie in the appreciation of means towards an acknowledged end, but in the indifference of persons in general to the end itself. If it were felt that the free development of individuality is one of the leading essentials of well-being; that it is not only a co-ordinate element with all that is designated by the terms civilization, instruction, education, culture, but is itself a necessary part and condition of all those things; there would be no danger that liberty should be undervalued, and the adjustment of the boundaries between it and social control would present no extraordinary difficulty. But the evil is, that individual spontaneity is hardly recognized by the common modes of thinking, as having any intrinsic worth, or deserving any regard on its own account. . . .

· · ·

He who lets the world, or his own portion of it, choose his plan of life for him, has no need of any other faculty than the ape-like one of imitation. He who chooses his plan for himself, employs all his faculties. He must use observation to see, reasoning and judgment to foresee, activity to gather materials for decision, discrimination to decide, and when he has decided, firmness and self-control to hold to his deliberate decision. And these qualities he requires and exercises exactly in proportion as the part of his conduct which he determines according to his own judgment and feelings is a large one. It is possible that he might be guided in some good path, and kept out of harm's way, without any of these things. But what will be his comparative worth as a human being? It really is of importance, not only what men do, but also what manner of men they are that do it. Among the works of man, which human life is rightly employed in perfecting and beautifying, the first in importance surely is man himself. Supposing it were possible to get houses built, corn grown, battles fought, causes tried, and even churches erected and prayers said, by machinery—by automatons in human form—it would be a considerable loss to exchange for these automatons even the men and women who at present inhabit the more civilized parts of the world, and who assuredly are but starved specimens of what nature can and will produce. Human nature is not a machine to be built after a model, and set to do exactly the work prescribed for it, but a tree, which requires to grow and develope itself on all sides, according to the tendency of the inward forces which make it a living thing.

. . .

. . . It will not be denied by anybody, that originality is a valuable element in human affairs. There is always need of persons not only to discover new truths, and point out when what were once truths are true no longer, but also to commence new practices, and set the example of more enlightened conduct, and better taste and sense in human life. This cannot well be gainsaid by anybody who does not believe that the world has already attained perfection in all its ways and practices. It is true that this benefit is not capable of being rendered by everybody alike: there are but few persons, in comparison with the whole of mankind, whose experiments, if adopted by others, would be likely to be any improvement on established practice. But these few are the salt of the earth; without them, human life would become a stagnant pool. Not only is it they who introduce good things which did not before exist; it is they who keep the life in those which already existed. . . .

. . .

Chapter 4: Of the Limits to the Authority of Society over the Individual

What, then, is the rightful limit to the sovereignty of the individual over himself? Where does the authority of society begin? How much of human life should be assigned to individuality, and how much to society?

Each will receive its proper share, if each has that which more particularly concerns it. To individuality should belong the part of life in which it is chiefly the individual that is interested; to society, the part which chiefly interests society.

Though society is not founded on a contract, and though no good purpose is answered by inventing a contract in order to deduce social obligations from it, every one who receives the protection of society owes a return for the benefit, and the fact of living in society renders it indispensable that each should be bound to observe a certain line of conduct towards the rest. This conduct consists, first, in not injuring the interests of one another; or rather certain interests, which, either by express legal provision or by tacit understanding, ought to be considered as rights; and secondly, in each person's bearing his share (to be fixed on some equitable principle) of the labours and sacrifices incurred for defending the society or its members from injury and molestation. These conditions society is justified in enforcing, at all costs to those who endeavour to withhold fulfilment. Nor is this all that society may do. The acts of an individual may be hurtful to others, or wanting in due consideration for their welfare, without going the length of violating any of their constituted rights. The offender may then be justly punished by opinion, though not by law. As soon as any part of a person's conduct affects prejudicially the interests of others, society has jurisdiction over it, and the question whether the general welfare will or will not be promoted by interfering with it, becomes open to discussion. . . .

. . . But neither one person, nor any number of persons, is warranted in saying to another human creature of ripe years, that he shall not do with his life for his own benefit what he chooses to do with it. He is the person most interested in his own well-being: the interest which any other person, except in cases of strong personal attachment, can have in it, is trifling, compared with that which he himself has; the interest which society has in him individually (except as to his conduct to others) is fractional, and altogether indirect: while, with respect to his own feelings and circumstances, the most ordinary man or woman has means of knowledge immeasurably surpassing those that can be possessed by any one else. The interference of society to overrule his judgment and purposes in what only regards himself, must be grounded on general presumptions; which may be altogether wrong, and even if right, are as likely as not to be misapplied to individual cases, by persons no better acquainted with the circumstances of such cases than those are who look at them merely from without. In this department, therefore, of human affairs, Individuality has its proper field of action. In the conduct of human beings towards one another, it is necessary that general rules should for the most part be observed, in order that people may know what they have to expect; but in each person's own concerns, his individual spontaneity is entitled to free exercise. Considerations to aid his judgment, exhortations to strengthen his will, may be offered to him, even obtruded on him, by others; but he himself is the final judge. All errors which he is likely to commit against advice and warning, are far outweighed by the evil of allowing others to constrain him to what they deem his good.

.   .   .

I fully admit that the mischief which a person does to himself, may seriously affect, both through their sympathies and their interests, those nearly connected with him, and in a minor degree, society at large. When, by conduct of this sort, a person is led to violate a distinct and assignable obligation to any other person or persons, the case is taken out of the self-regarding class, and becomes amenable to moral disapprobation in the proper sense of the term. . . .

But with regard to the merely contingent, or, as it may be called, constructive injury which a person causes to society, by conduct which neither violates any specific duty to the public, nor occasions perceptible hurt to any assignable individual except himself; the inconvenience is one which society can afford to bear, for the sake of the greater good of human freedom. . . .

. . .

Chapter 5: Applications

. . .

It was pointed out in an early part of this Essay, that the liberty of the individual, in things wherein the individual is alone concerned, implies a corresponding liberty in any number of individuals to regulate by mutual agreement such things as regard them jointly, and regard no persons but themselves. This question presents no difficulty, so long as the will of all the persons implicated remains unaltered; but since that will may change, it is often necessary, even in things in which they alone are concerned, that they should enter into engagements with one another; and when they do, it is fit, as a general rule, that those engagements should be kept. Yet in the laws, probably, of every country, this general rule has some exceptions. Not only persons are not held to engagements which violate the rights of third parties, but it is sometimes considered a sufficient reason for releasing them from an engagement, that it is injurious to themselves. In this and most other civilized countries, for example, an engagement by which a person should sell himself, or allow himself to be sold, as a slave, would be null and void; neither enforced by law nor by opinion. The ground for thus limiting his power of voluntarily disposing of his own lot in life, is apparent, and is very clearly seen in this extreme case. The reason for not interfering, unless for the sake of others, with a person's voluntary acts, is consideration for his liberty. His voluntary choice is evidence that what he so chooses is desirable, or at the least endurable, to him, and his good is on the whole best provided for by allowing him to take his own means of pursuing it. But by selling himself for a slave, he abdicates his liberty; he foregoes any future use of it, beyond that single act. He therefore defeats, in his own case, the very purpose which is the justification of allowing him to dispose of himself. He is no longer free; but is thenceforth in a position which has no longer the presumption in its favour, that would be afforded by his voluntarily remaining in it. The principle of freedom cannot require that he should be free not to be free. It is not freedom, to be allowed to alienate his freedom. . . .

.   .   .

Prolegomena to Ethics, Lectures on the Principles of Political Obligation, and Lecture on Liberal Legislation and Freedom of Contract

THOMAS HILL GREEN

Thomas Hill Green was born in 1836 and educated at Rugby and at Oxford, where he was a student, fellow, and tutor of Balliol College from 1855 to 1878. He then became Whyte's professor of moral philosophy at Oxford. While a fellow, and despite some reputation for radicalism, he was appointed assistant to a Royal commission on education in 1865, thus beginning a life-long work to extend educational opportunity. He later was the first college tutor to serve on the Oxford town council. As a tutor, he lectured on Greek philosophy and the New Testament, both lasting interests; throughout his life, he was absorbed in the reconciliation of faith and reason. Although his deepest philosophical sympathies lay with Kant and Hegel, he gave much attention to his British forerunners, especially Locke and Hume, both of whom he discussed critically in his introduction to Hume's Treatise of Human Nature *(1874). As professor of moral philosophy, Green lectured on ethics and, in 1879–1880, on the Principles of Political Obligation. He also delivered many public lectures, including "Liberal Legislation and Freedom of Contract" (1881). His* Prolegomena to Ethics *was nearly finished when he died suddenly in 1882.*

The following selections are reprinted from *Prolegomena to Ethics*, A. C. Bradley (Ed.), 5th ed. (Oxford: The Clarendon Press, 1906), by permission of the Clarendon Press, Oxford, and from volumes 2 and 3 of *Works of Thomas Hill Green*, R. L. Nettleship (Ed.) (London: Longman's, Green & Co. Ltd., 1906).

Prolegomena to Ethics
Book 3: The Moral Ideal and Moral Progress

Chapter 3: The Origin and Development of the Moral Ideal.

A. Reason as Source of the Idea of a Common Good.

. . .

202 . . . The conception of a moral law, in its strict philosophical form, is no doubt an analogical adaptation of the notion of law in the more primary sense—the notion of it as a command enforced by a political superior, or by some power to which obedience is habitually rendered by those to whom the command is addressed. But there is an idea which equally underlies the conception both of moral duty and of legal right; which is prior, so to speak, to the distinction between them; which must have been at work in the minds of men before they could be capable of recognising any kind of action as one that *ought* to be done, whether because it is enjoined by law or authoritative custom, or because, though not thus enjoined, a man owes it to himself or to his neighbour or to God. This is the idea of an absolute and a common good; a good common to the person conceiving it with others, and good for him and them, whether at any moment it answers their likings or no. As affected by such an idea, a man's attitude to his likes and dislikes will be one of which, in his inward converse, the "Thou shalt" or "Thou must" of command is the natural expression, though of law, in the sense either of the command of a political superior or of a self-imposed rule of life, he may as yet have no definite conception.

And so affected by it he must be, before the authority either of custom or of law can have any meaning for him. Simple fear cannot constitute the sense of such authority nor by any process of development, properly so called, become it. It can only spring from a conviction, on the part of those recognising the authority, that a good which is really their good, though in constant conflict with their inclinations, is really served by the power in which they recognise authority. Whatever force may be employed in maintaining custom or law, however "the interest of the stronger," whether an individual or the few or the majority of some group of people, may be concerned in maintaining it, only some persuasion of its contribution to a recognised common good can yield that sort of obedience to it which, equally in the simpler and the more complex stages of society, forms the social bond.

203. The idea, then, of a possible well-being of himself, that shall not pass away with this, that, or the other pleasure; and relation to some group of persons whose well-being he takes to be as his own, and in whom he is interested in being interested in himself—these two things must condition the life of any one who is to be a creator or sustainer either of law or of that prior authoritative custom out of which law arises. Without them there might be instruments of law and custom; intelligent co-operating subjects of law and custom there could not be. They are conditions at once of might being so exercised that it can be recognised as having right, and of that recognition itself. It is in this sense that the old language is justified, which speaks of Reason as the parent of Law. . . .

. . .

205. The foundation of morality, then, in the reason or self-objectifying consciousness of man, is the same thing as its foundation in the institutions of a common life—in these as directed to a common good, and so directed not mechanically but with consciousness of the good on the part of those subject to the institutions. Such institutions are, so to speak, the form and body of reason, as practical in men. Without them the rational or self-conscious or moral man does not exist, nor without them can any being have existed from whom such a man could be developed, if any continuity of nature is implied in development. No development of morality can be conceived, nor can any history of it be traced (for that would imply such a conception), which does not presuppose some idea of a common good, expressing itself in some elementary effort after a regulation of life. Without such an idea the development would be as impossible as it is impossible that sight should be generated when there is no optic nerve. With it, however restricted in range the idea may be, there is given "in promise and potency"

the ideal of which the realisation would be perfect morality, the ideal of a society in which every one shall treat every one else as his neighbour, in which to every rational agent the well-being or perfection of every other such agent shall be included in that perfection of himself for which he lives. And as the most elementary notion in a rational being of a personal good, common to himself with another who is as himself, is in possibility such an ideal, so the most primitive institutions for the regulation of a society with reference to a common good are already a school for the character which shall be responsive to the moral ideal.

• • •

B. The Extension of the Area of Common Good.

• • •

211. For an abstract expression of the notion that there is something due from every man to every man, simply as men, we may avail ourselves of the phrase employed in the famous definition of Justice in the Institutes:—"Justitia est constans et perpetua voluntas suum cuique tribuendi." [1] Every man both by law and common sentiment is recognised as having a "suum," whatever the "suum" may be, and is thus effectually distinguished from the animals (at any rate according to our treatment of them) and from things. He is deemed capable of having something of his own, as animals and things are not. He is treated as an end, not merely as a means. It is obvious indeed that the notion expressed by the "suum cuique," even when it carries with it the admission that every man, as such, has a "suum," is a most insufficient guide to conduct till we can answer the question what the "suum" in each case is, and that no such answer is deducible from the mere principle that every one has a "suum." In fact, of course, this principle is never wrought into law or general sentiment without very precise, though perhaps insufficient and ultimately untenable, determinations of what

---

[1] "Justice is the constant and perpetual will of rendering to one his due (*suum*)."—ED.

is due from one to another in the ordinary intercourse of those habitually associated. Particular duties to this man and that have been recognised long before reflection has reached the stage in which a duty to man as such can be recognised. How far upon reflection we can find in these particular duties—in the detail of conventional morality—a permanent and universal basis for right conduct, is a separate question. For the present we wish to follow out the effect exerted upon the responsive conscience by life in a society where a capacity for rights, some claim on his fellow-men, has come to be ascribed to every man. Given that readiness to recognise a duty and to act upon the recognition, which is the proper outcome in the individual of family and civil discipline as governed by an idea of common good, what sort of rule of conduct will the individual, upon unbiassed reflection, obtain for himself from the establishment in law and general sentiment of the principle that every man can claim something as his due? How will it tend to define for him the absolutely desirable, and the ideal of conduct as directed thereto?

212. The great result will be to fix it in his mind, as a condition of such conduct, that it should be *alike* for the real good of all men concerned in or affected by it, as estimated on the same principle. This rule has indeed become so familiarised to our consciences, however frequently we violate it, that at first sight it may seem to some too trivial to be worthy a philosopher's attention, while by others it may be remarked that, till we have decided what the real good of all men is, and have at least some general knowledge of the effect upon it, under certain conditions, of certain lines of conduct, the rule will not tell us how we ought to act in particular cases. Such a remark would be plainly true. For the present, however, we are considering the importance to the conscientious man of this recognition of a like claim in all men, taken simply by itself, irrespectively of those criteria of the good and of those convictions as to the means of arriving at it by which the recognition is in fact always accompanied. It is the source of the refinement in his sense of justice. It is that which makes him so over-curious, as it seems to the ordinary man of the world, in enquiring, as to any action that may suggest itself to him, whether the

benefit which he might gain by it for himself or for some one
in whom he is interested, would be gained at the expense of
any one else, however indifferent to him personally, however
separated from him in family, status, or nation. It makes the
man, in short, who will be just before he is generous; who will
not merely postpone his own interest to his friend's, but who,
before he gratifies an "altruistic" inclination, will be careful to
enquire how in doing so he would affect others who are not
the object of the inclination. This characteristic of the man who
is just in the full light of the idea of human equality is independent of any theory of well-being on his part. Whether he
has any theory on the matter at all, whether he is theoretically
an "Ascetic" or a "Hedonist," makes little practical difference.
The essential thing is that he applies no other standard in judging of the well-being of others than in judging of his own, and
that he will not promote his own well-being or that of one whom
he loves or likes, from whom he has received service or expects
it, at the cost of impeding in any way the well-being of one who
is nothing to him but a man, or whom he involuntarily dislikes;
that he will not do this knowingly, and that he is habitually on
the look-out to know whether his actions will have this effect
or not.

. . .

217 . . . Thus in the conscientious citizen of modern
Christendom reason without and reason within, reason as objective and reason as subjective, reason as the better spirit of
the social order in which he lives, and reason as his loyal recognition and interpretation of that spirit—these being but different aspects of one and the same reality, which is the operation
of the divine mind in man—combine to yield both the judgment,
and obedience to the judgment, which we variously express by
saying that every human person has an absolute value; that
humanity in the person of every one is always to be treated as
an end, never merely as a means; that in the estimate of that
well-being which forms the true good every one is to count for
one and no one for more than one; that every one has a "suum"
which every one else is bound to render him.

Lectures on the Principles of Political Obligation

.   .   .

G. Will, Not Force, Is the Basis of the State.

.   .   .

114. To ask why I am to submit to the power of the state, is to ask why I am to allow my life to be regulated by that complex of institutions without which I literally should not have a life to call my own, nor should be able to ask for a justification of what I am called on to do. For that I may have a life which I can call my own, I must not only be conscious of myself and of ends which I present to myself as mine; I must be able to reckon on a certain freedom of action and acquisition for the attainment of those ends, and this can only be secured through common recognition of this freedom on the part of each other by members of a society, as being for a common good. Without this, the very consciousness of having ends of his own and a life which he can direct in a certain way, a life of which he can make something, would remain dormant in a man. It is true that slaves have been found to have this consciousness in high development; but a slave even at his lowest has been partly made what he is by an ancestral life which was not one of slavery pure and simple, a life in which certain elementary rights were secured to the members of a society through their recognition of a common interest. He retains certain spiritual aptitudes from that state of family or tribal freedom. . . . Slavery, moreover, implies the establishment of some regular system of rights in the slave-owning society. The slave, especially the domestic slave, has the signs and effects of this system all about him. . . . Thus the appearance in slaves of the conception that they should be masters of themselves, does not conflict with the proposition that only so far as a certain freedom of action and acquisition is secured to a body of men through their recognition of the exercise of that freedom by each other as being for the common good, is there an actualisation of the individual's consciousness of having life and ends of his own. The exercise, manifestation,

expression of this consciousness through a freedom secured in the way described is necessary to its real existence, just as language of some sort is necessary to the real existence of thought, and bodily movement to that of the soul.

115. The demand, again, for a justification of what one is called on by authority to do presupposes some standard of right, recognised as equally valid for and by the person making the demand and others who form a society with him, and such a recognised standard in turn implies institutions for the regulation of men's dealings with each other, institutions of which the relation to the consciousness of right may be compared, as above, to that of language to thought. It cannot be said that the most elementary consciousness of right is prior to them, or they to it. They are the expressions in which it becomes real. As conflicting with the momentary inclinations of the individual, these institutions are a power which he obeys unwillingly; which he has to, or is made to, obey. But it is only through them that the consciousness takes shape and form which expresses itself in the question, "Why should I thus be constrained? By what right is my natural right to do as I like overborne?"

116. The doctrine that the rights of government are founded on the consent of the governed is a confused way of stating the truth, that the institutions by which man is moralised, by which he comes to do what he sees that he must, as distinct from what he would like, express a conception of a common good; that through them that conception takes form and reality; and that it is in turn through its presence in the individual that they have a constraining power over him, a power which is not that of mere fear, still less a physical compulsion, but which leads him to do what he is not inclined to because there is a law that he should.

Rousseau, it will be remembered, speaks of the "social pact" not merely as the foundation of sovereignty or civil government, but as the foundation of morality. Through it man becomes a moral agent; for the slavery to appetite he substitutes the freedom of subjection to a self-imposed law. If he had seen at the same time that rights do not begin till duties begin, and that if there was no morality prior to the pact there could not be rights, he might have been saved from the error which the notion of there being natural rights introduces into his theory.

But though he does not seem himself to have been aware of the full bearing of his own conception, the conception itself is essentially true. Setting aside the fictitious representation of an original covenant as having given birth to that common "ego" or general will, without which no such covenant would have been possible, and of obligations arising out of it, as out of a bargain made between one man and another, it remains true that only through a recognition by certain men of a common interest, and through the expression of that recognition in certain regulations of their dealings with each other, could morality originate, or any meaning be gained for such terms as "ought" and "right" and their equivalents.

117. Morality, in the first instance, is the observance of such regulations, and though a higher morality, the morality of the character governed by "disinterested motives," i.e., by interest in some form of human perfection, comes to differentiate itself from this primitive morality consisting in the observance of rules established for a common good, yet this outward morality is the presupposition of the higher morality. Morality and political subjection thus have a common source, "*political* subjection" being distinguished from that of a slave, as a subjection which secures rights to the subject. That common source is the rational recognition by certain human beings —it may be merely by children of the same parent—of a common well-being which is their well-being, and which they conceive as their well-being whether at any moment any one of them is inclined to it or no, and the embodiment of that recognition in rules by which the inclinations of the individuals are restrained, and a corresponding freedom of action for the attainment of well-being on the whole is secured.

• • •

M. The Right of the State to Promote Morality. 207. The right of the individual man as such to free life is constantly gaining on its negative side more general recognition. It is the basis of the growing scrupulosity in regard to punishments which are not reformatory, which put rights finally out of the reach of a criminal instead of qualifying him for their renewed exercise. But the only rational foundation for the ascription of this right is the ascription of capacity for free contribution to social good. We treat this capacity in the man whose crime has given proof of its having been overcome by anti-social tendencies, as yet giving him a title to a further chance of its development; on the other hand, we act as if it conferred no title on its possessors, before a crime has been committed, to be placed under conditions in which its realisation would be possible. Is this reasonable? Yet are not all modern states so acting? Are they not allowing their ostensible members to grow up under conditions which render the development of social capacity practically impossible? Was it not more reasonable, as in the ancient states, to deny the right to life in the human subject as such, than to admit it under conditions which prevent the realisation of the capacity that forms the ground of its admission? This brings us to the fourth of the questions that arose out of the assertion of the individual's right to free life. What is the nature and extent of the individual's claim to be enabled positively to realise that capacity for freely contributing to social good which is the foundation of his right to free life?

208. In dealing with this question, it is important to bear in mind that the capacity we are considering is essentially a free or (what is the same) a moral capacity. It is a capacity, not for action determined by relation to a certain end, but for action determined by a conception of the end to which it is relative. Only thus is it a foundation of rights. The action of an animal or plant may be made contributory to social good, but it is not therefore a foundation of rights on the part of an animal or plant, because they are not affected by the conception of the good to which they contribute. A right[2] is a power of

---

[2] I.e., a *moral* right. In Lecture A, § 27, Green says that only among "persons" can there come to be rights, which means, in the ethical sense, ". . . that rights are derived from the possession of personality as = a rational will (i.e., the capacity which man possesses of being determined to action by the conception of such a perfection of his being as involves the perfection of a society in which he lives) . . ." He goes on to say (§§ 29, 30) that "society should secure to the individual every power [as a right], that is necessary for realising this capacity." "Claims to such powers as are directly necessary to a man's acting as a moral person at all" may even be called "innate" or "natural"—not in the sense that they exist antecedently to society, "but that they arise out of, and are necessary for the fulfillment of, a moral capacity without which a man would not be a man."—ED.

acting for his own ends,—for what he conceives to be his good,—secured to an individual by the community, on the supposition that its exercise contributes to the good of the community. But the exercise of such a power cannot be so contributory, unless the individual, in acting for his own ends, is at least affected by the conception of a good as common to himself with others. The condition of making the animal contributory to human good is that we do not leave him free to determine the exercise of his powers; that we determine them for him; that we use him merely as an instrument; and this means that we do not, because we cannot, endow him with rights. We cannot endow him with rights because there is no conception of a good common to him with us which we can treat as a motive to him to do to us as he would have us do to him. It is not indeed necessary to a capacity for rights, as it is to true moral goodness, that interest in a good conceived as common to himself with others should be a man's dominant motive. It is enough if that which he presents to himself from time to time as his good, and which accordingly determines his action, is so far affected by consideration of the position in which he stands to others,—of the way in which this or that possible action of his would affect them, and of what he would have to expect from them in return,—as to result habitually, without force or fear of force, in action not incompatible with conditions necessary to the pursuit of a common good on the part of others. In other words, it is the presumption that a man in his general course of conduct will of his own motion have respect to the common good, which entitles him to rights at the hands of the community. The question of the moral value of the motive which may induce this respect—whether an unselfish interest in common good or the wish for personal pleasure and fear of personal pain—does not come into the account at all. An agent, indeed, who could only be induced by fear of death or bodily harm to behave conformably to the requirements of the community, would not be a subject of rights, because this influence could never be brought to bear on him so constantly, if he were free to regulate his own life, as to secure the public safety. But a man's desire for pleasure to himself and aversion from pain to himself, though dissociated from any desire for a higher object, for any object that is desired because good for others, may constitute a capacity for rights, if his imagination of pleasure and pain is so far affected by sympathy with the feeling of others about him as to make him, independently of force or fear of punishment, observant of established rights. In such a case the fear of punishment may be needed to neutralise anti-social impulses under circumstances of special temptation, but by itself it could never be a sufficiently uniform motive to qualify a man, in the absence of more spontaneously social feelings, for the life of a free citizen. The qualification for such a life is a spontaneous habit of acting with reference to a common good, whether that habit be founded on an imagination of pleasures and pains or on a conception of what ought to be. In either case the habit implies at least an understanding that there is such a thing as a common good, and a regulation of egoistic hopes and fears, if not an inducing of more "disinterested" motives, in consequence of that understanding.

209. The capacity for rights, then, being a capacity for spontaneous action regulated by a conception of a common good, either so regulated through an interest which flows directly from that conception, or through hopes and fears which are affected by it through more complex channels of habit and association, is a capacity which cannot be generated—which on the contrary is neutralised—by any influences that interfere with the spontaneous action of social interests. Now any direct enforcement of the outward conduct, which ought to flow from social interests, by means of threatened penalties—and a law requiring such conduct necessarily implies penalties for disobedience to it—does interfere with the spontaneous action of those interests, and consequently checks the growth of the capacity which is the condition of the beneficial exercise of rights. For this reason the effectual action of the state, i.e., the community as acting through law, for the promotion of habits of true citizenship, seems necessarily to be confined to the removal of obstacles. Under this head, however, there may and should be included much that most states have hitherto neglected, and much that at first sight may have the appearance of an enforcement of moral duties, e.g., the requirement that parents have their children taught the elementary arts. To educate one's children is no doubt a moral duty, and it is not

one of those duties, like that of paying debts, of which the neglect directly interferes with the rights of someone else. It might seem, therefore, to be a duty with which positive law should have nothing to do, any more than with the duty of striving after a noble life. On the other hand, the neglect of it does tend to prevent the growth of the capacity for beneficially exercising rights on the part of those whose education is neglected, and it is on this account, not as a purely moral duty on the part of a parent, but as the prevention of a hindrance to the capacity for rights on the part of children, that education should be enforced by the state. It may be objected, indeed, that in enforcing it we are departing in regard to the parents from the principle above laid down; that we are interfering with the spontaneous action of social interests, though we are doing so with a view to promoting this spontaneous action in another generation. But the answer to this objection is, that a law of compulsory education, if the preferences, ecclesiastical or otherwise, of those parents who show any practical sense of their responsibility are duly respected, is from the beginning only felt as compulsion by those in whom, so far as this social function is concerned, there is no spontaneity to be interfered with; and that in the second generation, though the law with its penal sanctions still continues, it is not felt as a law, as an enforcement of action by penalties, at all.

210. On the same principle the freedom of contract ought probably to be more restricted in certain directions than is at present the case. The freedom to do as they like on the part of one set of men may involve the ultimate disqualification of many others, or of a succeeding generation, for the exercise of rights. This applies most obviously to such kinds of contract or traffic as affect the health and housing of the people, the growth of population relatively to the means of subsistence, and the accumulation or distribution of landed property. In the hurry of removing those restraints on free dealing between man and man, which have arisen partly perhaps from some confused idea of maintaining morality, but much more from the power of class-interests, we have been apt to take too narrow a view of the range of persons—not one generation merely, but succeeding generations—whose freedom ought to be taken into account, and of the conditions necessary to their freedom

("freedom" here meaning their qualification for the exercise of rights). Hence the massing of population without regard to conditions of health; unrestrained traffic in deleterious commodities; unlimited upgrowth of the class of hired labourers in particular industries which circumstances have suddenly stimulated, without any provision against the danger of an impoverished proletariate in following generations. Meanwhile, under pretence of allowing freedom of bequest and settlement, a system has grown up which prevents the landlords of each generation from being free either in the government of their families or in the disposal of their land, and aggravates the tendency to crowd into towns, as well as the difficulties of providing healthy house-room, by keeping land in a few hands. It would be out of place here to consider in detail the remedies for these evils, or to discuss the question how far it is well to trust to the initiative of the state or of individuals in dealing with them. It is enough to point out the directions in which the state may remove obstacles to the realisation of the capacity for beneficial exercise of rights, without defeating its own object by vitiating the spontaneous character of that capacity.

Lecture on Liberal Legislation and Freedom of Contract

. . .

We shall probably all agree that freedom, rightly understood, is the greatest of blessings; that its attainment is the true end of all our effort as citizens. But when we thus speak of freedom, we should consider carefully what we mean by it. We do not mean merely freedom from restraint or compulsion. We do not mean merely freedom to do as we like irrespectively of what it is that we like. We do not mean a freedom that can be enjoyed by one man or one set of men at the cost of a loss of freedom to others. When we speak of freedom as something to be so highly prized, we mean a positive power or capacity of doing or enjoying something worth doing or enjoying, and that, too, something that we do or enjoy in common with others. We mean by it a power which each man exercises through the help or security given him by his fellow-men, and which he in turn helps to secure for them. When we measure the progress of a society by its growth in freedom, we measure it by the increasing development and exercise on the whole of those powers of contributing to social good with which we believe the members of the society to be endowed; in short, by the greater power on the part of the citizens as a body to make the most and best of themselves. Thus, though of course there can be no freedom among men who act not willingly but under compulsion, yet on the other hand the mere removal of compulsion, the mere enabling a man to do as he likes, is in itself no contribution to true freedom. In one sense no man is so well able to do as he likes as the wandering savage. He has no master. There is no one to say him nay. Yet we do not count him really free, because the freedom of savagery is not strength, but weakness. The actual powers of the noblest savage do not admit of comparison with those of the humblest citizen of a law-abiding state. He is not the slave of man, but he is the slave of nature. Of compulsion by natural necessity he has plenty of experience, though of restraint by society none at all. Nor can he deliver himself from that compulsion except by submitting to this restraint. So to submit is the first step in true freedom, because the first step towards the full exercise of the faculties with which man is endowed. But we rightly refuse to recognise the highest development on the part of an exceptional individual or exceptional class, as an advance towards the true freedom of man, if it is founded on a refusal of the same opportunity to other men. . . .

If I have given a true account of that freedom which forms the goal of social effort, we shall see that freedom of contract, freedom in all the forms of doing what one will with one's own, is valuable only as a means to an end. That end is what I call freedom in the positive sense: in other words, the liberation of the powers of all men equally for contributions to a common good. No one has a right to do what he will with his own in such a way as to contravene this end. It is only through the guarantee which society gives him that he has property at all, or, strictly speaking, any right to his possessions. This guarantee is founded on a sense of common interest. Every one has an interest in securing to every one else the free use and enjoyment and disposal of his possessions, so long as that freedom on the part of one does not interfere with a like freedom on the part of others, because such freedom contributes to that equal development of the faculties of all which is the highest good for all. This is the true and the only justification of rights of property. Rights of property, however, have been and are claimed which cannot be thus justified. We are all now agreed that men cannot rightly be the property of men. The institution of property being only justifiable as a means to the free exercise of the social capabilities of all, there can be no true right to property of a kind which debars one class of men from such free exercise altogether. We condemn slavery no less when it arises out of a voluntary agreement on the part of the enslaved person. A contract by which any one agreed for a certain consideration to become the slave of another we should reckon a void contract. Here, then, is a limitation upon freedom of contract which we all recognise as rightful. No contract is valid in which human persons, willingly or unwillingly, are dealt with as commodities, because such contracts of necessity defeat the end for which alone society enforces contracts at all.

Are there no other contracts which, less obviously perhaps but really, are open to the same objection? In the first place, let us consider contracts affecting labour. Labour, the economist tells us, is a commodity exchangeable like other commodities. This is in a certain sense true, but it is a commodity which attaches in a peculiar manner to the person of man. Hence restrictions may need to be placed on the sale of this commodity which would be unnecessary in other cases, in order to prevent labour from being sold under conditions which make it impossible for the person selling it ever to become a free contributor to social good in any form. This is most plainly the case when a man bargains to work under conditions fatal to health, e.g., in an unventilated factory. Every injury to the health of the individual is, so far as it goes, a public injury. It is an impediment to the general freedom; so much deduction from our power, as members of society, to make the best of ourselves. Society is, therefore, plainly within its right when it limits freedom of contract for the sale of labour, so far as is done by our laws for the sanitary regulations of factories, workshops, and mines. It is equally within its right in prohibiting the labour of women and young persons beyond certain hours. If they work beyond those hours, the result is demonstrably physical deterioration; which, as demonstrably, carries with it a lowering of the moral forces of society. For the sake of that general freedom of its members to make the best of themselves, which it is the object of civil society to secure, a prohibition should be put by law, which is the deliberate voice of society, on all such contracts of service as in a general way yield such a result. The purchase or hire of unwholesome dwellings is properly forbidden on the same principle. Its application to compulsory education may not be quite so obvious, but it will appear on a little reflection. Without a command of certain elementary arts and knowledge, the individual in modern society is as effectually crippled as by the loss of a limb or a broken constitution. He is not free to develop his faculties. With a view to securing such freedom among its members it is as certainly within the province of the state to prevent children from growing up in that kind of ignorance which practically excludes them from a free career in life, as it is within its province to require the sort of building and drainage necessary for public health.

Our modern legislation then with reference to labour, and education, and health, involving as it does manifold interference with freedom of contract, is justified on the ground that it is the business of the state, not indeed directly to promote moral goodness, for that, from the very nature of moral goodness, it cannot do, but to maintain the conditions without which a free exercise of the human faculties is impossible. It does not indeed follow that it is advisable for the state to do all which it is justified in doing. We are often warned nowadays against the danger of over-legislation; or, as I heard it put in a speech of the present home [3] secretary in days when he was sowing his political wild oats, of "grandmotherly government." There may be good ground for the warning, but at any rate we should be quite clear what we mean by it. The outcry against state interference is often raised by men whose real objection is not to state interference but to centralisation, to the constant aggression of the central executive upon local authorities. . . . But there are some political speculators whose objection is not

[3] Sir William Vernon-Harcourt.

merely to centralisation, but to the extended action of law altogether. They think that the individual ought to be left much more to himself than has of late been the case. . . . Might not all the rules, . . . which legislation of the kind we have been discussing is intended to attain, have been attained without it; not so quickly, perhaps, but without tampering so dangerously with the independence and self-reliance of the people?

Now, we shall probably all agree that a society in which the public health was duly protected, and necessary education duly provided for, by the spontaneous action of individuals, was in a higher condition than one in which the compulsion of law was needed to secure these ends. But we must take men as we find them. Until such a condition of society is reached, it is the business of the state to take the best security it can for the young citizens' growing up in such health and with so much knowledge as is necessary for their real freedom. In so doing it need not at all interfere with the independence and self-reliance of those whom it requires to do what they would otherwise do for themselves. . . . But it was not their case that the laws we are considering were especially meant to meet. It was the overworked women, the ill-housed and untaught families, for whose benefit they were intended. And the question is whether without these laws the suffering classes could have been delivered quickly or slowly from the condition they were in. Could the enlightened self-interest or benevolence of individuals, working under a system of unlimited freedom of contract, have ever brought them into a state compatible with the free development of the human faculties? No one considering the facts can have any doubt as to the answer to this question. Left to itself, or to the operation of casual benevolence, a degraded population perpetuates and increases itself. . . .

As there is practically no danger of a reversal of our factory and school laws, it may seem needless to dwell at such length on their justification. I do so for two reasons; partly to remind the younger generation of citizens of the great blessing which they inherited in those laws, and of the interest which they still have in their completion and extension; but still more in order to obtain some clear principles for our guidance when we approach those difficult questions of the immediate future. . . .

· · ·

JOHN RAWLS

John Rawls was born in 1921, earned his A.B. at Princeton University in 1943, and, after studying at Cornell University, returned to Princeton for his Ph.D. in 1950. He spent the next two years teaching at Princeton, a year as a Fulbright Fellow at Oxford, and then taught at Cornell, Harvard, and M.I.T. until 1962, when he became professor of philosophy at Harvard. He is the author of a number of influential papers, including "Outline of a Decision Procedure for Ethics," "Two Concepts of Rules," "Justice as Fairness," "Constitutional Liberty and the Concept of Justice," "The Sense of Justice," "Distributive Justice," "Distributive Justice: Some Addenda," and "Justification of Civil Disobedience."

Chapter 1: Justice as Fairness

. . .

3. The Main Idea of the Theory of Justice.   My aim is to present a conception of justice which generalizes and carries to a higher level of abstraction the familiar theory of the social contract as found, say, in Locke, Rousseau, and Kant.[1] In order

The following selections are reprinted by permission of the publishers from John Rawls' *A Theory of Justice* (Cambridge, Mass.: The Belknap Press of Harvard University Press, Copyright, 1971, by the President and Fellows of Harvard College).

[1] As the text suggests, I shall regard Locke's *Second Treatise of Government*, Rousseau's *The Social Contract*, and Kant's ethical works beginning with *The Foundations of the Metaphysics of Morals* as definitive of the contract tradition. For all of its greatness, Hobbes's *Leviathan* raises special problems. . . .

to do this we are not to think of the original contract as one to enter a particular society or to set up a particular form of government. Rather, the guiding idea is that the principles of justice for the basic structure of society are the object of the original agreement. They are the principles that free and rational persons concerned to further their own interests would accept in an initial position of equality as defining the fundamental terms of their association. These principles are to regulate all further agreements; they specify the kinds of social cooperation that can be entered into and the forms of government that can be established. This way of regarding the principles of justice I shall call justice as fairness.

Thus we are to imagine that those who engage in social cooperation choose together, in one joint act, the principles which are to assign basic rights and duties and to determine the division of social benefits. Men are to decide in advance how they are to regulate their claims against one another and what is to be the foundation charter of their society. Just as each person must decide by rational reflection what constitutes his good, that is, the system of ends which it is rational for him to pursue, so a group of persons must decide once and for all what is to count among them as just and unjust. The choice which rational men would make in this hypothetical situation of equal liberty, assuming for the present that this choice problem has a solution, determines the principles of justice.

In justice as fairness the original position of equality corresponds to the state of nature in the traditional theory of the social contract. This original position is not, of course, thought of as an actual historical state of affairs, much less as a primitive condition of culture. It is understood as a purely hypothetical situation characterized so as to lead to a certain conception of justice. Among the essential features of this situation is that no one knows his place in society, his class position or social status, nor does any one know his fortune in the distribution of natural assets and abilities, his intelligence, strength, and the like. I shall even assume that the parties do not know their conceptions of the good or their special psychological propensities. The principles of justice are chosen behind a veil of ignorance. This ensures that no one is advantaged or disadvantaged in the choice of principles by the outcome of natural chance or the contingency of social circumstances. Since all are similarly situated and no one is able to design principles to favor his particular condition, the principles of justice are the result of a fair agreement or bargain. For given the circumstances of the original position, the symmetry of everyone's relations to each other, this initial situation is fair between individuals as moral persons, that is, as rational beings with their own ends and capable, I shall assume, of a sense of justice. The original position is, one might say, the appropriate initial status quo, and thus the fundamental agreements reached in it are fair. This explains the propriety of the name "justice as fairness": it conveys the idea that the principles of justice are agreed to in an initial situation that is fair. The name does not mean that the concepts of justice and fairness are the same, any more than the phrase "poetry as metaphor" means that the concepts of poetry and metaphor are the same.

Justice as fairness begins, as I have said, with one of the most general of all choices which persons might make together, namely, with the choice of the first principles of a conception of justice which is to regulate all subsequent criticism and reform of institutions. Then, having chosen a conception of justice, we can suppose that they are to choose a constitution and a legislature to enact laws, and so on, all in accordance with the principles of justice initially agreed upon. Our social situation is just if it is such that by this sequence of hypothetical agreements we would have contracted into the general system of rules which defines it. Moreover, assuming that the original position does determine a set of principles (that is, that a particular conception of justice would be chosen), it will then be true that whenever social institutions satisfy these principles those engaged in them can say to one another that they are cooperating on terms to which they would agree if they were free and equal persons whose relations with respect to one another were fair. They could all view their arrangements as meeting the stipulations which they would acknowledge in an initial situation that embodies widely accepted and reasonable constraints on the choice of principles. The general recognition of this fact would provide the basis for a public acceptance of the corresponding principles of justice. No society can, of course, be a scheme of cooperation which men enter voluntarily in a literal sense; each person finds himself placed at birth in some particular position in some particular society, and the nature of this position materially affects his life prospects. Yet a society satisfying the principles of justice as fairness comes as close as a society can to being a voluntary scheme, for it meets the principles which free and equal persons would assent to under circumstances that are fair. In this sense its members are autonomous and the obligations they recognize self-imposed.

One feature of justice as fairness is to think of the parties in the initial situation as rational and mutually disinterested. This does not mean that the parties are egoists, that is, individuals with only certain kinds of interests, say in wealth, prestige, and domination. But they are conceived as not taking an interest in one another's interests. They are to presume that even their spiritual aims may be opposed, in the way that the aims of those of different religions may be opposed. Moreover, the concept of rationality must be interpreted as far as possible in the narrow sense, standard in economic theory, of taking the most effective means to given ends. I shall modify this concept to some extent, as explained later (§ 25), but one must try to avoid introducing into it any controversial ethical elements. The initial situation must be characterized by stipulations that are widely accepted.

In working out the conception of justice as fairness one main task clearly is to determine which principles of justice would be chosen in the original position. To do this we must describe this situation in some detail and formulate with care the problem of choice which it presents. These matters I shall take up in the immediately succeeding chapters. It may be observed, however, that once the principles of justice are thought of as arising from an original agreement in a situation of equality, it is an open question whether the principle of utility would be acknowledged. Offhand it hardly seems likely that persons who view themselves as equals, entitled to press their claims upon one another, would agree to a principle which may require lesser life prospects for some simply for the sake of a greater sum of advantages enjoyed by others. Since each desires to protect his interests, his capacity to advance his conception of the good, no one has a reason to acquiesce in an enduring loss for himself in order to bring about a greater net balance of satisfaction. In the absence of strong and lasting benevolent impulses, a rational man would not accept a basic structure merely because it maximized the algebraic sum of advantages irrespective of its permanent effects on his own basic rights and interests. Thus it seems that the principle of utility is incompatible with the conception of social cooperation among equals for mutual advantage. It appears to be inconsistent with the idea of reciprocity implicit in the notion of a well-ordered society. Or, at any rate, so I shall argue.

I shall maintain instead that the persons in the initial situation would choose two rather different principles: the first requires equality in the assignment of basic rights and duties, while the second holds that social and economic inequalities, for example inequalities of wealth and authority, are just only if they result in compensating benefits for everyone, and in particular for the least advantaged members of society. These principles rule out justifying institutions on the grounds that the hardships of some are offset by a greater good in the aggregate. It may be expedient but it is not just that some should have less in order that others may prosper. But there is no injustice in the greater benefits earned by a few provided that the situation of persons not so fortunate is thereby improved. The intuitive idea is that since everyone's well-being depends upon a scheme of cooperation without which no one could have a satisfactory life, the division of advantages should be such as to draw forth the willing cooperation of everyone taking part in it, including those less well situated. Yet this can be expected only if reasonable terms are proposed. The two principles mentioned seem to be a fair agreement on the basis of which those better endowed, or more fortunate in their social position, neither of which we can be said to deserve, could expect the willing cooperation of others when some workable scheme is a necessary condition of the welfare of all.[2] Once we decide to look for a conception of justice that nullifies the accidents of natural endowment and the contingencies of social circumstance as counters in quest for political and economic advantage, we are led to these principles. They express the result of leaving aside those aspects of the social world that seem arbitrary from a moral point of view.

[2] For the formulation of this intuitive idea I am indebted to Allan Gibbard.

The problem of the choice of principles, however, is extremely difficult. I do not expect the answer I shall suggest to be convincing to everyone. It is, therefore, worth noting from the outset that justice as fairness, like other contract views, consists of two parts: (1) an interpretation of the initial situation and of the problem of choice posed there, and (2) a set of principles which, it is argued, would be agreed to. One may accept the first part of the theory (or some variant thereof), but not the other, and conversely. The concept of the initial contractual situation may seem reasonable although the particular principles proposed are rejected. To be sure, I want to maintain that the most appropriate conception of this situation does lead to principles of justice contrary to utilitarianism and perfectionism, and therefore that the contract doctrine provides an alternative to these views. Still, one may dispute this contention even though one grants that the contractarian method is a useful way of studying ethical theories and of setting forth their underlying assumptions.

Justice as fairness is an example of what I have called a contract theory. Now there may be an objection to the term "contract" and related expressions, but I think it will serve reasonably well. Many words have misleading connotations which at first are likely to confuse. The terms "utility" and "utilitarianism" are surely no exception. They too have unfortunate suggestions which hostile critics have been willing to exploit; yet they are clear enough for those prepared to study utilitarian doctrine. The same should be true of the term "contract" applied to moral theories. As I have mentioned, to understand it one has to keep in mind that it implies a certain level of abstraction. In particular, the content of the relevant agreement is not to enter a given society or to adopt a given form of government, but to accept certain moral principles. Moreover, the undertakings referred to are purely hypothetical: a contract view holds that certain principles would be accepted in a well-defined initial situation.

The merit of the contract terminology is that it conveys the idea that principles of justice may be conceived as principles that would be chosen by rational persons, and that in this way conceptions of justice may be explained and justified. The theory of justice is a part, perhaps the most significant part, of the theory of rational choice. Furthermore, principles of justice deal with conflicting claims upon the advantages won by social cooperation; they apply to the relations among several persons or groups. The word "contract" suggests this plurality as well as the condition that the appropriate division of advantages must be in accordance with principles acceptable to all parties. The condition of publicity for principles of justice is also connoted by the contract phraseology. Thus, if these principles are the outcome of an agreement, citizens have a knowledge of the principles that others follow. It is characteristic of contract theories to stress the public nature of political principles. Finally there is the long tradition of the contract doctrine. Expressing the tie with this line of thought helps to define ideas and accords with natural piety. There are then several advantages in the use of the term "contract." With due precautions taken, it should not be misleading.

· · ·

Chapter 2: The Principles of Justice

11. Two Principles of Justice. I shall now state in a provisional form the two principles of justice that I believe would be chosen in the original position. In this section I wish to make only the most general comments, and therefore the first formulation of these principles is tentative. As we go on I shall run through several formulations and approximate step by step the final statement to be given much later. I believe that doing this allows the exposition to proceed in a natural way.

The first statement of the two principles reads as follows.

First: each person is to have an equal right to the most extensive basic liberty compatible with a similar liberty for others.

Second: social and economic inequalities are to be arranged so that they are both (a) reasonably expected to be to everyone's advantage, and (b) attached to positions and offices open to all.

There are two ambiguous phrases in the second principle, namely "everyone's advantage" and "equally open to all." Determining their sense more exactly will lead to a second formulation of the principle in § 13. . . .

By way of general comment, these principles primarily apply, as I have said, to the basic structure of society. They are to govern the assignment of rights and duties and to regulate the distribution of social and economic advantages. As their formulation suggests, these principles presuppose that the social structure can be divided into two more or less distinct parts, the first principle applying to the one, the second to the other. They distinguish between those aspects of the social system that define and secure the equal liberties of citizenship and those that specify and establish social and economic inequalities. The basic liberties of citizens are, roughly speaking, political liberty (the right to vote and to be eligible for public office) together with freedom of speech and assembly; liberty of conscience and freedom of thought; freedom of the person along with the right to hold (personal) property; and freedom from arbitrary arrest and seizure as defined by the concept of the rule of law. These liberties are all required to be equal by the first principle, since citizens of a just society are to have the same basic rights.

The second principle applies, in the first approximation, to the distribution of income and wealth and to the design of organizations that make use of differences in authority and responsibility, or chains of command. While the distribution of wealth and income need not be equal, it must be to everyone's advantage, and at the same time, positions of authority and offices of command must be accessible to all. One applies the second principle by holding positions open, and then, subject to this constraint, arranges social and economic inequalities so that everyone benefits.

These principles are to be arranged in a serial order with the first principle prior to the second. This ordering means that a departure from the institutions of equal liberty required by the first principle cannot be justified, or compensated for, by greater social and economic advantages. The distribution of wealth and income, and the hierarchies of authority, must be consistent with both the liberties of equal citizenship and equality of opportunity.

It is clear that these principles are rather specific in their content, and their acceptance rests on certain assumptions that I must eventually try to explain and justify. A theory of justice depends upon a theory of society in ways that will become evident as we proceed. For the present, it should be observed that the two principles (and this holds for all formulations) are a special case of a more general conception of justice that can be expressed as follows.

> All social values—liberty and opportunity, income and wealth, and the bases of self-respect—are to be distributed equally unless an unequal distribution of any, or all, of these values is to everyone's advantage.

Injustice, then, is simply inequalities that are not to the benefit of all. Of course, this conception is extremely vague and requires interpretation.

As a first step, suppose that the basic structure of society distributes certain primary goods, that is, things that every rational man is presumed to want. These goods normally have a use whatever a person's rational plan of life. For simplicity, assume that the chief primary goods at the disposition of society are rights and liberties, powers and opportunities, income and wealth. (Later on in Part Three the primary good of self-respect has a central place.) These are the social primary goods. Other primary goods such as health and vigor, intelligence and imagination, are natural goods; although their possession is influenced by the basic structure, they are not so directly under its control. Imagine, then, a hypothetical initial arrangement in which all the social primary goods are equally distributed: everyone has similar rights and duties, and income and wealth are evenly shared. This state of affairs provides a benchmark for judging improvements. If certain inequalities of weath and organizational powers would make everyone better off than in this hypothetical starting situation, then they accord with the general conception.

Now it is possible, at least theoretically, that by giving up some of their fundamental liberties men are sufficiently compensated by the resulting social and economic gains. The general conception of justice imposes no restrictions on what sort of inequalities are permissible; it only requires that everyone's position be improved. We need not suppose anything so drastic as consenting to a condition of slavery. Imagine instead that men forego certain political rights when the economic returns are significant and their capacity to influence the course of policy by the exercise of these rights would be marginal in any case. It is this kind of exchange which the two principles as stated rule out; being arranged in serial order they do not permit exchanges between basic liberties and economic and social gains. The serial ordering of principles expresses an underlying preference among primary social goods. When this preference is rational so likewise is the choice of these principles in this order.

In developing justice as fairness I shall, for the most part, leave aside the general conception of justice and examine instead the special case of the two principles in serial order. The advantage of this procedure is that from the first the matter of priorities is recognized and an effort made to find principles to deal with it. One is led to attend throughout to the conditions under which the acknowledgment of the absolute weight of liberty with respect to social and economic advantages, as defined by the lexical order of the two principles, would be reasonable. Offhand, this ranking appears extreme and too special a case to be of much interest; but there is more justification for it than would appear at first sight. Or at any rate, so I shall maintain (§ 82). Furthermore, the distinction between fundamental rights and liberties and economic and social benefits marks a difference among primary social goods that one should try to exploit. It suggests an important division in the social system. Of course, the distinctions drawn and the ordering proposed are bound to be at best only approximations. There are surely circumstances in which they fail. But it is essential to depict clearly the main lines of a reasonable conception of justice; and under many conditions anyway, the two principles in serial order may serve well enough. When necessary we can fall back on the more general conception.

The fact that the two principles apply to institutions has certain consequences. Several points illustrate this. First of all, the rights and liberties referred to by these principles are those which are defined by the public rules of the basic structure. Whether men are free is determined by the rights and duties established by the major institutions of society. Liberty is a certain pattern of social forms. The first principle simply requires that certain sorts of rules, those defining basic liberties, apply to everyone equally and that they allow the most extensive liberty compatible with a like liberty for all. The only reason for circumscribing the rights defining liberty and making men's freedom less extensive than it might otherwise be is that these equal rights as institutionally defined would interfere with one another.

Another thing to bear in mind is that when principles mention persons, or require that everyone gain from an inequality, the reference is to representative persons holding the various social positions, or offices, or whatever, established by the basic structure. Thus in applying the second principle I assume that it is possible to assign an expectation of well-being to representative individuals holding these positions. This expectation indicates their life prospects as viewed from their social station. In general, the expectations of representative persons depend upon the distribution of rights and duties throughout the basic structure. When this changes, expectations change. I assume, then, that expectations are connected: by raising the prospects of the representative man in one position we presumably increase or decrease the prospects of representative men in other positions. Since it applies to institutional forms, the second principle (or rather the first part of it) refers to the expectations of representative individuals. As I shall discuss below, neither principle applies to distributions of particular goods to particular individuals who may be identified by their proper names. The situation where someone is considering how to allocate certain commodities to needy persons who are known to him is not within the scope of the principles. They are meant to regulate basic institutional arrangements. We must not assume that there is much similarity from the standpoint of justice between an administrative allotment of goods to specific persons and the appropriate design of society. Our common sense intuitions for the former may be a poor guide to the latter.

Now the second principle insists that each person benefit from permissible inequalities in the basic structure. This means that it must be reasonable for each relevant representative man defined by this structure, when he views it as a going concern, to prefer his prospects with the inequality to his prospects without it. One is not allowed to justify differences in income or organizational powers on the ground that the disadvantages of those in one position are outweighed by the greater advantages of those in another. Much less can infringements of liberty be counterbalanced in this way. Applied to the basic structure, the principle of utility would have us maximize the sum of expectations of representative men (weighted by the number of persons they represent, on the classical view); and this would permit us to compensate for the losses of some by the gains of others. Instead, the two principles require that everyone benefit from economic and social inequalities. It is obvious, however, that there are indefinitely many ways in which all may be advantaged when the initial arrangement of equality is taken as a benchmark. How then are we to choose among these possibilities? The principles must be specified so that they yield a determinate conclusion. I now turn to this problem.

12. *Interpretations of the Second Principle.* I have already mentioned that since the phrases "everyone's advantage" and "equally open to all" are ambiguous, both parts of the second principle have two natural senses. Because these senses are independent of one another, the principle has four possible meanings. Assuming that the first principle of equal liberty has the same sense throughout, we then have four interpretations of the two principles. These are indicated in the table below.

	"Everyone's advantage"	
"Equally open"	Principle of efficiency	Difference principle
Equality as careers open to talents	System of Natural Liberty	Natural Aristocracy
Equality as equality of fair opportunity	Liberal Equality	Democratic Equality

I shall sketch in turn these three interpretations: the system of natural liberty, liberal equality, and democratic equality. . . .

   The first interpretation . . . I shall refer to as the system of natural liberty. In this rendering the first part of the second principle is understood as the principle of efficiency adjusted so as to apply to institutions or, in this case, to the basic structure of society; and the second part is understood as an open social system in which, to use the traditional phrase, careers are open to talents. I assume in all interpretations that the first principle of equal liberty is satisfied and that the economy is roughly a free market system, although the means of production may or may not be privately owned. The system of natural liberty asserts, then, that a basic structure satisfying the principle of efficiency and in which positions are open to those able and willing to strive for them will lead to a just distribution. Assigning rights and duties in this way is thought to give a scheme which allocates wealth and income, authority and responsibility, in a fair way whatever this allocation turns out to be. The doctrine includes an important element of pure procedural justice which is carried over to the other interpretations.

. . .

In the system of natural liberty the initial distribution is regulated by the arrangements implicit in the conception of careers open to talents (as earlier defined). These arrangements presuppose a background of equal liberty (as specified by the first principle) and a free market economy. They require a formal equality of opportunity in that all have at least the same legal rights of access to all advantaged social positions. But since there is no effort to preserve an equality, or similarity, of social conditions, except insofar as this is necessary to preserve the requisite background institutions, the initial distribution of assets for any period of time is strongly influenced by natural and social contingencies. The existing distribution of income and wealth, say, is the cumulative effect of prior distributions of natural assets—that is, natural talents and abilities—as these have been developed or left unrealized, and their use favored or disfavored over time by social circumstances and such chance contingencies as accident and good fortune. Intuitively, the most obvious injustice of the system of natural liberty is that it permits distributive shares to be improperly influenced by these factors so arbitrary from a moral point of view.

The liberal interpretation, as I shall refer to it, tries to correct for this by adding to the requirement of careers open to talents the further condition of the principle of fair equality of opportunity. The thought here is that positions are to be not only open in a formal sense, but that all should have a fair chance to attain them. Offhand it is not clear what is meant, but we might say that those with similar abilities and skills should have similar life chances. More specifically, assuming that there is a distribution of natural assets, those who are at the same level of talent and ability, and have the same willingness to use them, should have the same prospects of success regardless of their initial place in the social system, that is, irrespective of the income class into which they are born. In all sectors of society there should be roughly equal prospects of culture and achievement for everyone similarly motivated and endowed. The expectations of those with the same abilities and aspirations should not be affected by their social class.

The liberal interpretation of the two principles seeks, then, to mitigate the influence of social contingencies and natural fortune on distributive shares. To accomplish this end it is necessary to impose further basic structural conditions on the social system. Free market arrangements must be set within a framework of political and legal institutions which regulates the overall trends of economic events and preserves the social conditions necessary for fair equality of opportunity. The elements of this framework are familiar enough, though it may be worthwhile to recall the importance of preventing excessive accumulations of property and wealth and of maintaining equal opportunities of education for all. Chances to acquire cultural knowledge and skills should not depend upon one's class position, and so the school system, whether public or private, should be designed to even out class barriers.

While the liberal conception seems clearly preferable to the system of natural liberty, intuitively it still appears defective. For one thing, even if it works to perfection in eliminating the influence of social contingencies, it still permits the distribution of wealth and income to be determined by the natural distribution of abilities and talents. Within the limits allowed by the background arrangements, distributive shares are decided by the outcome of the natural lottery; and this outcome is arbitrary from a moral perspective. There is no more reason to permit the distribution of income and wealth to be settled by the distribution of natural assets than by historical and social fortune. Furthermore, the principle of fair opportunity can be only imperfectly carried out, at least as long as the institution of the family exists. The extent to which natural capacities develop and reach fruition is affected by all kinds of social conditions and class attitudes. Even the willingness to make an effort, to try, and so to be deserving in the ordinary sense is itself dependent upon happy family and social circumstances. It is impossible in practice to secure equal chances of achievement and culture for those similarly endowed, and therefore we may want to adopt a principle which recognizes this fact and also mitigates the arbitrary effects of the natural lottery itself. That the liberal conception fails to do this encourages one to look for another interpretation of the two principles of justice.

Before turning to the conception of democratic equality, we should note that of natural aristocracy. On this view no attempt is made to regulate social contingencies beyond what is required by formal equality of opportunity, but the advantages of persons with greater natural endowments are to be limited to those that further the good of the poorer sectors of society. The aristocratic ideal is applied to a system that is open, at least from a legal point of view, and the better situation of those favored by it is regarded as just only when less would be had by those below, if less were given to those above.[3] In this way the idea of *noblesse oblige* is carried over to the conception of natural aristocracy.

Now both the liberal conception and that of natural aristocracy are unstable. For once we are troubled by the influence of either social contingencies or natural chance on the determination of distributive shares, we are bound, on reflection, to be bothered by the influence of the other. From a moral standpoint the two seem equally arbitrary. So however we move away from the system of natural liberty, we cannot be satisfied short of the democratic conception. . . .

[3] . . . I am indebted to Robert Rodes for pointing out to me that natural aristocracy is a possible interpretation of the two principles of justice and that an ideal feudal system might also try to fulfill the difference principle.

13. *Democratic Equality and the Difference Principle.* The democratic interpretation, as the table suggests, is arrived at by combining the principle of fair equality of opportunity with the difference principle. This principle removes the indeterminateness of the principle of efficiency by singling out a particular position from which the social and economic inequalities of the basic structure are to be judged. Assuming the framework of institutions required by equal liberty and fair equality of opportunity, the higher expectations of those better situated are just if and only if they work as part of a scheme which improves the expectations of the least advantaged members of society. The intuitive idea is that the social order is not to establish and secure the more attractive prospects of those better off unless doing so is to the advantage of those less fortunate. . . .

•   •   •

To illustrate the difference principle, consider the distribution of income among social classes. Let us suppose that the various income groups correlate with representative individuals by reference to whose expectations we can judge the distribution. Now those starting out as members of the entrepreneurial class in property-owning democracy, say, have a better prospect than those who begin in the class of unskilled laborers. It seems likely that this will be true even when the social injustices which now exist are removed. What, then, can possibly justify this kind of initial inequality in life prospects? According to the difference principle, it is justifiable only if the difference in expectation is to the advantage of the representative man who is worse off, in this case the representative unskilled worker. The inequality in expectation is permissible only if lowering it would make the working class even more worse off. Supposedly, given the rider in the second principle concerning open positions, and the principle of liberty generally, the greater expectations allowed to entrepreneurs encourages them to do things which raise the long-term prospects of laboring class. Their better prospects act as incentives so that the economic process is more efficient, innovation proceeds at a faster pace, and so on. Eventually the resulting material benefits spread throughout the system and to the least advantaged. I shall not consider how far these things are true. The point is that something of this kind must be argued if these inequalities are to be just by the difference principle.

. . .

17. The Tendency to Equality.

. . .

. . . We see then that the difference principle represents, in effect, an agreement to regard the distribution of natural talents as a common asset and to share in the benefits of this distribution whatever it turns out to be. Those who have been favored by nature, whoever they are, may gain from their good fortune only on terms that improve the situation of those who have lost out. The naturally advantaged are not to gain merely because they are more gifted, but only to cover the costs of training and education and for using their endowments in ways that help the less fortunate as well. No one deserves his greater natural capacity nor merits a more favorable starting place in society. But it does not follow that one should eliminate these distinctions. There is another way to deal with them. The basic structure can be arranged so that these contingencies work for the good of the least fortunate. Thus we are led to the difference principle if we wish to set up the social system so that no one gains or loses from his arbitrary place in the distribution of natural assets or his initial position in society without giving or receiving compensating advantages in return.

In view of these remarks we may reject the contention that the injustice of institutions is always imperfect because the distribution of natural talents and the contingencies of social circumstance are unjust, and this injustice must inevitably carry over to human arrangements. Occasionally this reflection is offered as an excuse for ignoring injustice, as if the refusal to acquiesce in injustice is on a par with being unable to accept death. The natural distribution is neither just nor unjust; nor is it unjust that men are born into society at some particular position. These are simply natural facts. What is just and unjust is the way that institutions deal with these facts. Aristocratic and caste societies are unjust because they make these contingencies the ascriptive basis for belonging to more or less enclosed and privileged social classes. The basic structure of these societies incorporates the arbitrariness found in nature. But there is no necessity for men to resign themselves to these contingencies. The social system is not an unchangeable order beyond human control but a pattern of human action. In justice as fairness men agree to share one another's fate. In designing institutions they undertake to avail themselves of the accidents of nature and social circumstance only when doing so is for the common benefit. The two principles are a fair way of meeting the arbitrariness of fortune; and while no doubt imperfect in other ways, the institutions which satisfy these principles are just.

A further point is that the difference principle expresses a conception of reciprocity. It is a principle of mutual benefit. We have seen that, at least when chain connection holds, each representative man can accept the basic structure as designed to advance his interests. The social order can be justified to everyone, and in particular to those who are least favored; and in this sense it is egalitarian. But it seems necessary to consider in an intuitive way how the condition of mutual benefit is satisfied. Consider any two representative men A and B, and let B be the one who is less favored. Actually, since we are most interested in the comparison with the least favored man, let us assume that B is this individual. Now B can accept A's being better off since A's advantages have been gained in ways that improve B's prospects. If A were not allowed his better position, B would be even worse off than he is. The difficulty is to show that A has no grounds for complaint. Perhaps he is required to have less than he might since his having more would result in some loss to B. Now what can be said to the more favored man? To begin with, it is clear that the well-being of each depends on a scheme of social cooperation without which no one could have a satisfactory life. Secondly, we can ask for the willing cooperation of everyone only if the terms of the scheme are reasonable. The difference principle, then, seems to be a fair basis on which those better endowed, or more fortunate in their social circumstances, could expect others to collaborate with them when some workable arrangement is a necessary condition of the good of all.

There is a natural inclination to object that those better situated deserve their greater advantages whether or not they are to the benefit of others. At this point it is necessary to be clear about the notion of desert. It is perfectly true that given a just system of cooperation as a scheme of public rules and the expectations set up by it, those who, with the prospect of improving their condition, have done what the system announces that it will reward are entitled to their advantages. In this sense the more fortunate have a claim to their better situation; their claims are legitimate expectations established by social institutions, and the community is obligated to meet them. But this sense of desert presupposes the existence of the cooperative scheme; it is irrelevant to the question whether in the first place the scheme is to be designed in accordance with the difference principle or some other criterion.

Perhaps some will think that the person with greater natural endowments deserves those assets and the superior character that made their development possible. Because he is more worthy in this sense, he deserves the greater advantages that he could achieve with them. This view, however, is surely incorrect. It seems to be one of the fixed points of our considered judgments that no one deserves his place in the distribution of native endowments, any more than one deserves one's initial starting place in society. The assertion that a man deserves the superior character that enables him to make the effort to cultivate his abilities is equally problematic; for his character depends in large part upon fortunate family and social circumstances for which he can claim no credit. The notion of desert seems not to apply to these cases. Thus the more advantaged representative man cannot say that he deserves and therefore has a right to a scheme of cooperation in which he is permitted to acquire benefits in ways that do not contribute to the welfare of others. There is no basis for his making this claim. From the standpoint of common sense, then, the difference principle appears to be acceptable both to the more advantaged and to the less advantaged individual. Of course, none of this is strictly speaking an argument for the principle, since in a contract theory arguments are made from the point of view of the original position. But these intuitive considerations help to clarify the nature of the principle and the sense in which it is egalitarian.

. . .

A further merit of the difference principle is that it provides an interpretation of the principle of fraternity. In comparison with liberty and equality, the idea of fraternity has had a lesser place in democratic theory. It is thought to be less specifically a political concept, not in itself defining any of the democratic rights but conveying instead certain attitudes of mind and forms of conduct without which we would lose sight of the values expressed by these rights. Or closely related to this, fraternity is held to represent a certain equality of social esteem manifest in various public conventions and in the absence of manners of deference and servility. No doubt fraternity does imply these things, as well as a sense of civic friendship and social solidarity, but so understood it expresses no definite requirement. We have yet to find a principle of justice that matches the underlying idea. The difference principle, however, does seem to correspond to a natural meaning of fraternity: namely, to the idea of not wanting to have greater advantages unless this is to the benefit of others who are less well off. The family, in its ideal conception and often in practice, is one place where the principle of maximizing the sum of advantages is rejected. Members of a family commonly do not wish to gain unless they can do so in ways that further the interests of the rest. Now wanting to act on the difference principle has precisely this consequence. Those better circumstanced are willing to have their greater advantages only under a scheme in which this works out for the benefit of the less fortunate.

The ideal of fraternity is sometimes thought to involve ties of sentiment and feeling which it is unrealistic to expect between members of the wider society. And this is surely a further reason for its relative neglect in democratic theory. Many have felt that it has no proper place in political affairs. But if it is interpreted as incorporating the requirements of the difference principle, it is not an impracticable conception. It does seem that the institutions and policies which we most confidently think to be just satisfy its demands, at least in the sense that the inequalities permitted by them contribute to the well-being of the less favored. Or at any rate, so I shall try to make plausible in Chapter 5. On this interpretation, then, the principle of fraternity is a perfectly feasible standard. Once we accept it we can associate the traditional ideas of liberty, equality, and fraternity with the democratic interpretation of the two principles of justice as follows: liberty corresponds to the first principle, equality to the idea of equality in the first principle together with equality of fair opportunity, and fraternity to the difference principle. In this way we have found a place for the conception of fraternity in the democratic interpretation of the two principles, and we see that it imposes a definite requirement on the basic structure of society. The other aspects of fraternity should not be forgotten, but the difference principle expresses its fundamental meaning from the standpoint of social justice.

Now it seems evident in the light of these observations that the democratic interpretation of the two principles will not lead to a meritocratic society. This form of social order follows the principle of careers open to talents and uses equality of opportunity as a way of releasing men's energies in the pursuit of economic prosperity and political dominion. There exists a marked disparity between the upper and lower classes in both means of life and the rights and privileges of organizational authority. The culture of the poorer strata is impoverished while that of the governing and technocratic elite is securely based on the service of the national ends of power and wealth. Equality of oppor tunity means an equal chance to leave the less fortunate behind in the personal quest for influence and social position.[4] Thus a meritocratic society is a danger for the other interpretations of the principles of justice but not for the democratic conception. For, as we have just seen, the difference principle transforms the aims of society in fundamental respects. This consequence is even more obvious once we note that we must when necessary

[4] For elaborations of this point to which I am indebted, see John Schaar, "Equality of Opportunity and Beyond," Nomos IX: Equality, ed. by J. R. Pennock and J. W. Chapman (New York, Atherton Press, 1967); and B. A. O. Williams, "The Idea of Equality,' in Philosophy, Politics and Society, ed. Peter Laslett and W. G. Runciman (Oxford, Basil Blackwell, 1962), pp. 125–129.

take into account the essential primary good of self-respect and the fact that a well-ordered society is a social union of social unions (§ 79). It follows that the confident sense of their own worth should be sought for the least favored and this limits the forms of hierarchy and the degrees of inequality that justice permits. Thus, for example, resources for education are not to be allotted solely or necessarily mainly according to their return as estimated in productive trained abilities, but also according to their worth in enriching the personal and social life of citizens, including here the less favored. As a society progresses the latter consideration becomes increasingly more important.

.   .   .

Index of Names and Subjects

Italicized page numbers indicate passages in the readings.

Socrates, 8, 24

Sovereignty. *See* General will as sovereign, Individual as sovereign, *and* State as sovereign

Spencer, Herbert, 163

State, Aristotle's concept of, 7–8, 10–14; and church, 19–20; Cicero's version of, 14–18; citizens of, *124;* and civil law, *66;* and civil society, 155–56; classical model of, 20; and constitutionalism, 12–13; and Declaration of Independence, 22–23; defined, 5–6, 21–22, *62;* democratic, 12, *65;* deontological view of, 24–25; and despotism, *120–21, 190–91;* formation of, 29, *61–62, 123–26;* function of, 41–42; and the good life, 8–9; and government, *139;* Hobbes' view of, 29–33, *62–65;* and ideology, 23; individualist philosophy of, 29, 31–32; institution of, *63;* kingship, 12, 19–20, *65;* laws of, *133–36;* and liberty, *65–66;* Locke's view of, 36; and morality, 4, 32, *209–14;* and nation, 20; obligations to, 41–42; organic theory of, 152; Plato's concept of, 7–10, 12–14; and polis, 13, 21, 49; and political order, 4; rationality of, 153–54; republican form of, *134–35;* and right, 32; and rights, *63–64, 66;* ruin of, *139–41;* Saint Thomas' concept of, 18–20; scientific theory of, 24–25, 30–31; and slavery, *207–8;* and social order, 6; subjects of, *124;* and suffrage, *141–44,* 157–58; teleological view of, 24–25; theories of, 23; and tyranny, 12, 18, 33, *87, 112, 114, 125,* 161, *188–89;* and will, *207–9. See also* Government

State as defender of natural rights, 33–37. *See also* Government, State, *and* State of Nature

State as sovereign, 4–7, 29–33, *62–65, 124–25. See also* State

State of nature, 4–5, 34–35; community formed from, *78–79;* and equality, *68–69;* and freedom, *68;* and government, *72–73, 82–85;* and justice, *101;* and liberty, *69;* Locke on, *68–73;* passage to civil state from, *125–26;* powers of man in, 70, *84;* preservation of mankind, *69, 71, 84;* and reparation for transgressions, *70–71, 84;* and self-preservation, *71, 84;* and war, *73–74. See also* Human nature

State of war, Hobbes on, *54–57, 61, 65;* Locke on, *73–74;* in state of nature, *73–74*

Stephen, L., 171

Stewart, J. B., 51

Stoics, 14–15

Strauss, L., 27

Sumner, William Graham, 163

Sutton, F. X., 1 n

Thomas, Saint. *See* Aquinas, Saint Thomas

Thorne, Samuel, 20 n

Tucker, R. C., 158 n

Tyranny. *See* State

Ulpian, 145, 166

Utilitarianism, 25–26, 37–43, 50, 159–63, *224;* criticism of, 161–63; fatal objection to, 164; and freedom, 163; and greatest happiness principle, 43, 159–61, 164; and justice, 150–51; and laissez-faire, 161; and moral equality, 164–69; and scientific hedonism, 161; and self-government, 162; and self-preference principle, 160–61; and social legislation, 161; and socialism, 162; and subservience, 164; and suffrage, 161

Voltaire, 46 n

War. *See* State of war

Warrender, H., 51

Weber, Max, 5–6, 21–22

Weldon, T. D., 27

Woodbine, G. E., 20 n